THE PEOPLE
CALLED QUAKERS

THE PEOPLE
CALLED QUAKERS

by / D. Elton Trueblood

PROFESSOR OF PHILOSOPHY
EARLHAM COLLEGE

HARPER & ROW, PUBLISHERS

NEW YORK

LIBRARY OF CONGRESS CATALOG CARD NUMBER: 66-15046

E-S

Dedicated
to the two
Samuel J. Truebloods
between whom I stand

Contents

Preface

This book is my contribution to the pursuit of an ecumenical ideal. The ideal is for all Christians, operating in true humility, to be willing and able to learn from one another. There is nothing wrong with the continued existence of historic communions, provided each one is humble enough to realize that it has something to learn from the others and is willing to make some effort to do so. But such mutual learning is possible only if each group makes publicly available its own spiritual treasures. To a surprising degree, these treasures are borrowable.

What follows is, in no sense, a history of the Quaker Movement, which covers more than three hundred years. That history has been written and capably written, as the Annotated Bibliography in Appendix B is intended to show. The present volume is more philosophical than historical because it is an effort to depict a people who represent one experiment in radical Christianity, with emphasis on their ways of thinking. Accordingly, historical events are mentioned only when the understanding of the ideas requires it. In any case, it is not the intention to talk of Quakers exclusively in the past tense. Though it may be a surprise to some readers to discover it, Quakerism is a practical alternative for contemporary men and women. Far from being historically interesting and no more, it is a live option.

Since the time when I began to write seriously for publication, more than thirty years ago, it has been part of my hope that I might someday be able to write a full-length book on Quaker ideas. This hope has been strengthened through the years by what I have learned in teaching a course in Quakerism, first at Haverford College and later at Earlham College. The publication of the book coincides not only with the completion of twenty years of academic responsibility at Earlham, but also with my official retirement. Though I was often tempted to write on this subject earlier, I am glad, now, that I did not do so. I needed the discipline of teaching and of engagement in other kinds of writing as preparation for this welcome task.

This book is part payment on a debt. The debt goes back a long way, to Arnold Trueblood who died in prison in Lincoln in 1658, as a persecuted member of the then infant Quaker Movement. It involves an unbroken heritage for which I am not responsible, but for which I am profoundly grateful. It involves the many influences, particularly in England and in America, which have enriched my life, intellectually, culturally, and emotionally. I am grateful to the strong groups of Friends in Iowa, in New England, in North Carolina, in Baltimore, in Philadelphia, and in Indiana, among all whom I have been fortunate enough to live and work.

The Quaker Way of Life is something with which I have been intimately acquainted from my earliest memories. Very soon, as a small boy, I learned that the heritage in which I was reared was a rich one. Though, in the intervening years, other heritages have appealed to me as precious, I have never ceased to value my own. I soon learned that, with no inconsistency whatever, a person may value his own communion and yet, at the same time, see its weaknesses as well as its strengths and also the strengths of others. Therefore the mood in which this book has been conceived is that of a combination of involvement and detachment. It is possible to care deeply and yet, in accordance with the scholarly ideal, to look critically at ourselves and at those whom we love.

In view of what has just been written, the thoughtful reader will understand that it is never my intention to produce propaganda for any Quaker organization. I am highly conscious of the possible justification of the judgment of Dr. Samuel Johnson when, in a conversation with his friend James Boswell, in 1776, he said that he liked individual Quakers, but not the sect. My practical purpose, rather than being sectarian, is the much larger one of aiding in the revival of true religion. And my deep conviction is that any important revival of true religion must be the result of a fresh recognition and acceptance of certain principles, some of which happen to be the very ones upon which the entire Quaker faith rests. About these principles there is a surprising amount of ignorance, but I have come to see that this ignorance is not necessary. My hope, therefore, is to reach friendly readers, most of whom may never call themselves Quakers, but who are gratefully aware of some of the principles and practices of those who *are* called Quakers. There are, it is probable, many who are Quakers without knowing that they are.

The time for an exposition and examination of Quaker ideas seems to me to be ripe. This is partly because ours is a time of extreme unsettlement and consequent searching. Though the prosperous period of the churches is clearly over, the period of honest searching for religious truth is by no means over. My book is, accordingly, addressed to the Seekers of the latter third of the twentieth century.

The title of the book has been chosen in the hope that it will make the reader expect to find within it the depiction of a way of life, as well as of a way of thought. The phrase employed is one which was used by both Barclay and Penn. They did not write of the Quaker Church or of the Society of Friends, but of *The People Called Quakers*.

If there is anything unique in this book it is the effort of the author to deal with Quaker ideas as a whole, rather than from the point of view of one geographical area or of one theological section of the total Quaker community. My intention is to be fair to all parties and to see Quakerism as an entire movement, even though it contains contrasting and complementary emphases within it.

D.E.T.

Earlham College
February, 1966

THE PEOPLE
CALLED QUAKERS

1 / The Quaker Explosion

The rise of the people called Quakers is one of the
memorable events in the history of man.

GEORGE BANCROFT

There are not many popular images which are more distorted than
that of Quakers. According to the popular conception, Quakers are
an exceedingly mild and harmless people, largely given to silence,
totally unaggressive, with a religion that is neither evangelical in
content nor evangelistic in practice. It is generally understood that
the appearance of Quakers has something of the benign character
of the man pictured on the Quaker Oats box, and many identify
Quakers with contemporary "plain people." Even those who
realize that there have been changes in dress and manner of life
still suppose that Quakers are prudent in all their ways and
moderate in all their views. It is understood that they are good and
kind, but also ineffective. Above all, it is believed that Quakerism
is a faith which, being essentially antique, is irrelevant to the life
of modern men and women. Many, who hear of the Quaker faith,
are not sure whether it is Christian, and few look upon it as a live
option for themselves today. Some even believe that Quakerism is
something into which it is necessary for people to be born.

The important thing to say about this image is that it is
erroneous at almost every point. The conventional image has little
fidelity in relation to contemporary Quakers, while it has none at
all in relation to the Quakers of three hundred years ago, when the
Movement was marked by an amazing vitality. It is important, in
the cause of truth, to set the record straight and to this end, this
and subsequent chapters are devoted. It is necessary to correct a

1

false image, if Quakerism is to have any relevance to the needs and perplexities of contemporary men and women. Not many will pay serious attention to Quakerism, or see it as a live option, if they think of Quakers as a queer little sect, marked, indeed, by the integrity which gives credence to the commercial advertisements in which the name Quaker appears, but also marked by insipidity.

In counteracting the erroneous stereotype, there is some help from an unexpected quarter, namely, humor. The Quaker jokes, which are numerous and much admired, are genuinely helpful, since nearly all of them secure their point by an unexpected turn of events, in which the supposed softness of the Quaker is shown to be either deceptive or nonexistent. Good as the jokes are, however, the only adequate corrective to the false Quaker image is that which is produced by direct confrontation with the explosive life of the earliest Friends, which often comes as a shock to the modern inquirer.

The Quaker explosion occurred during the forty exciting years between 1650 and 1690. In this period, Quakerism began in England and spread rapidly to various parts of the world, including most of the English colonies on the western shore of the Atlantic Ocean. Starting from nothing, or almost nothing, first in the experience of George Fox and then in that of those who were enkindled by his brightly burning fire, Quakerism was, for a while, the fastest-growing movement of the Western world. Thousands of Quakers, both men and women, suffered cruel imprisonment; many were whipped and beaten; and four, including one woman, were hanged on Boston Common. Nearly all, in spite of wide differences of ability and of education, engaged in preaching to anyone who would listen, and even some jailers were convinced by the persuasiveness of the message. Kings were addressed; governments were influenced; books and pamphlets were published in fantastic numbers. Whatever else Quakers were, they were not a harmless sect. If they had been such, the persecution, even in a savage age, would have been incomprehensible. The great mark of the new Movement was an undoubted dynamism. If we could know what sort of message produced such dynamism, we should know something truly important and perhaps something relevant to our own sorely troubled time. Since human needs have not changed, in spite of changes in technology, it is wholly possible that the message relevant to one time may, if it is truly understood, be seen as relevant to another.

First of all, then, the thoughtful reader must understand that the Quaker Movement, at its inception and for a full forty years thereafter, presented many of the characteristics of a cultural and religious storm. Far from being moderate, the first Quakers exhibited the kind of "excessiveness" which Professor Whitehead has assured us is "a necessary element in all greatness."[1] The truly moderate man is not likely to achieve very much, but this was not the Quaker danger. Whatever the theological spectrum was, Quakers were not in the middle of it. This is what Harold Loukes means by saying that the Quaker theme is the "extreme statement of the Reformation."[2] One evidence of the extreme character of Quakerism was the fact that the new breed of preachers were disturbers of the peace. They spoke in church services where they had captive audiences, they shocked officials by treating them as equals rather than with obsequious manners, they treated women as the equals of men, they sang in prison, and they made an effective witness behind prison walls.

Far from separating themselves from the world, the first Quakers established one important colony and were influential members of legislatures in several others. Indeed, the English colonies in America were so deeply affected by the Quaker Movement that one cannot understand their story apart from some reference to the new faith. Not only was Pennsylvania established

[1] Alfred North Whitehead, *Adventures of Ideas* (New York: The Macmillan Company, 1933), p. 138.
[2] *The Quaker Contribution* (New York: The Macmillan Company, 1965), p. 15.

as a Quaker experiment in government; Quaker influence was earlier significant in at least three other colonies. In Rhode Island, Quaker governors held office for thirty-six successive terms. Robert Barclay, the greatest of the early Quaker thinkers, was appointed the first governor of East Jersey. In North Carolina, with a Quaker, John Archdale, as Governor, Quakers controlled at one time half of all of the seats in the Assembly.

The influence on the world and the attempt to redress evils by vigorous action did not end with the first or classic period. Quakers were the first people of the Western world to make a direct assault on the institution of slavery, with the result that, sixty years before the Emancipation Proclamation, there was not one Quaker slaveholder in America. The Quaker grandparents of living people underwent great personal risks, in the middle of the nineteenth century, in conducting the underground railroad, secretly conveying slaves from the Border States to the Canadian frontier.

The recitation of such facts gives us a start on the correction of the generally accepted image, but we reach a deeper understanding of the contrast when we begin to acquaint ourselves with the language of the first Quakers, as preserved in their flood of writings. We are soon aware of a style of life in which there was terrific gusto, uninhibited by the fear of seeming extreme. Quakers did not hesitate, for example, to speak of their Movement as "Primitive Christianity Revived." The recognition of the danger of immodesty seems to have played absolutely no part in the early nomenclature. Thus, there was no hesitation, among the early Quakers, particularly the dynamic men of the north of England, in calling themselves "First Publishers of the Truth." Another immodest name was "Children of the Light," such language being adapted boldly from the New Testament (I Thess. 5:5, Luke 16:8, John 12:36, Eph. 5:8). Even the word "Friends," which later developed into an official name, "The Religious Society of Friends," was an adaptation of the words of Christ, "I have called you friends" (John 15:15).

Because of the long-standing Quaker emphasis on the sinfulness of war, an emphasis in which Quakers were, for a while, unique, though they are so no longer, many of our own day picture the Quakers as wholly nonmilitant in mood. It is really shocking to such persons to learn how far from the truth this conception is. The early Quakers, being steeped in the language of the New Testament, and therefore familiar with the military metaphors with which the New Testament abounds, did not hesitate to employ them. Knowing the Epistles as they did, they felt no embarrassment in speaking of "the breastplate of faith and love," or "for an helmet, the hope of salvation" (I Thess. 5:8). When they were thrown into foul prisons, it helped them immensely to remember one who had said, "Endure hardness, as a good soldier of Jesus Christ" (II Tim. 2:3). Militant language was so congenial to Quakers in general that they tended to refer to their entire struggle as the "Lamb's War." Such was, indeed, the title of a book by the most eloquent and most maligned of all first-generation Quakers, James Nayler. This reference was also Biblical, being based on Revelation 17:14.

Perhaps the strangest part of the present distorted image of Quakers is the idea that Quakers are excessively reticent and therefore uninterested in making converts. There may be such Quakers today, but it is doubtful if there was one such in the first forty years of the Quaker explosion. All tried to make converts and they tried all of the time. The clarity of Robert Barclay on this point is indicated by his unapologetic defense of proselytizing when he wrote, "We desire therefore all that come among us to be proselyted."[3] They even took the opportunities provided by fairs and by wrestling matches. Any situation was a proper one in the Lamb's War.

Closely allied to the notion that Quakerism is intrinsically un-evangelistic is the equally erroneous notion that Quakerism is not tied to the Christian heritage. Some even suppose that Quakerism

[3] Barclay's *Apology*, XI, 7.

is a kind of religion-in-general, without a direct commitment to Jesus Christ. There may, indeed, be living Quakers who feel this way about it, but their position is not even remotely similar to that of Friends in the period of greatest dynamism. Not only were the earliest Quakers conscious of commitment to Jesus Christ; the same has been true of the mainstream of Quakers ever since and is certainly true of the majority of those who call themselves Quakers today. Even in his lifetime, Fox felt the necessity to take cognizance of the rumor or slander that the movement which stemmed from his preaching was not specifically Christian. This caused him, in 1671, to write in his *Journal*:

Whereas many scandalous lies and slanders have been cast upon us, to render us odious; as that we do deny God, and Christ Jesus, and the Scriptures of truth, etc. This is to inform you that all our books and declarations, which for these many years have been published to the world, do clearly testify the contrary.

One of the best evidences that the image which Fox and his associates conveyed to their contemporaries was a dynamic one, is that provided by the nickname Quaker, which, though originally given as an intended insult, has long been proudly adopted. That it was already accepted gladly and without apology by the end of the classic period is shown by the fact that William Penn, when he wrote his famous Preface to the official edition of the *Journal of George Fox*, called his story "The Rise and Progress of the People Called Quakers," thus using the phrase already used by Barclay in his *Apology*. The nickname Quaker was really an unintended compliment. It was a way of admitting that these people were not insipid, but were, instead, the movers and shakers of the established order. Such was the meaning of Thomas Carlyle when, in referring to Fox when making his famous suit of leather, with his own crude instruments, he wrote:

Stitch away, thou noble Fox: every prick of that little instrument is pricking into the heart of Slavery, and World-worship, and the Mammon-god. Thy elbows jerk, as in strong swimmer-strokes, and

every stroke is bearing thee across the Prison-ditch, within which
Vanity holds her Workhouse and Ragfair, into lands of true Liberty;
were the work done, there is in broad Europe one Free Man, and thou
art he.[4]

Fox, thought Carlyle, could not be satisfied with conventional
satisfactions and rewards, because his life was profoundly shaken.

There are two early accounts of the origin of the name Quaker,
one in the *Journal* of George Fox and another in Barclay's *Apology*. Though not identical, they bear equal witness to the fact that
the faith of early Friends so took hold of them that they actually
seemed to be shaken. "The priest scoffed at us," wrote Fox, "and
called us Quakers. But the Lord's power was so over them, and the
word of life was declared in such authority and dread to them, that
the priest began trembling himself; and one of the people said,
'Look how the priest trembles and shakes, he is turned a Quaker
also.' "[5] According to Fox, the first individual who called the
members of the new Movement Quakers was Justice Bennet of
Derby. He coined the term, Fox reported, "because we bid them
tremble at the word of the Lord. This was in the year 1650."
Though there was once a time when members of the Movement
preferred to be called Friends, there is a growing tendency, in the
latter half of the twentieth century, to accept the opprobrious
nickname and even to rejoice in it. This is particularly true as we
leave off vestiges of the quietistic period and understand better the
extreme vitality of the original Movement. Contemporary Friends
are not ashamed of the fact that they are part of a Movement in
which men and women were once so shaken that they trembled;
on the contrary, they are becoming ashamed of the fact that they
are so little shaken themselves. It is hard, for example, to read the
words of Robert Barclay, describing his own experience of three
centuries ago, without interpreting them as a standing challenge to
subsequent lack of the power to which he bore witness.

[4] *Sartor Resartus*, Bk. III, Chap. 1.
[5] *Journal*, 1652.

For not a few have come to be convinced of the truth after this manner, of which I myself, in part, am a true witness, who not by strength of arguments, or by a particular disquisition of each doctrine, and convincement of my understanding thereby, came to receive and bear witness of the truth, but by being secretly reached by this life; for when I came into the silent assemblies of God's people, I felt a secret power among them, which touched my heart, and as I gave way unto it, I found the evil weakening in me, and the good raised up, and so I became thus knit and united unto them, hungering more and more after the increase of this power and life, whereby I might feel myself perfectly redeemed. And indeed this is the surest way to become a Christian, to whom afterwards the knowledge and understanding of principles will not be wanting, but will grow up so much as is needful, as the natural fruit of this good root.[6]

These people, in this amazing phenomenon, were not trying to set up a new church or a denomination, for such an aim would have seemed to them to be low and unworthy. Since it was their intention to be universal rather than sectarian, they called *all men.* What is amazing in the light of contemporary aims, is the ambitiousness of their expectations. Indeed, they expected nothing less than the transformation of the whole nation. Even beyond this, they confidently hoped to reach men all over the world. "The field is the world," they read in Matthew 13:38, and they believed it.

The boldness of the vision, which had so much to do with the willingness to face persecution, as well as the passionate evangelization, is expressed in Penn's account of the vision which came to Fox on Pendle Hill in 1652. "He had," wrote Penn, "a vision of the great work of God in the earth, and of the way that he was to go forth in a public ministry, to begin it. He saw people thick as motes in the sun, that should in time be brought home to the Lord, that there might be but one Shepherd and one sheepfold in all the earth."[7] We do not understand the expectancy of the

---

[6] Barclay's *Apology*, XI, 7.
[7] *Rise and Progress of the People Called Quakers* (Philadelphia: Friends Book Store, 1947), p. 53, 54.

early Quakers until we realize that it was total. Their message was
not for the peculiar people, but for all mankind.

Though the message of these people who gathered about
George Fox was total in the sense just mentioned, it was also total
in a far more important sense. The really surprising fact was that
the first Quakers were seldom mere followers; they were all
involved as participators in what seemed to them an important
undertaking. Other Christian leaders, including Martin Luther,
had announced the priesthood of every believer as a doctrine, but
these new people came close to demonstrating it as a fact. The
most striking single aspect of the new Movement was what might
be called the "priesthood of every member." Each, as he was
shaken, undertook to shake others; each little fire accepted the
grave responsibility of starting other fires in other human hearts.

We expect, in any movement, but particularly in a new movement, to observe a wide chasm between leader and followers. This
can be noted in the work of many great men, including St.
Francis, Martin Luther, and John Wesley. In the Quaker Movement this chasm is almost nonexistent. Not only men like Barclay
and Penington, but large numbers of now forgotten men and
women had experiences similar to those of George Fox. This is one
profound reason why there was never a serious temptation to call
the new people "Foxites." This conception of total involvement
has been seen in part by a number of scholars, but the one who
has expressed it most clearly is Professor Hugh Barbour. "Each
Friend himself," writes Barbour, "came to know the same direct
power which George Fox had announced. Several hundred Friends
shared fully in Fox's own roles as preacher, tract-writer, and
gatherer of Quaker Meetings. Above all, Friends shared Fox's
experience of the total world."[8]

When we speak of the explosion of Quakerism this is a large

[8] *The Quakers in Puritan England* (New Haven and London: Yale
University Press, 1964), p. 1.

part of what we mean. There was not much novelty of doctrine, and the organization, which came later, was really unimpressive, but total involvement is so rare that it will always be striking and it necessarily involves radical consequences. If Fox had been merely a great speaker, he might soon have been forgotten, and if he had been merely a great organizer, he would have left behind a conventional church or denomination, but the phenomenon in question was much more than that of inspired and persuasive leadership.

We get some idea of the phenomenon of total involvement when we learn that Friends had produced, by 1715, about 2,750 tracts. In the first thirteen years after the start of 1652, Quakers were responsible for at least 25,000 printed pages. In spite of terrible hardships, including cruel imprisonments and other punishments, these people were writing, speaking, and traveling with a fertility that is hard to match in the history, not merely of any religious movement, but of any movement of any kind. These simple people naturally amaze us, as we consider their story in perspective, but it is worthwhile to know that they themselves were also amazed.

The prophethood of every member did not mean that all were equal in power or in persuasiveness. Indeed, Fox and a few others were known as public Friends, but the important point is that they rejected the leader principle as it is ordinarily understood. Fox quoted the aspiration of Moses, "Would [God that] all the people were prophets," as a kind of golden text. The private Friends were to be preachers just as truly as the public Friends. "Come tradesmen, tent-makers, physicians and customs men, what can you say for God?" During the period of Cromwell's rise to power, England was seething with new religious movements. Several of these were well represented in Cromwell's "New Model Army" which is still regarded as one of the wonders of military history. These soldiers discussed religious ideas endlessly, and regiments even formed themselves into "gathered churches." We know the names of the new movements, not because they survived, but only because of the accounts of contemporary historians. The important fact to note is that nearly all of these movements *died*. They did not outlive, or did not long outlive, the vigorous influences of their founders. To the detached observer, the young George Fox appeared to be just another of these fervid innovators. Why, when so many new movements died quickly, did the one which was inspired by Fox flourish and survive?

The essential persuasiveness of the early Quaker message is not easily understood. This is true, not only for outsiders, but for practicing Quakers of our generation. Much of the difficulty arises from the tendency of modern liberal Quakers to see early Friends as similar to themselves. Since a good many today are mildly mystical, the natural tendency is to interpret early Quakers as equally mystical, but this is clearly an error, as any careful study of the available literature will reveal.

The characteristic writings of early Friends are marked, not by a mood of quiet contemplation, as modern man has been led to expect, but by confidence and gusto. In no one set of writings is this mood more evident than in the works of Edward Burrough (1633–1663) who, because of his combination of vitality and tenderness, was called, by his associates, a Son of Thunder and Consolation. Words poured from him, in both written and spoken form, like a torrent. This attractive young man, who was born at Underbarrow, between Kendal and Windermere, early became a strong Puritan and, at the age of seventeen, was vividly aware of God's presence. The big change came when, at the age of nineteen, he first heard Fox, during Fox's initial success in the north. After eleven years of feverish missionary activity, Burrough was imprisoned at Newgate in London and died there at the age of thirty. His account of the vitality of the fellowship helps us to understand its true character.

We obeyed the Light of Christ in us, and took up the Cross to all earthly glories, crowns and ways, and denied ourselves, our relations, and all that stood in the way betwixt us and the Lord. And while waiting upon the Lord in silence, as often we did for many hours together, we received often the pouring down of the Spirit upon us and our hearts were made glad, and our tongues loosed, and our mouths opened . . . and the glory of the Father was revealed; and then began we to sing praises to the Lord God Almighty and to the Lamb forever, who has redeemed us to God, and brought us out of the captivity and bondage of the world, and put an end to sin and death.[9]

It is hard to know which of the associates of Fox was the most eloquent in describing the corporate experience of the presence of Christ in the midst of their Movement. Perhaps, however, the most brilliant statement of the theme was provided by Francis Howgill (1618-1669). The crowning passage is:

The Kingdom of Heaven did gather us and catch us all, as in a net, and his heavenly power at one time drew many hundreds to land. We came to know a place to stand in and what to wait in; and the Lord appeared daily to us, to our astonishment, amazement and great admiration, insomuch that we often said one unto another with great joy of heart: "What, is the Kingdom of God come to be with men? And will he take up his tabernacle among the sons of men, as he did of old? Shall we, that were reckoned as the outcasts of Israel, have this honour of glory communicated amongst us, which were but men of small parts and of little abilities, in respect of many others, as amongst men?" And from that day forward, our hearts were knit unto the Lord and one unto another in true and fervent love, in the covenant of Life with God; and that was a strong obligation or bond upon all our spirits, which united us one unto another. We met together in the unity of the Spirit, and of the bond of peace, treading down under our feet all reasoning about religion. And holy resolutions were kindled in our hearts as a fire which the Life kindled in us to serve the Lord while we had a being, and mightily did the Word of God grow amongst us, and the desires of many were after the Name of the Lord. O happy day! O blessed day! the memorial of which can never pass out of my mind. And thus the Lord, in short, did form us to be a people for his praise in our generation.[10]

The literary fecundity of the first and second generation of Friends is amazing. This is particularly true of the records of those

9 *The Memorable Works of a Son of Thunder*, 1672, preliminary leaves.
10 *Ibid.*, "Testimony of Francis Howgill concerning Edward Burrough."

who were committed to prisons, either under Cromwell or after the royal Restoration of 1660. One of the most attractive of the early Quaker preachers was William Dewsbury, who had been a trumpeter in the army of Oliver Cromwell. Recalling his long years of imprisonment at Warwick, he wrote, about a week before he died:

> For this I can say I never since played the coward, but joyfully entered prisons as palaces, telling mine enemies to hold me there as long as they could; and in the prison house I sung praises to my God and esteemed the bolts and locks put upon me as jewels; and in the name of the eternal God I alway got the victory, for they could keep me no longer than the determined time of my God.[11]

William Dewsbury was a humble man, while Isaac Penington was the son of the one-time Lord Mayor of London, but the reported experiences of the two breathe the same spirit. Of his prison days Penington wrote:

> I have had experience myself of the Lord's goodness and preservation of me in my suffering . . . for the testimony of His truth, who made my bonds pleasant to me, and my noisome prison (enough to have destroyed my weakly and tender-educated nature) place of pleasure and delight, where I was comforted by my God night and day and filled with prayers for His people, as also with love to, and prayers for, those who had been the means of outwardly afflicting me and others upon the Lord's account.

A Friend who had, on several occasions, been a fellow prisoner with Isaac Penington, wrote that he never saw the man cast down or dejected in spirit. "O, the remembrance of the glory that did often overshadow us in the place of confinement, so that, indeed, the prison was made by the Lord unto us . . . as a pleasant place."[12]

The persecution on the part of the old religious establishment in

---

[11] Dewsbury, "The faithful testimony of that ancient servant of the Lord in his books, epistles and writings," 1689, preliminary unnumbered page.

[12] The writer is Robert Jones, whose testimony appears at the beginning of Penington's *Collected Works*.

England might have been expected, but the paradox is that the most severe persecution arose in the New World, in the new establishment of Massachusetts. A law was made which provides later generations with an unintentional yet unmistakable evidence of the vitality of the infant Quaker Movement. The law, which was to the effect that Quakers who were banished and who returned, would be put to death, showed how deep and almost frantic the fear of the Quakers was. The strange thing is the degree to which the law failed in its main purpose, which was to put fear in the hearts of the Quaker preachers. Four were actually hanged, William Leddra, Marmaduke Stephenson, Mary Dyer, and William Robinson. The dates were 1659, 1660, and 1661. Few documents make us understand the essence of the bursting life which Quakerism represented better than the words written by the simple Yorkshireman, Marmaduke Stephenson, on the night before the Boston authorities hanged him and his companion. Like a true scientist, he simply gives the record of experience, as follows:

In the beginning of the year 1655, I was at the plough in the east parts of Yorkshire in Old England, near the place where my outward being was; and as I walked after the plough, I was filled with the love and presence of the living God, which did ravish my heart when I felt it, for it did increase and abound in me like a living stream, so did the life and love of God run through me like precious ointment giving a pleasant smell, which made me to stand still. And, as I stood a little still, with my heart and mind stayed upon the Lord, the word of the Lord came to me in a still, small voice, which I did hear perfectly, saying to me in the secret of my heart and conscience, "I have ordained thee a prophet unto the nations," and, at the hearing of the word of the Lord, I was put to a stand, seeing that I was but a child for such a weighty matter. So, at the time appointed, Barbados was set before me, unto which I was required of the Lord to go and leave my dear and loving wife and tender children; for the Lord said unto me, immediately by His Spirit, that He would be as an husband to my wife and as a father to my children, and they should not want in my absence, for He would provide for them when I was gone. And I believed the Lord would perform what He had spoken, because I was made willing to give up myself to His work and service, to leave all and follow Him, whose presence and life is with me, where I rest in peace and quietness of spirit, with my dear brother (William Robinson) under the shadow of His wings, who hath made us willing to lay down our lives for His name's sake, if unmerciful men be suffered to take them from us.[13]

Wenlock Christison, who had also been banished, came into the Massachusetts court at the moment when William Leddra was being sentenced. A few days later, when he, in turn, was tried, Christison spoke words to the judges which express the secret of the Quaker phenomenon better than most. "Do not think," he said, "to weary out the living God by taking away the lives of His servants. What do you gain by it? For the last man you put to death, here are five come in his room. And if you have power to take my life from me, God can raise up the same principle of life in ten of His servants and send them among you in my room."

It is not very surprising to the modern reader to learn that a movement so highly charged led, in some instances, to extremes of fanatacism and to sharp personal conflicts. The most moving example of this came within the first few years, in the experience of the highly gifted preacher, James Nayler (1617?–1660). For a while this remarkable man exhibited an unbalanced mind, but the end of the story is so glorious that it is impossible to call it a tragedy. Out of the pain and turmoil of Nayler's experience there came finally the most eloquent words of the entire Quaker story.

James Nayler was a Yorkshire farmer who was aroused by the first wave of Quaker enthusiasm and promptly became an eloquent exponent. Nayler's sense of a firsthand encounter with the Living God brought great vitality to his words, but, before long, he came to identify himself so closely with Christ that he allowed his deluded followers to give to him honor similar to that given to Christ in the triumphal entry into Jerusalem. In the year 1656, physically and mentally overstrained, Nayler rode into the city of

[13] Joseph Besse, A *Collection of the Sufferings of the people called Quakers*, 1753, Vol. 2, pp. 201–2.

Bristol, allowing his flatterers to strew garments in his way as they sang "Holy, holy, holy, Lord God of Israel." Nayler was examined in the House of Commons where he claimed, in evident sincerity, that the honor was not done to him as an individual but "as to a sign of Christ's second coming and being revealed in His saints." By a narrow majority Nayler escaped the death penalty, but a terrible sentence, with which Cromwell did not concur, was passed. After being severely flogged in the streets, Nayler was set in the pillory for two hours, his forehead was branded with a B, as a blasphemer, and his tongue, the instrument of his brilliant speech, was bored through with a hot iron. After all this he was imprisoned. At this time he was forty years old, being Fox's senior by eight years.

After his release from prison, Nayler lived only a short time, but it was long enough for full atonement. He recognized the harm that he had done to his fellows, saying that "the Lord knows it was never in my heart to cause you to mourn, whose sufferings is my greatest sorrow that ever yet came upon me." Again large numbers flocked to hear his preaching in London before he set out on foot for his old home in the north, where he was found dying in a field. Shortly before he died he wrote what has come to be regarded as the most beautiful record of Christian experience which any Quaker has written in more than three centuries. The key words are:

There is a spirit which I feel that delights to do no evil nor to revenge any wrong, but delights to endure all things in hope to enjoy its own in the end. Its hope is to out-live all wrath and contention and to weary out all exaltations and cruelty of whatever is of a nature contrary to itself. It sees to the end of all temptations. As it bears no evil in itself, so it conceives none in thoughts to any other. If it be betrayed, it bears it, for its ground and spring is the mercies and forgiveness of God. Its crown is meekness, its life is everlasting love unfeigned; and takes its kingdom with entreaty and not with contention, and keeps it by lowliness of mind. In God alone it can rejoice, though none else regard it, or can own its life.[14]

[14] "The Examination of James Nayler at Appleby," 1716.

Not all of the first Quaker generation could write as James Nayler wrote, and not all of the troubles of the new Movement ended as gloriously as did the Nayler episode. The very rejection of the leader principle, which was intrinsic to the movement, led naturally to dissension, most of which is not of sufficient importance to record. The conviction that the Light of Christ could shine directly in each heart led some Friends to a position which can only be termed spiritual anarchy. Within twenty years of the beginning, Fox realized that the Movement had to have some formal structure, especially that which is involved in regular times and places of meeting. A few religious anarchists opposed this development and caused a small division which was reflected even in America, particularly in the Southern colonies in the 1670's.

The first great burst of new life came to an end with the cessation of persecution and with the death of Barclay and Fox in 1690 and 1691. There was still much greatness after the initial period, some of which will be mentioned in later chapters of this book, but Quaker life in the second period was inevitably different. Without the clear and present danger of imprisonment Friends became a more quiet people and soon began to illustrate some of the features which are part of the familiar caricature of the mild and decent Quaker who gets rich by honest dealing and by tending to his own business. Since the number of Quakers in the colonies soon outnumbered those in the mother country, the spiritual center of gravity tended to move westward. With widespread locations, from which it was not easy to keep in close touch with Friends in London, the Quakers of different areas naturally began to move in different directions. One important counterbalance to local aberrations was the beneficent practice of almost constant visiting, a practice brilliantly illustrated in John Woolman's visit to Friends in North Carolina.

Important and effective as the traveling ministry was, deep differences began to arise and it was soon evident that opposing groups of Friends were on a collision course. The result was a disastrous division between what we may term "liberal" and "orthodox" Friends in 1827. Because this division has been so largely transcended in our generation there is little value in detailed discussion of the unhappy events which came to a climax midway in the three hundred years of Quaker history, but it is important to say that all of the divisions have arisen out of a particular or exclusive emphasis on some one aspect of the basic Quaker faith, to the consequent neglect of other elements of the total faith. Always, it has been possible for each side in a controversy to quote something or somebody from the earliest period of vitality, precisely because it was so rich in its ingredients.

Of all the surprising features of Quakerism, one of the most surprising is that of the wide inequality between Quaker numbers and Quaker influence. By ordinary standards, Quakers have never been numerous and, even though there are some vigorous attempts at renewal today, the Quaker population is not keeping pace with the general population growth. It is not easy to know how many professed Quakers there are today, but it can be confidently stated that the number hardly exceeds 200,000. This number seems pitifully small, yet the influence has, by any valid standard of measurement, been enormous. The literary references, the scientific influences, the attacks on social evils, the educational impact— all these have made a tremendous difference in the world and continue to make a difference. Why is this true?

We have part of an answer when we realize that, implicit in the Quaker Way of Life, there has always, or nearly always, been what may be termed a holy worldliness. The words of Christ about salt, light, and leaven have been taken seriously. The ultimate test of the Quaker Movement is not to be found in the efficiency of its own organization, which is sometimes almost nonexistent, but rather in the difference made in governments, schools, economics, and social habits. Because William Penn is the best-known representative of the People Called Quakers, far better known, indeed, than is the founder, it is reasonable to listen to him as he tries to state the essence of this answer.

2 / The Achievement of George Fox

> Many sons have done virtuously in this day; but, dear George, thou excellest them all.
>
> WILLIAM PENN

By any reasonable standard of judgment, George Fox was a remarkable man. Though Quakerism is not merely the lengthened shadow of this man, it could never have been started without him. He grew up far from centers of population and influence; he had very little education; he possessed no important connections except those which he created. Nevertheless, he became a powerful influence and he has certainly left his mark to this day. He was a strong man, and a good man, and he had something to say which was able to reach not only those who were unlettered like himself, but also people of privilege and education.

It was one of these privileged persons, the son of Admiral Penn, who wrote, soon after Fox died, the Preface to Fox's inimitable *Journal*. Penn's Preface is a brilliant piece of writing, the high point coming when the younger man seeks to assess the older man's character.

And truly I must say, that though God had visibly clothed him with a divine preference and authority, and indeed his very presence expressed a religious majesty, yet he never abused it, but held his place in the church of God with great meekness, and a most engaging humility and moderation. For upon all occasions, like his blessed Master, he was a servant to all; holding and exercising his eldership in the invisible power that had gathered them, with reverence to the head

20

The Christian convent and monastery are within, where the soul encloistered from sin; and in this religious house the true followers Christ carry about with them, who exempt not themselves from th conversation of the world, though they keep themselves from the ev of the world in their conversation. . . . True godliness don't turn me out of the world, but enables them to live better in it and excites the endeavors to mend it.[15]

The Quaker Movement has had some low periods, eithe through dissension or through apathy, but it has also demonstrate a truly remarkable ability for self-criticism and for renewal on th inside. In some places contemporary Quakerism is dead or dying but in others there is powerful fermenting process. One of th chief reasons for the fermenting process, where it is occurring, i the rediscovery of the essential message which led to the origina Quaker explosion in the second half of the seventeenth century. I is important, as our contemporary rediscovery proceeds, that we d not succumb to the temptation to idolize the earliest Quake period. The past cannot be repeated and ought not to be repeated even if it were possible. What is important is that the vision o greatness demonstrated in an earlier time may help men and women of this generation to know how to discover the secret of an equal vitality, with relevance to the contemporary situation.

[15] The Witness of William Penn, ed. Frederick B. Tolles and E. Gordon Alderfer (New York: The Macmillan Company, 1957), p. 48.

and care over the body; and was received, only in that spirit and power of Christ, as the first and chief elder in this age: who, as he was therefore worthy of double honour, so for the same reason it was given by the faithful of this day, because his authority was inward and not outward, and that he got it and kept it by the love of God, and power of an endless life. I write my knowledge, and not report, and my witness is true; having been with him for weeks and months together on divers occasions, and those of the nearest and most exercising nature; and that by night and by day, by sea and by land; in this and in foreign countries: and I can say I never saw him out of his place, or not a match for every service or occasion.

If Penn's witness had stood alone it would be very impressive, but it does not stand alone for it is supported by the reports of many others. It is clear that Fox was a natural leader, but there have been many natural leaders in human history. What is really amazing is that he did not become or seek to become the bishop of a new church. Instead he was satisfied to perform *function* without seeking *status*. That this was true is the chief point of Penn's analysis. Penn recognized that Fox was "the first instrument" of "that despised people, that God has in his great mercy gathered and united by his own blessed Spirit," and "whose fellowship I value above all worldly greatness," but he also recognized that Fox did not obtain or even seek any official position.

This combination of strength and humility is so rare that it would make an impact in any generation. The moral and intellectual genius of Fox has been recognized by a great variety of thinkers and historians, including Thomas Carlyle and George Bancroft. William James used Fox as a star witness in his Gifford Lectures, *The Varieties of Religious Experience*, showing how the young man was, for a time, deeply disturbed, but became highly effective when his new conviction produced integration in his personality.

The essentials of the life of Fox can be quickly told. He was born in a humble, reverent home at Drayton-in-the-Clay, now called Fenny Drayton, a tiny village of Leicestershire, in 1624. It helps us to keep our historical perspective if we remember that Fox was born one year before Charles I became King. When he was nearly twenty years old Fox experienced spiritual longings and great misgivings which he could neither explain nor deny. It seemed natural to him to go to the "priests," the state-appointed pastors of the national church, but they were singularly unhelpful. Clearly, they thought Fox was slightly deranged, and they were too superficial to understand a man who was trying to find out the very basis of a vital faith. What the priests could not give him Fox was able to find alone, by direct experience. "Then the Lord," wrote Fox later, "did let me see why there was none upon the earth that could speak to my condition, namely, that I might give Him all the glory." By the age of twenty-three, in 1647, Fox had arrived at a faith, grounded not in tradition or on the reports of other men, but in an immediate divine-human encounter, to which he referred by saying, "and this I knew experimentally."

After five years of wandering over England, talking with many, thinking much, convincing a few, and being imprisoned twice, Fox came to real maturity in the early summer of 1652. He climbed a hill on the border of Lancastershire and Yorkshire, part of the Pennine range, and there, on a beautifully clear day, arrived at a wholly new conception of his work in the world. In his vivid report he said, "the Lord let me see a-top of the hill in what places He had a great people to be gathered." From that day forward, Fox was both resolute and successful. To the north he found, especially in Westmorland, people who were called Seekers and who were only too glad to know someone who could make them into Finders. The people were as kindling, while Fox was the spark to ignite them. Soon he was speaking at Sedbergh, where there was a fair, and on Firbank Fell, a wild desolate place where Fox addressed more than a thousand people, standing on a rock and speaking for three hours.

From this time on, Fox was not alone. Many of those who heard him in 1652 became vigorous missionaries almost overnight. Some went out two by two, like the Apostles and also like those mentioned in the tenth chapter of Luke's Gospel. Fox was probably influenced by the Gospel parallel in estimating that there were seventy ministers whom the Lord raised up and sent out of the north country. At first, says Fox, the religious leaders were not seriously disturbed when they observed this powerful missionary effort, since they prophesied that "within a month we should be all scattered again and come to nothing." Far from this prediction coming true, these people inspired by Fox went to many parts of the world, including various sections of the European continent and nearly all of the English colonies in America.

In the same summer Fox, with some companions, traveled to Ulverston, in that remote part of Lancashire which lies northwest of Morecambe Bay, and there Fox first met the remarkable family named Fell. Though Judge Fell never became a Quaker, his wife Margaret did and was, indeed, the most influential woman of the new Movement. Her great house, Swarthmore Hall, provided the wandering Quaker preachers with a base, to which they could return when worn out in the field. Because of Judge Fell's great influence, Quakers were relatively safe from severe persecution and imprisonment if they were known to be his guests.

For the next few years Fox traveled almost constantly. He had no money, but this represented no problem, because those who were not immediately involved in missionary labors supported those who were. There was not much organization, but very little was needed, for all thought of themselves as parts of a missionary band. A meeting was established at Swarthmore, but it was expected that most of the members would be away most of the time. The fellowship was real, but it was not primarily geographic or residential.

The *Journal* of Fox, one of the famous books of the world, is chiefly a record of his missionary journeys. He suffered eight imprisonments, two prior to the Pendle Hill experience and six afterward. His longest imprisonment, amounting to two years and eight months (1664–1666), was at Lancaster and Scarborough, for refusal to take the oath of Supremacy and Allegiance. His most terrible punishment was at Launceton in Cornwall, in 1656, where he was put "into Doomsdale, a nasty stinking place where they said few people came out alive; where they used to put witches and murderers before their execution; where the prisoners' excrement had not been carried out for scores of years, as it was said. It was all like mire, and in some places at the top of the shoes."[1] Doomsdale had neither toilet facilities nor chimney. Though the prisoners would have been willing to clean the foul place, they were not permitted to do so, and the jailer would not allow them to have beds or straw on which to lie.

The fact that Fox could survive eight imprisonments, as well as many beatings, is some indication of the ruggedness of his physique. Though somewhat depleted in strength at the end, Fox continued to speak and to write to the day of his death. In 1669, at the age of forty-five, Fox married Margaret Fell, the widow of Judge Fell, and, after this, considered Swarthmore his home, though he was not often able to enjoy its comforts.

The journeys of Fox, outside his native land, were to Ireland in 1669, to the Barbados, Jamaica, and the American colonies for two years (1671–1673), to Holland and Germany for three months in 1677, and to Holland for seven weeks in 1684. In his first visit to Holland Fox was accompanied by several of his strongest associates, particularly Robert Barclay, William Penn, and George Keith. In the long American journey Fox visited groups of Friends in Maryland, on Long Island, in Rhode Island, and in the Southern colonies of Virginia and North Carolina. His major American base was the eastern shore of Maryland, where Friends gathered in great numbers, coming chiefly by boat. The entire journey was marked by almost incredible hardships. For example, Fox went ashore at Point Comfort, but, he wrote, "the weather

[1] *Journal of George Fox*, ed. John L. Nickalls (Cambridge: The University Press, 1952), p. 252.

was so cold, that though we made a good fire in the woods to lie by, our water, that we had got for our use, was frozen near the fireside."[2] Soon after his return from America, and before he could accompany his wife to their home, Fox suffered his last imprisonment, amounting to fourteen months.

He died on the 13th of January, 1691 (Eleventh Month, 1690, Old Style), and was buried in the Friends burial ground, near Bunhill Fields, in London, in the presence of about four thousand people. A few days earlier, as Fox came out of his last meeting, in which he spoke with great power, he remarked, "Now I am clear, I am fully clear."

George Fox lived in a great age, but he did not know it. Those who have read and appreciated Alfred North Whitehead's Lowell Lectures, *Science and the Modern World*, have been struck by the characterization of the seventeenth century as "The Century of Genius." The more we contemplate this age the more we recognize the accuracy of Professor Whitehead's pithy expression.

It is the one century which consistently, and throughout the whole range of human activities, provided intellectual genius adequate for the greatness of its occasions. The crowded stage of this hundred years is indicated by the coincidences which mark its literary annals. At its dawn Bacon's *Advancement of Learning* and Cervantes' *Don Quixote* were published in the same year [1605]. . . . The first quarto edition of Hamlet appeared in the preceding year. Shakespeare and Cervantes died on the same day, April 23, 1616. In the spring Harvey expounded the circulation of blood.[3]

The century was glorious in philosophy, in natural science, in literature, and in religious thought. Any sensitive visitor to the seventeenth-century room of the National Portrait Gallery in London is bound to be deeply and favorably impressed. The century was adorned by Descartes, Locke, Spinoza, and many

[2] The text used here is that of the Tercentenary edition, ed. Norman Penney (Everyman's Library, 1924), p. 303.
[3] *Science and the Modern World* (New York: The Macmillan Company, 1948), pp. 58, 59.

more in philosophy. In science we encounter the names of Galileo, Boyle, and Newton, with the founding of the Royal Society. In literature we have the gigantic figure of John Milton, but he did not stand alone. In religious thought we can be grateful for Blaise Pascal, Richard Baxter, Jeremy Taylor, John Bunyan, and many more. Part of the paradox is that most literate people would add here the name of George Fox.

The nature of Fox's training and experience was such that he was not directly influenced by the great ideas of his time. Robert Barclay could quote the Cambridge Platonists and William Penn was aware of a rich literary inheritance, but Fox belonged to another order. The spiritual life, as he saw it, was nearly extinct. The clergymen whom he met were superficial in their understanding both of his problems and of their own vocation. Most of them, he thought, had entered the pastorate as a trade, without any sense of urgency or any real commitment to the cause of Christ. Since he was apparently not much of a reader, he probably was unaware of the works of Bunyan and Baxter, but his friend, Nayler, did write an *Answer to Baxter*.

It is important to know that, though Fox may have been ignorant of the writings of Baxter, Baxter knew about the followers of Fox and, while objecting to their theology, admired their courage. Quakers often bore the brunt of persecution arising from the Quaker Act of 1662 and the Conventicle Acts of 1664 and 1670, because they continued to meet openly, while the ordinary nonconformists avoided imprisonment by meeting secretly. That this was well understood by Richard Baxter is shown as follows:

The fanatics called Quakers did greatly relieve the sober people for a time; for they were so resolute, and gloried in their constancy and sufferings that they assembled openly and were dragged away daily to the Common Gaol, and yet desisted not, but the rest came the next day nevertheless, so that the Gaol at Newgate was filled with them. Abundance of them died in prison and yet they continued their assemblies still—yea many turned Quakers because the Quakers kept their meetings openly and went to prison for it cheerfully.[4]

[4] *Reliquiae Baxterianae*, Pt. II, p. 437.

Most periods include elements of both darkness and light, but the seventeenth century shows them in extreme. The low opinion held by Fox about the general level of the clergy was probably accurate, but there were a few men of the very highest intellectual and spiritual stature and there was a great ferment among the common people. However dull the church life may have been, there was magnificent religious interest in the army and in all ordinary people whose minds were influenced by the last great wave of Puritanism. It has not been standard practice to think of Fox as a Puritan, and in one sense he was not, but there is no chance, whatever, of understanding this powerful man apart from his Puritan heritage. This is why Hugh Barbour's doctoral dissertation at Yale, now published as *The Quakers in Puritan England*, is so important for scholarship.

"Puritanism," says Barbour with conviction, "has been the greatest religious movement in English history,"[5] and there is much evidence to support this claim. It is highly unfortunate that, at the present time in the latter part of the twentieth century, it is still conventional to sneer at Puritanism. Puritans are caricatured as dull men, destructive of art and literature, who neither have any fun themselves nor want anyone else to have any. Such a caricature is possible only for the ignorant. How, for example, can the conventional sneer be made consistent with any genuine understanding of Milton?

The Puritan Movement, while it could never be identified with any one organization, was a dominant influence in England for a full century and did much to set the stage for what we now see as the emergence of genius in various areas of human endeavor. Puritanism was the plain man's revolt against the evils of priestcraft and all religion which centers in mere ceremonialism. The statues were removed, not primarily in order to destroy art, but because, in many instances, they had become idols. The Puritan started with a deep conviction of the sovereignty of God and ended with a daily life of Goodness, not because of his own merit,

[5] *Op. cit.*, p. 2.

but as a reasonable response to God's mercy. Believing that God had directly changed his life, the characteristic Puritan saw that the consequence had to be a changed society, whether in the army, or a daily vocation, or the state. Each man, he thought, must, on his pilgrim way in this short life, seek to find the life to which God has called him. Here is a marvelous antidote to any cult of self-indulgence and the empty freedom of self-expression. A Puritan was a soldier under orders, whose task it was to learn what the orders were and to follow them. It is no wonder that Cromwell's army seemed irresistible.

Efforts to connect the development of George Fox's ideas with medieval mysticism have failed, but there can be no doubt of the influence of the entire climate of opinion which Puritanism made ubiquitous, and which included mystical elements of its own. As early as 1628 there was, in England, an English translation of the famous *Theologia Germanica*, made by John Everard. This book, admired by Luther, was a classic statement of the possibility of the real encounter of God with the human soul. The respect for the godly layman, the hatred of ecclesiastical hierarchy, the emphasis on plain dress, even the use of "thee" and "thou" in place of the fashionable "you"—all these are in the mood of a pervasive Puritan mentality. The Quaker Movement went beyond this inheritance, but that it was truly an inheritance is foolish to deny. There were evils and dangers in Puritanism, as there are evils and dangers in Quakerism, but the grandeur of the Puritan conception of human dignity is almost overwhelming when seriously studied and understood.

Fox came to young manhood in the period of outstanding Puritan victories. The Civil War broke out in 1642, when Fox was only eighteen. How much the young man of Drayton understood of the war we do not know, but it is impossible to suppose that he was totally unaffected by it. At first King Charles was successful in opposing those who sought to have a constitutional government, because he had command of the army, but, after a year of defeat, the Long Parliament called to their aid the Scotch. The Scottish price meant a real victory for Puritanism in general, since the "Solemn League and Covenant" of 1643 involved the agreement to establish Presbyterianism as the religion of England. Archbishop Laud, the most hated of the royal ecclesiastics, was executed, and the way seemed open to the establishment of a noble experiment in government, not radically different in spirit from that which Penn tried, forty years later, to set up in Pennsylvania. The general purpose, in the words of the Covenant, states "that we and our posterity after us may, as brethren, live in faith and love, and the Lord may delight to dwell in the midst of us." When Fox, a little later, said that Christ had come to teach His people Himself, he was, in part, claiming that what had been seen as a hope had actually, in one phase of society, come to pass in sober fact.

The military victory of Parliament was won by the amazing discipline and courage of Cromwell's army, made up so largely of men who sought God's rule in their own lives. Charles I was executed in 1649, the same year that was marked, in the life of Fox, by imprisonment for the first time.

The great religious burst of the seventeenth century, including that in the mind of George Fox, came, not in a period of calmness, but during the strain and stress of a terrible civil war. The war, as might be expected, stirred up new ideas and also led to moral and spiritual decay. The scene of vitality and of discouragement seems to have provided an ideal seedbed for the thinking of young Fox. Richard Baxter, himself a member of Cromwell's army, was honest enough to see the spiritual dangers inherent in the turmoil, though he entertained no doubt concerning the justice of the Parliamentary cause.

It is as natural for both wars and private contention to produce errors, schisms, contempt of magistracy, ministers and ordinances, as it is for a dead carrion to breed worms and vermin. Believe it from one that hath too many years experience of both in armies and garrisons, it

is as hard a thing to maintain, even in your people, a sound understanding, a tender conscience, a lively, gracious, heavenly frame of
spirit, and an upright life in a way of war and contention, as to keep
your candle lighted in the greatest storms or under the water.[6]

Part of the explanation of the achievement of George Fox is
that he was affected by the civil war and yet was not directly
involved in it. He missed the corruption of army and garrison life,
so vividly described by Richard Baxter, but he nevertheless participated in the general upheaval of ideas. Though not highly literate,
and certainly not a reader of the learned works of his time nor of
very many of the printed sermons of the Puritan preachers, which
poured from the press in a steady stream, young Fox was bound to
be affected by the exciting ideas which were major causes of the
civil war and which led to the execution of the King, with the
emergence of Oliver Cromwell as the dominant figure.

Early in 1646, when Fox was only twenty-one years old, he
traveled to Coventry and, as he entered the city, had his first great
insight, which started the process by which he was changed from a
Seeker into a Finder. On the surface this insight seems fairly
simple, but it did not seem simple to him. The insight was
extremely basic for it was really his answer to the question "What
is a Christian?" Christians, he saw, are believers, but there is a
world of difference between the appearance and the reality. The
mark of a true believer is a changed life! Many, therefore, who say
that they are believers really are not and they never are unless they
are changed from death to life. Therefore, no person can become
a Christian by a mere ceremony, however beautiful or however
ancient; the reality of the new life is all that counts. If we have the
reality, nothing else is required, and if we do not have the reality,
nothing else will suffice. Seen in its full implication, the emphasis
on reality, and nothing but reality, is a powerful starting point.

As Fox's first insight was an answer to what it means to be a
Christian, his second insight was an answer to what it means to be

---

[6] *The Saints Everlasting Rest*, Pt. 3, Chap. 14, 10.

a minister. Because it was the common belief of the people, said Fox, he had assumed uncritically that the ministry was a trade or an occupation, like any other, and that a man could qualify for it by attending a trade school, in this case Oxford or Cambridge. Fox saw, in a blazing light, that a theological education was not sufficient for a true ministry, and in his own career he proved that it was not necessary.[7]

A minister, Fox saw, is one who ministers, and again the touchstone is reality. Therefore all externals, such as ordination, apostolic succession, laying on of hands, etc., seemed to the clear mind of Fox as nothing. What a man is cannot be changed by what is done to him externally. If the ministry is a holy calling rather than a trade, it is naturally open to all, whether male or female. It was no accident that so many of the strong Quaker preachers were women, for in Christ there is neither male nor female, as there is neither lay nor clerical. If God really sets a man on fire, he will ignite others, and that, Fox thought, is what the ministry means. It is something that occurs, not something that can be arranged artificially.[8]

The third major insight, which came soon after the first two, was an answer to another fundamental question, "What is the Church?" Though people generally referred to a building as a church, young Fox quickly saw that this usage was erroneous. God, he was assured, does not dwell in temples made with hands. Earlier he had accepted the general view of his neighbors, both lay and clerical, that there is such a thing as holy ground, and that the church building is a holy place, which houses or commercial

[7] Barbour, op. cit., p. 2.

[8] That Fox was not alone, in his time, in saying that a university training cannot make a minister is shown by one of the writings of John Milton, Considerations Touching the Likeliest Way to Remove Hirelings out of the Church (1659). In it Milton says: "It is a fond error, though too much believed among us, to think that the university makes a minister of the Gospel: what it may conduce to other arts or sciences I dispute not now, but that which makes fit a minister the Scripture can but inform us to be only from above."

buildings are not. Fox, in his third insight, challenged the popular view directly. "But the Lord shewed me, so that I did see clearly," he said, "that he did not dwell in these temples which men had commanded and set up, but in people's hearts."[9]

The church meant a great deal to Fox, so much so, indeed, that he could not identify it either with bricks and stones or with an ecclesiastical hierarchy. Again he was concerned with reality and the major reality, he was convinced, was the living fellowship. This, of course, was the logical conclusion of the general Puritan conception of the church, but it was left to Fox to envision it with absolute clarity. One consequence of this insight was a change in language. No longer would Fox call an ecclesiastical building a "church." Instead it was a "steeple-house." This insight also affected subsequent Quaker practice and is the deepest reason why Quaker places of worship, when later they were built, were normally called meetinghouses. By such terminology Quakers have sought to avoid the suggestion that there is any distinction between holy places and secular places. The meetinghouse is not sacred, but is merely a convenience. God can reach men in barns or in prisons or anywhere. In the language of the late Martin Buber, "All real life is meeting."

The early twenties of his life were for Fox times of inner turmoil as well as of intellectual excitement, when he got very little assistance from other men. His greatest help came from an almost constant study of the Bible. What we call insights he called "openings," and he was delighted when these supported one another in a coherent picture or were consistent with what he discovered in the Scriptures. "When I had openings, they answered one another and answered the Scriptures, for I had great openings of the Scriptures; and when I was in troubles, one trouble also answered to another."[10]

Of the major insights which brought some order into the

---

[9] *Journal*, ed. John L. Nickalls, p. 8.
[10] *Ibid.*, p. 9.

outlook of Fox in his early twenties, the fourth was the most important. The heart of this was the realization that he could base his faith, not merely upon reasonings, and not on reports of the experience of other men in other ages, but rather upon a firsthand acquaintance with Jesus Christ in the living present. If Christ is a *cause* living reality, and not a merely historical figure, He can be known directly, here and now, as truly as He was known by Peter and John in Galilee. This was, to Fox, an extremely exciting and clarifying idea. It meant that his religion did not need to rest upon anything secondhand. His fourth insight was absolutely crucial to what is called The Quaker Way, in so far as that "way" is fundamentally empirical rather than speculative. Like science, Quakerism is, and always has been, since the young manhood of George Fox, more a method than a system of beliefs. Even though beliefs are important, it is missing the point to ask "What does a Quaker believe?" What is far more relevant is to ask how a Quaker seeks to relate to that on which he ultimately depends. Fox sought to be a follower of Christ and he learned, in experience, rather than in speculation, that he could know Christ directly, in his own inner consciousness. To make the point abundantly clear he added the sentence to which allusion has already been made, "This I knew experimentally." It would have meant the same if he had written "experientially." The crucial passage in the *Journal*, describing the fourth insight, refers to what occurred at the age of twenty-three, as follows:

Now after I had that opening from the Lord that to be bred at Oxford or Cambridge was not sufficient to fit a man to be a minister of Christ, I regarded the priests less, and looked more after the dissenting people. Among them I saw there was some tenderness, and many of them came afterwards to be convinced, for they had some openings. But as I had forsaken the priests, so I left the Separate preachers also, and those called the most experienced people; for I saw there was none among them all that could speak to my condition. And when all my hopes in them and in all men were gone, so that I had nothing outwardly to help me, nor could I tell what to do, then, Oh! then, I heard a voice which said, "There is one, even Christ Jesus, that can speak to thy condition; and when I heard it my heart did leap for joy."[11]

It is not difficult to see how revolutionary this concept was. If the experience recorded by Fox was veridical, he was bound to have a new attitude toward the Bible, toward sacraments, toward tradition, toward the whole problem of how to live. If genuine firsthand religious experience is possible, there still remain many questions to be answered, but we have a tremendous place from which to start. Here was the fulcrum of Archimedes, comparable to that so termed by Descartes in his *Discourse on Method*. If Christ can be known directly, many of the things which men have thought necessary begin to take second place. It was not strange that, after this, Fox did not feel the further necessity of consulting the priests. He had learned that he could go to the Source!

Once Fox had received his four basic insights, he had the essentials of a message which was destined to make a great difference in the world, but not until he was twenty-eight did the whole thing come together in his mind in a truly effective manner. Meantime, he reported that he had great temptations and his inward sufferings were severe. "I could find none to open my condition to but to the Lord alone, unto whom I cried night and day." He seems to have been sorely troubled by what we should call the problem of evil. His conclusion was that, while the evil was real, it was not ultimate. "I saw also that there was an ocean of darkness and death, but an infinite ocean of light and love, which flowed over the ocean of darkness. In that also I saw the infinite love of God; and I had great openings."[12]

Many have sought to know what happened in the summer of 1652 to produce a radical change in the achievement of Fox. The best guess is that he suddenly saw the way in which his separate

[11] P. 11.
[12] *Ibid.*, p. 19.

convictions could be parts of a unified whole and that this whole was something for which other people were waiting. He sensed that many, besides himself, were dissatisfied with secondhand religion and suddenly he saw how he could provide the word which people longed to hear.

The essence of this new word was that Christ can be encountered in the Present Tense. Suddenly Fox realized that men are not fully satisfied with knowing what once *was*, just as they are not satisfied with hopes of the distant future. The continuous, immediate present is the most exciting of all tenses, because the present is really all that we have. As Fox approached Pendle Hill, in the late spring of 1652, he was conscious of a divine message to the effect that power would come, not merely from knowing the Scriptures, but rather from participating in the same spirit from which the Scriptures arose. Any person, he saw, who could, in the present, stand where the prophets and Apostles once stood, would, as a consequence, shake all the country for ten miles around. Suddenly he recognized the vast difference between *knowledge about* and *acquaintance with*. With this conception fresh in his mind, Fox climbed Pendle Hill where, says Penn, he had his ecumenical vision. After this he had something powerful to say and at last he knew how to say it.

The first important result of the Pendle Hill experience came at Sedbergh, where Fox made his first public use of the idea of Christ as the present *Teacher*. "There I declared the everlasting Truth of the Lord and the word of life for several hours, and that the Lord Christ Jesus was come to teach his people himself, and bring them off all the world's ways and teachers to Christ their way to God."[13] When he addressed the great crowd on Firbank Fell, the next Sunday, Fox centered on the same moving theme to the effect that it was possible to have an experience of Christ in the living present. He told the multitude that they "might all come to

[13] *Ibid.,* p. 107.

know Christ, their teacher, their counsellor, their shepherd to feed them, and their bishop to oversee them, and to know their bodies to be the temples of God and Christ for them to dwell in."[14]

Clearly this was heady stuff. It was extremely moving to the rank and file, who could see how different from conventional religion all this was. But it was also highly disturbing to the priests who rightly recognized that, if what Fox said was true, their function was not necessary, as had previously been supposed. If we have access to the Head Teacher, why do we need the lesser ones?

The conception of the possibility of the *present* experience of Christ is more fundamental than any other in the entire system of Quaker thought. Even the famous conception of the inner light was understood to be the Light of Christ in the individual human heart now. This is why Fox rejected the premillennial predictions about Christ coming to reign a thousand years. The mistake of these deluded people, he said, was that "they looked upon this reign to be outward, when He was come inwardly in the hearts of His people, to reign and rule there."

During his worst imprisonment, in 1656, Fox made the clearest emphasis on the living present, employing the older English form of the present perfect tense, and saying, "Christ is come." Obviously influenced by the metaphor of the everlasting knocking (Rev. 3:20), Fox's message from prison was "But Christ is come, and doth dwell in the hearts of His people and reigns there. And thousands, at the door of whose hearts he hath been knocking, have opened to him, and he is come in, and doth sup with them and they with him."[15]

While in prison in 1656, Fox wrote a remarkable exhortation to "Friends in the ministry," which included an attractive phrase which has had wide use in the twentieth century. A major task of a minister, he wrote, is that of "answering." By this he apparently

[14] *Ibid.*, p. 109.
[15] *Ibid.*, p. 261.

meant that it is possible to nurture and to bring to fulfillment the vague yearnings toward the divine, which are in all men, but which are often underdeveloped. The minister, then, is the one who helps to make actual what otherwise is only potential. The Quaker ministers were urged to *answer* "that of God in them all," even their adversaries. The multiple task, he wrote, included "*spreading* the Truth abroad, *awakening* the witness, *confounding* deceit, *gathering*."[16] The consequence, Fox promised, is that "you will come to walk cheerfully over the world, answering that of God in every one." Only a very remarkable man could write from such a foul prison about "walking cheerfully over the world."

To many of his contemporaries who heard about Fox he undoubtedly appeared to be merely another of the wild-eyed men who adorned the left wing of the Puritan Movement. Some of the things which he said still sound very much like those reported by William Haller in his brilliant book, *The Rise of Puritanism*. Like many of the Puritan preachers, Fox was a bold or even harsh controversialist, and the titles of his tracts sound equally bitter. When, after his debate with Roger Williams in Rhode Island, Fox entitled his report *The Boasting Baptist Badly Beaten*, he was operating with a familiar pattern. Henry Burton was haled before the privy council, in 1627, for publishing a pamphlet called *The Baiting of the Pope's Bull* and was imprisoned, in 1629, for publishing another: *Babel no Bethel*. Even many of Fox's expressions were common elements of the Puritan ethic, that concerning the children of the light being a fair example. In 1636, Thomas Goodwin had published a volume of sermons entitled A *Child of Light Walking in Darkness*.

The two great figures of speech of the Puritan mood, both vividly portrayed in the literary works of John Bunyan, were those of the *pilgrim* and the *warrior*. It seems almost inevitable that a man, with Bunyan's genius and background, should have written *Pilgrim's Progress* and *The Holy War*. The Puritans even had the

[16] *Ibid.*, p. 263. Italics added.

practice of allowing several to speak in a religious meeting, rather than depending on one man. How, then, was the achievement of Fox different from theirs?

Clearly Fox was different from the scholarly Puritans who poured out from Cambridge for so many years, because he was not and did not claim to be a learned man. Superficially, therefore, he was classed with the riffraff of ranters. One of the most vocal of these was Lodowick Muggleton, a London tailor turned preacher, who claimed to have great revelations. He and his cousin John Reeve announced, in 1652, the same year that Fox had his Pendle Hill experience, that they were the two witnesses of Revelation 11. The sect which they founded, called Muggletonians, lingered on in a feeble way for two hundred years, before it finally died. What is there in the message of Fox which has made the Movement which he founded so much more dynamic and enduring than theirs?

The answer is undoubtedly complex, but we know what some of the elements of it are. A very important part of Fox's achievement was that he was able to create a living fellowship, with a vivid life of its own, apart from its dependence on his personal magnetism. Though not an educated man himself, he was able to win men who were well educated, as in the examples of Barclay and Penn, and he was also able to make such persons feel that they could learn from the fellowship of men and women less privileged than themselves. The thousands of committed persons who were gathered first by Fox, and then by the help of many others, were not merely dedicated men; they were members of a truly redemptive group. They actually shared one another's burdens. When one man was taken to prison, the others, without even any discussion, supported his family. When all of the adults, in some meetings, were in prison, the children kept the meetings going, and the officers did not have the temerity to arrest them. Something of this mutual sharing has always been part of the Quaker Way and has been one of the reasons for its continuance.

The achievement of George Fox is to be measured by the group which he left when he died, a group distinguished, not only by its temporary dynamism, and not only by its ability to survive in comfort, as also in persecution, but even more by its ability to grow, if not in numbers, at least in social sensitivity. In the unlettered Fox, and in his immediate followers, the Puritan stock had sprouted a new branch. There is still the moral earnestness, there is still the dream of a holy nation, there is still the desire to know what one's divine calling is, but there is an added lightness and gaiety and there is manifest affection which transcends the hardness of the Puritan ethic. Part of the glory of George Fox was that he knew how to walk cheerfully over the world.

3 / The Quaker Aristocrats

> Fox made some converts to whom he was immeasurably
> inferior in everything except the energy of his conviction.
>
> LORD MACAULAY

Quakers have never had, or wanted to have, any shrines, because
all places can be equally holy, but the nearest approach to a
Quaker shrine is Jordans, about twenty miles west of London in
Buckinghamshire. Here is a small meetinghouse, in a country
setting, dating from the seventeenth century. Just outside the door
lie the graves of the Peningtons and the Penns. Between the
meetinghouse and the hostel there are other graves and an old
barn. Professor Rendel Harris thought that the beams of this barn,
which are evidently ship's beams, were taken from the *Mayflower*
when it was dismembered.

The whole scene is one of peace and simple beauty, and it is
associated with great people. About a mile away is the home called
the Grange, occupied, in the seventeenth century, by Isaac and
Mary Penington. At the other corner of an equilateral triangle is
Chalfont St. Giles, where stands what is known as Milton's
Cottage, an attractive place to which the blind poet repaired
during the Fire of London. It is a repository today for important
Milton documents and is managed by a knowledgeable director.
The walk on any part of the triangle is still delightful, even though
some of the rural atmosphere is rapidly being lost. Not far from
the attractive meetinghouse is the modern Jordans Village, and, a
few miles in the opposite direction, lies Stoke Poges, the scene of
Gray's *Elegy Written in a Country Churchyard*. The area is

important to Quakers, not only because of its present vitality, but also because of the reminders of events three hundred years ago, when it was the scene of important developments. Here grew up Gulielma Springett, daughter of Mary Penington, who became the first wife of William Penn.

In her book, *The Roman Way*, Edith Hamilton explained, with her customary clarity, her method of presenting Roman life, when she wrote: "What the Romans did has always interested me much less than what they were, and what the historians have said they were is beyond all comparison less interesting to me than what they themselves said." The same principle applies in understanding the People called Quakers. The Quaker Way of life has been produced, not primarily by a system of church government nor by the affirmation of a creed, but by the actual life of a people. Fortunately these people have been among the most prolific of writers, and of no local group is this more true than those who were connected, in one way or another, with Jordans. The total volume of the published writings of the Peningtons, Ellwood, and Penn is immense. Some of their writing was done, however, not in the beautiful setting of Buckinghamshire, but in prisons.

Though the earliest of those aroused by the stinging message of George Fox were exceedingly humble men and women, often with little or no education, this situation was soon altered, and it was altered first in the person of Isaac Penington. When Penington began to make acquaintance with any Quakers, he was repelled by them as individuals and disappointed in their message. They seemed to him, he said, "a poor, weak, silly, contemptible generation who had some smatterings of truth in them." The rudeness of the first Quakers whom he met deeply offended this sensitive man. "How ridiculous," he wrote, "was their manner of coming forth and appearance to the eye of man! About what poor, trivial circumstances, habits, gestures and things did they seem to lay great weight and make great matters of moment. . . . I cannot wonder that any wise man, or sort of professors, did, or do yet despise them." But when this fastidious gentleman heard George Fox, he changed his mind.

Isaac Penington was born in 1616, the eldest son of Sir Isaac Penington, Lord Mayor of London at the outbreak of the Civil War (1642–1643), and representative of the City of London in the Long Parliament. In 1649, the elder Penington was one of the judges of King Charles I, though he declined to sign the death warrant. The Peningtons represented the finest and purest strain of those who were loyal to the Puritan ethic. Nevertheless, young Penington became dissatisfied with the official religion and, for a time, joined himself with an Independent congregation. Soon he parted with the Congregationalists and admitted that he was a Seeker, looking for help everywhere. The first of the Quaker writings which met his eye repelled him. As early as 1649, Penington was showing himself an expert writer, producing "Glimpses of the Heart of Man. . . . drawn with a dark pencill by a dark hand in the midst of Darkness." In 1650, he published "Several Fresh inward Openings," and a year later "Life of a Christian." His books were essentially a continuation of the torrent of Puritan writings which provided the material for Professor William Haller's great book. It was of this stream of writing, to which Penington's early work belongs, that Haller could say, "I have not been able to read them without renewed amazement at the extraordinary vitality of Puritan thought and character or without feeling that I have drawn near to the central fire which still burns in the pages of Milton."[1]

A major event in Penington's life was his marriage, in 1654, to Mary Proud Springett, widow of Sir William Springett and mother of the future wife of William Penn. This gifted woman, who had been a widow for eleven years, had already gone through many stages of religious turmoil. When she and her first husband

[1] *The Rise of Puritanism* (New York: Harper & Row, Torchbook edition, 1957), Preface.

THE QUAKER ARISTOCRATS / 43

were married in 1641, their Puritan convictions were so intense
that they refused even the use of a ring. They also refused the
singing of the Psalms in metre and the use of bread and wine in
Holy Communion. The earnest young mother, when the child,
Gulielma, was born, would not permit her to be baptized. "I was
so vehement in prayer," she wrote, "that I chose the more remote
places to pray in, that I might not be heard to pray, and could not
but be loud in the earnest pouring out of my soul." For a while,
before marrying Penington, she despaired of finding religious truth
and turned to frivolity. This remarkable woman, with a striking
literary flair, wrote her *Experiences*, but the book was not published in her lifetime. Part of the manuscript lay concealed for
nearly forty years behind the wainscoting in a room of William
Penn's house at Worminghurst in Sussex.

Not long after her second marriage, when Mary Penington was
walking in a park with her new husband, a Quaker stopped the
aristocratic couple, reproved them for their gay clothing, and then
gave witness to the new life which he had experienced. This was a
vivid example of the bold faithfulness in witness on the part of the
earliest Quaker missionaries. They took advantage of all opportunities and ran, consequently, the risk of having to suffer insult-
ing rebuffs. Isaac Penington quickly outargued the man, but two
others, better qualified, came to see the Peningtons on the following day, after which Mary reported that "their solid and weighty
carriage struck a dread over me."

Being of a high social position, the Peningtons had much to lose
by the decision to become Quakers. The most obvious marks of
the new way of life, which was at the same time both attractive
and repellent to them, were those of "hat honor" and the "plain
language." Most Quakers, convinced of the ultimate equality of
men before God, refused to use flattering titles in addressing
supposed superiors or to doff the hat. We must remember that, in
the seventeenth century, when the hat was commonly worn in the
house, it was a clear mark of deference to be uncovered. This is

why Quaker men were careful to remove their hats during prayer, though their stout egalitarianism would not let them give other men what they reserved for Almighty God. Since "you" was the polite form of the second personal pronoun, it was expected to be used by inferiors while addressing superiors. If a servant addressed his master as "thou," this constituted a gross affront, an act of insubordination. Fox and his followers determined to use the singular of the second person in all cases, not in order to be queer, but in order to make a witness about something significant in the relationship between man and man. It is important for us to understand that this was not a piece of capricious trifling. The practice of saying "thou" put every would-be Quaker to the test, since each one who refused to engage in conventional flattery ran a serious risk of seeming to be crude or even insolent.

Both Penn and Barclay, in upholding the Quaker practice of not giving greater respect to people of high station, made use of a passage in a letter to the Roman matron Celantia, attributed to Jerome.

Heed not thy nobility, nor let that be a reason for thee to take place of any; repute not those of meaner extraction to be thy inferiors, our religion admits no respect of persons, nor doth it lead us to value the outward condition of men, but their inward frame and spirit: it is hereby that we pronounce men noble or base. With God, not to serve sin is the only freedom, and to excel in virtue is to be noble. . . . Besides it is a folly for any to boast his gentility, since all are equally esteemed by God. . . . Nor is it material to what estate a man is born, since all are equally new creatures in Christ.

Perhaps the boldest application of this principle is that of Robert Barclay in his address to King Charles II, which introduced his famous *Apology*. Barclay said "thee" to the King, exactly as he would have done to an equal or to a supposed inferior. Warning the King against temptations, Barclay wrote:

Against which snare, as well as the temptation of those that may or do feed thee, and prompt thee to evil, the most excellent and prevalent remedy will be, to apply thyself to that Light of Christ, which shineth in thy conscience; which neither can nor will flatter thee, nor suffer thee to be at ease in thy sins; but doth and will deal plainly and faithfully with thee, as those that are followers thereof have also done.

The time came when the Peningtons decided to make the big break with their former way of life and to become known openly as Quakers. In January, 1658, a General Meeting of Friends was held in Buckinghamshire, from which it was reported, "Isaac Penington and his wife grow in the knowledge of the truth: they were there and others of his family." The major step came in May, 1658, when Penington publicly joined the new Movement, apparently under the powerful influence of Fox, who was present, and immediately he felt that he had reached the end of a long and tortuous spiritual journey. The works of both Isaac and Mary Penington are filled with some of the most vivid and persuasive reports of firsthand religious experiences which are to be found in any literature of any generation.

As was to prove true in the experience of Penn and other privileged persons on turning Quaker, Penington was faced at once with bitter hostility on the part both of his father and of his closest associates. His father wrote to say that he no longer had any comfort in him, but Penington was not in the least deterred. He had advanced beyond the situation in which his religion was a matter of convention or even of inference, to the place in which he was convinced by what seemed to him to be direct *experience*. We are fortunate that he had the gift of writing in glowing words and that he was, therefore, able to give classic expression to the central Quaker experience of knowing the God and Father of Jesus Christ. His words, which are clearly independent of changing fashions of theology, are as follows:

At last, after all my distresses, wanderings and sore travels, I met with some writings of this people called Quakers, which I cast a slight eye upon and disdained, as falling very short of that wisdom, light, life and power, which I had been longing for and searching after. . . . After a long time, I was invited to hear one of them (as I had been often, they in tender love pitying me and feeling my want of that which they possessed). . . . When I came, I felt the presence and power of the Most High among them, and words of truth from the Spirit of truth reaching to my heart and conscience, opening my state as in the presence of the Lord. Yea, I did not only feel words and demonstrations from without, but I felt the dead quickened, the seed raised; insomuch as my heart, in the certainty of light and clearness of true sense, said: "This is he: this is he; there is no other; this is he whom I have waited for and sought after from my childhood, who was always near me, and had often begotten life in my heart, but I knew him not distinctly, nor how to receive him or dwell with him." And then in this sense (in the melting and breakings of my spirit), was I given up to the Lord, to become his, both in waiting for the further revealing of his seed in me, and to serve him in the life and power of his seed.

But some may desire to know what I have at last met with. I answer, "I have met with the Seed." Understand that word, and thou wilt be satisfied and inquire no further. I have met with my God, I have met with my Saviour, and he hath not been present with me without his Salvation, but I have felt the healings drop upon my soul from under his wings. I have met with the Seed's Father, and in the Seed I have felt him my Father; there I have read his nature, his love, his compassions, his tenderness, which have melted, overcome and changed my heart before him.

Now that Penington had found a solid rock of conviction and was a Finder rather than a mere Seeker, his writings flowed in greater volume than before. With him began that adequate literary expression of the Quaker Faith which continued with Penn, Ellwood, and Barclay. Without these men the rugged apostles from the north would still have been great men, but it is very unlikely that we would ever have heard of them. It was the men of learning and literary ability who kept the Quaker Movement going, by giving it a larger and more nearly universal appeal. All of them admired Fox, but all had abilities which the rugged preacher did not have. Without them, Fox might easily have been forgotten, as happened to many of the men who made a stir during the period of the Commonwealth. The forgotten ones were like Theudas and Judas the Galilean, mentioned by the Pharisee Gamaliel in the Jewish Council. Of many a man like Fox it could have been said with truth, "he also perished, and all who followed him were scattered" (Acts 5:37). One of the major differences between Fox and Muggleton, who likewise called his followers "Friends," was that Fox could appeal, as Muggleton could not, to people of the character of the Peningtons, while they, in turn, could appeal to the world. Penington did not live, as did the others mentioned in this chapter, to see the end of persecution, for he died in 1679, at the age of sixty-three.

About fifteen miles from Jordans, at Crowell, in Oxfordshire, there lived a young gentleman named Thomas Ellwood, who became a friend of the Peningtons. At a farm called the Grove, not far from the Penington estate, Ellwood attended a Quaker meeting for the first time in December, 1659. Both Edward Burrough and James Nayler were present, this being more than three years after Nayler's fall and subsequent cruel punishment. Nayler had been released from Bridewell in September. Ellwood, only twenty years old at the time, was mightily impressed, especially by Edward Burrough. "I drank in his words with desire," he wrote later, "for they not only answered my understanding but warmed my heart with a certain heat, which I had not till then felt from the ministry of any man."

Ellwood went to the Grange, as the Peningtons' guest, in the evening, where, after supper, the servants were called in. After a short silence, Burrough began to speak about the universal free grace of God to all mankind. Ellwood's father was present and argued for Calvinistic tenets, but Nayler, now greatly restored to intellectual power, answered him effectively. After the Ellwoods had returned to Crowell, the young man finally decided to make an open break, which was indicated by his refusal to say "you" to a single person, "contrary," he said, "to the pure plain, and single language of truth." It must be understood that he and others stressed this practice as a matter of honesty. To use the plural when addressing only one was, they thought, simply dishonest.

Soon Ellwood's father, a county magistrate, sent the young man on legal business to Oxford, where he met his old school fellows. These young men saluted Ellwood in the usual manner, putting off their hats, bowing, and saying, "Your humble servant, Sir." When Ellwood stood without moving his cap or bending the knee, one acquaintance, much amused, clapped him on the shoulder, saying, "What, Tom, a Quaker?" Ellwood says that he readily and cheerfully replied, "Yes, a Quaker." He reports that, as these words were uttered, he felt joy in his heart "for I rejoiced that . . . I had strength and boldness given me to confess myself to be one of that despised people." When, after another visit to the Grange, he returned home, he said to his father, "Isaac Penington and his wife remember their loves to thee," which made his father angry. The next morning, when young Ellwood stood before his father with his hat on, it was too much, and the father beat the son with his fists, plucking off his hat and throwing it away. On one occasion the father said, "Sirrah, if ever I hear you say 'thou' or 'thee' to me again, I'll strike your teeth down your throat." Soon after this, Thomas Ellwood left Crowell for London, where he became a reader to the blind Milton. When Milton came to live at Chalfont St. Giles he was coming to the area which Ellwood, his secretary, knew well and in which Ellwood's most radical changes had occurred.

Though Thomas Ellwood rendered many services to the Quaker Movement, his most signal service was that of editing the *Journal* of George Fox, soon after the death of Fox in 1691. The original *Journal* as dictated by Fox was an exceedingly crude piece of writing, though containing elements of power. The leading Friends could easily see that a vast amount of editorial work was needed and this Ellwood, as a skilled writer, provided. Consequently, the standard edition of the *Journal* is called the Ellwood edition, published in 1694.

The publication of Fox's *Journal* was a big event in the life of Quakers. Because there was a rugged greatness about Fox, the uniqueness of his autobiography was guaranteed, but decent publications required the assistance of men whose gifts were different from his own. Thus assistance came largely from two men who had the capacity to take the fresh ideas of Fox and to make them understandable to the larger, literate public. These two men, Ellwood and Penn, represented the Jordans group which owed so much to Isaac Penington. The younger men, of similar gifts, carried on after Penington's death and were at the height of their intellectual powers when Fox died. The work of Ellwood in editing the mass of manuscript was of great value, but the work of the other, William Penn, was of almost equal value. The long Preface which he wrote for the *Journal*, called by him "Rise and Progress of the People Called Quakers," is really a little book. It was written when the famous colonist was back in England at almost fifty years of age, and with ample time at his disposal. The work was evidently produced in a spirit of great intensity, for three reasons: first, as a testimony to the faith of his youth, second, as a recognition of the despised people who had suffered so much, and, third, as a way of doing honor to the humble man who had been "the first instrument" of the Movement. Penn did not hesitate to call Fox "The great and blessed apostle of our day."

William Penn was far and away the best-known Quaker who ever lived. Born in 1644, the year of Milton's *Areopagitica*, he was twenty years younger than Fox, to whom he accordingly looked up as to a spiritual father. Penn's own father, Admiral Sir William Penn, was a person of distinction who played an important role in the growing British Empire. The Admiral owned vast estates in Ireland, belonged to high social circles in London, and stood in favor of the Court of Charles II. He clearly hoped that his gifted son would do him honor in following pursuits similar to his own. He was, therefore, bitterly disappointed when his son turned Quaker, and he could not have guessed that this bitter disappointment was a step toward a fabulous development in the course of which one of the finest of the English colonies would be named for himself, by his King.

A crucial event in the life of William Penn came when he was only twelve, at his father's house in County Cork, Ireland. There he heard one of the wandering Quaker preachers, Thomas Loe, a man who was a moving speaker and transparently good. The boy thought to himself, "What, if they would all be Quakers?" At sixteen, the Admiral's son was entered at Christ Church, Oxford, but a year later, in the autumn of 1661, he was expelled, much to the chagrin of the father. The primary cause of the expulsion was the production of an essay which offended the College authorities. Penn and some others were under the influence of the former Dean, John Owen, who, at the Restoration, had lost his place. Penn and a few other students held prayer meetings among themselves, not wholly different from those which the Wesleys were to hold in the following century in the same University. As a result, they were fined for their nonconformity. A mood was building up which finally made Penn the foremost champion of religious liberty in England.

"Bitter usage," said Penn, "I underwent when I returned to my father, whipping, beating and turning out of doors." In 1662, the Admiral, not knowing what else to do with his difficult son, sent him to France to finish his education among people of quality. For a while, on his return to London, Penn was a law student at Lincoln's Inn; later he tried out sea life by sailing with the fleet in April, 1665. In 1666, his father sent him to the brilliant court of the Duke of Ormonde in Ireland, where his best-known portrait, in a suit of armor, was painted. Because he was put in charge of his father's Irish estates, Penn was in Cork when Thomas Loe, whom he had heard eleven years earlier, visited again and spoke.

What Loe said about faith struck Penn deeply. Like almost all Protestants, Penn believed that men are saved by faith, but Thomas Loe showed that there are radically different *kinds* of faith. This was a new twist and exactly what Penn needed to hear. The question, he saw, is not *whether* a man has a religion, but *what kind*. "There is a faith," began Loe, "that overcomes the world; and there is a faith that is overcome by the world." At the end of the sermon the twenty-three-year-old courtier was in tears. Soon he was arrested, with others, because he attended a meeting. The Earl of Orrery released the young man, but wrote such a strong letter to the Admiral that Penn was ordered home to England. In December, 1667, Pepys wrote in his *Diary* that the younger Penn "is a Quaker again or some very melancholy thing."

The Admiral was incensed at the course of events, telling his son that, if he would leave off this Quaker foolishness, he was fitted, by training, to be one of the King's ministers. The father even tried to be tolerant, saying that the son could "thee and thou" anyone he pleased, with the exception of the King, the Duke of York, and himself. One of the first things the converted courtier did was to go to Court, in the summer of 1668, on behalf of persecuted and suffering Quakers. His inspiring mentor, Thomas Loe, died in October, 1668, but before he died he gave Penn the theme of the Cross, which was soon to be developed. "Taking me by the hand," says Penn, "he spoke thus, 'Dear heart, bear thy cross, stand faithful for God, and bear thy testimony in thy day and generation; and God will give thee an eternal crown of glory, that none shall ever take from thee. There is not another way.' "[2]

The first and natural public result of Penn's conversion was authorship, in a book *Sandy Foundations Shaken,* a controversial and superficial treatment of the doctrine of the Trinity. As a result of this first book, Penn was imprisoned in the Tower of London, which was close to his birthplace, on Tower Hill. Imprisonment in the Tower gave Penn a chance to write his second book, one of the famous works produced in prison. He called it *No Cross No Crown.* Much later, in 1682, just before sailing for America to found his colony, Penn brought out the matured edition, by which the book is best known. The book is not exciting to the modern reader, but it gives some indication of Penn's subsequent genius

[2] Maria Webb, *The Penns and Peningtons o fthe Seventeenth Century* (Philadelphia: Henry Longstreth, 1868), p. 198.

and makes strongly the point that the way of the Cross "is the only door to true Christianity." Since his formerly estranged father had died before the second edition was completed, it included a moving reference to him and to his changed spirit at the end. The Admiral's final words to his famous son were, "Son William, if you and your friends keep to your plain way of preaching, and keep to your plain way of living, you will make an end of the priests to the end of the world. Bury me by my mother: live all in love: shun all manner of evil: and I pray God to bless you all; and He will bless you."[3]

The second edition of *No Cross No Crown* includes one of the best of Penn's autobiographical fragments, as follows:

Christ's Cross is Christ's way to Christ's Crown. This is the subject of the following Discourse, first written during my confinement in the Tower of London, in the year 1668, now reprinted with great enlargements of matter and testimonies, that thou, Reader, mayest be won to Christ; and if won already, brought nearer to Him. It is a path, God, in His everlasting kindness, guided my feet into in the flower of my youth, when about twenty-two years of age: then He took me by the hand, and led me out of the pleasures, vanities and hopes of the world. I have tasted of Christ's judgments and mercies, and of the world's frowns and reproaches: I rejoice in my experience, and dedicate it to thy service in Christ. It is a debt I have long owed, and has been long expected: I have now paid it and delivered my soul.[4]

These words were dated at Worminghurst in Sussex, the First of the 6th Month, 1682. Worminghurst was Penn's home while he was planning his imaginative *Frame of Government*, and while he enjoyed a large degree of royal favor. At this time he attended Quaker meeting in a building called the Blue Idol, which still stands and which is now a guest house. On the wall, at the Blue Idol, is a letter, signed by George Fox, which furnishes a humorous indication of the fact that, in spite of his announced willingness to

---

[3] As this testimony indicates, Pepys was probably incorrect in his report that Admiral Penn was an atheist.
[4] *No Cross No Crown*, 2nd ed., Preface.

accept the way of the Cross, Penn was severely criticized by some other Quakers because of his supposed worldliness of dress and manner of life. Especially was he criticized by one woman for wearing a wig. The letter of Fox to this woman, which can be seen at the Blue Idol, makes three points: first, that William had no hair and that, therefore, in the winter his head was cold, second, it was a very modest wig, and, third, no matter how bad a wig may be, censoriousness is worse.[5]

Penn's life was never peaceful. He was forced to stay away from his beloved colony for many years, fighting in England for the life of the colony and his own political life. Because of his friendship with King James II, he was widely suspected of being a clandestine Roman Catholic and, after the glorious Revolution and the coming of William of Orange, was forced to live in retirement. He had to face a strong attack from his fellow Quakers in the Yearly Meeting of 1698, and the closing years of his life were harassed ones, because of both colonial difficulties and financial embarrassments. The colony, for all its stunning success, was a severe drain on Penn's financial resources, which were endangered, in any case, by his own lack of business efficiency. His second and final residence in Pennsylvania was of less than two years' duration (December 1, 1699-November 3, 1701), because he was called home to England to face the proposals in Parliament for annexing to the Crown the proprietary colonial governments.[6]

The most satisfying phase of Penn's life was clearly that of his preaching, which took him on demanding journeys, particularly to the European continent. The most ambitious of the travels in the ministry was made to Holland and Germany in 1677 when Fox was fifty-three, Penn was thirty-three, and Robert Barclay was

[5] Penn lost most of his hair as a result of an illness when he was three years of age. Fox called Penn's wig "a very short civil thing," costing only five shillings.

[6] Penn, with much help from his friends, had been given, in 1694, a regrant of Pennsylvania from the Crown, on conditions, the most important of which dealt with military defense.

twenty-eight. Their ship arrived in Holland with great fanfare and they seem to have made something of a stir. This was written up by Penn in his book of *Travels in Holland and Germany*. The part of the journey which seems to have pleased Penn most, inasmuch as he never ceased to be a courtier, was the visit which he, in company with Robert Barclay, made to the seat of Princess Elizabeth and Countess Horne, two highborn ladies whose religious experience resembled his own.

Princess Elizabeth of the Rhine, a cousin of King Charles II and a more distant cousin of Barclay, maintained a brilliant Court, with a constant encouragement of intellectual and spiritual life. That this influence had gone on for years is shown by the fact that Descartes, who died in 1650, dedicated his *Principles of Philosophy* to this patroness of learning. The Princess, who died in 1680, never became a Quaker, but she was glad to have the Quaker preachers hold a meeting in her castle and carried on a vigorous correspondence, particularly with Barclay. One tangible result of Penn's visit to the Rhineland was his interest in the persecuted Christian minorities of the area and the eventual decision to give them asylum in his new colony. This has given rise to the creation of one of the best-known and most admired subcultures of America, that of the so-called "Pennsylvania Dutch."

The interest of Penn in the persecuted minorities of Germany was a reflection of his passionate interest in religious freedom in England. One of his major reasons for establishing a colony, when the Stuart indebtedness to the Penn family made this feasible, was his desire to demonstrate religious freedom in action. It is a paradox that the Revolution of 1689, which sealed the case for religious freedom, should have led to Penn's disfavor at Court. This disfavor arose, not because of his principles, but because of his known friendship for the Roman Catholic King. King James II asked Penn for assistance in return for past favors, and the letter in which he asked this became known. Penn, while denying any part in the effort to oppose the accession of William and Mary, was honest enough to admit his personal love for the late King. He "supposed," he wrote, "King James would have him to endeavour his restitution; and that, though he could not decline the suspicion, yet he could avoid the guilt. And, since he had loved King James in his prosperity, he should not hate him in his adversity; yea, he loved him still for many favours he had conferred on him, though he would not join with him in what concerned the state of the kingdom."

The greatest single blow which Penn delivered in the cause of religious freedom came in his early years, in the course of what has come to be seen, in retrospect, as a famous and crucial trial. In August, 1670, when Penn was only twenty-six, he attended a Quaker meeting held in Gracechurch Street which was so large that "it was more like a tumult than a solid assembly," according to one participant. Penn did most of the speaking and, to prevent disturbance, promised the arresting soldiers that he would come to them at the conclusion of the meeting. Accordingly, Penn and a linen draper, named William Meade, were committed. The fact that the two men were indicted for riot, rather than for disobedience of the Conventicle Act, give them the benefit of jury. The surprising event was that the bench, which was highly prejudiced, wholly failed in their efforts to browbeat not only the prisoners, but, what is more important, the jury.

A truly independent jury was, at that time, a genuine novelty. The members of the jury listened as witnesses reported that they had seen Penn speaking, though, because of the noise, they could not hear what he said. When Penn said that no power on earth could divert him from worshiping God, and then demanded production of the law which he had allegedly broken, the leaders of the court became so rude that even the Lord Mayor shouted, "Take him away, take him away, turn him into the bail-dock." The eloquent Penn replied, by pointed questions: "Is this justice or true judgment? Must I therefore be taken away because I plead for the fundamental laws of England? However, this I leave upon your consciences who are of the jury, and my sole judges, that if these ancient fundamental laws which relate to liberty and property, and are not limited to particular persuasiveness in matter of religion, must not be indispensably maintained and observed, who can say he hath right to the coat on his back?"

Penn's strategy of relating the case to the wider field of liberty in general, combined with his direct appeal to the jurymen, was effective. To the amazement and chagrin of the gentlemen of the bench, the jury brought in for Meade a verdict of Not Guilty and for Penn "Guilty of speaking in Gracious Street." This was the key to the whole trial, because everyone knew that it was no crime to talk on the street. The angry Recorder said to the jury, "Gentlemen, you shall not be dismissed till we have a verdict that the Court will accept; and you shall be locked up, without meat, drink, fire, and tobacco; you shall not think thus to abuse the Court; we will have a verdict by the help of God or you shall starve for it." Penn looked the jurymen in the face, as the court broke up, and said, "You are Englishmen; mind your privilege; give not away your right."

Sunday found the jury resolute in spite of their confinement. The Lord Mayor was enraged and abused them by saying, "Have you no more wit than to be led by such a pitiful fellow? I will cut his nose." On Monday, since the verdict was still refused, the brave jurymen brought in a new verdict of Not Guilty for both defendants. The sad and shocking consequence of this was a fine levied on each juryman with imprisonment until paid, but the eventual outcome was an important victory in the entire struggle for freedom. After some imprisonment, and a year's suspense, the judges in the Court of Common Pleas agreed that *no jury can be fined for its verdict.* This revolutionary decision refers to what is known as *Bushell's Case,* since Bushell was the brave foreman of the jury. Admiral Penn was on his deathbed at the time of the trial, and the older man's admiration for his son's stand seems to have led to a reconciliation shortly before he died.

The two things for which William Penn will be remembered longest are his colonization and his writing, though in his lifetime he was known also as a brilliant preacher. The colonization was the maturing of a boyhood dream, which, he said, inspired even his Oxford days. It was one which many shared, though few could hope to see it materialized. In February, 1682, Penn and eleven other Quakers bought East Jersey (what we call northern New Jersey) from the widow of Sir George Carteret. Twelve other persons, including Robert Barclay, were associated in the proprietorship and Barclay was made Governor. East Jersey was a natural step to the land west of the Delaware River. Admiral Penn had made a dying request to the Duke of York to use his influence with the King to help and protect his son. The grant of Pennsylvania was accordingly arranged, partly to discharge a debt of sixteen thousand pounds, owed to Admiral Penn's estate, the Duke of York throwing in Delaware for good measure. Penn's conceptions of colonial government were largely Utopian, in that he held the widely shared idea that new lands could start a civilization free from the encrusted evils of the old world, provided the start was right. Accordingly, Penn worked feverishly on his colonial plans.

That Penn was a man of powerful political ideas there is no doubt. What he proposed was, indeed, a "Holy Experiment." Though he was convinced that religion, far from being something separated from political life, is rightly its driving inspiration, he nevertheless upheld separation of church and state. His *Frame of Government* exists today, in Penn's own handwriting, interlined with comments by John Locke and Viscount Sidney. Penn exerted an undoubted influence on the entire American development by means of his suggestions, presented to the Royal Commission in 1697, that there be a union of the colonies. He even proposed that two representatives be elected from each colony in a "congress," thus helping to prepare the plan of the Senate almost a hundred years in advance. Penn's genius as a political theorist is also shown by the fact that he was one of the first to envisage some kind of a Union of Nations. His *Essay Towards the Present and Future Peace of Europe*, 1693, offered a concrete plan of world order.

Penn found time, in his busy life, to do a great deal of writing for publication. One of the most fruitful times for writing came when he was back in England and under a political cloud because of his known friendship for King James II. Then, in forced retirement in lieu of arrest, he wrote *Some Fruits of Solitude*. This is a collection of aphorisms, chiefly original, many of which are highly quotable. For example, it is easy to remember that "the very trimming of the vain world would clothe all the naked one."[7]

Penn's Preface to the Ellwood edition of the *Journal of George Fox* was a task exactly suited to the great man's powers, with time to write and an agreeable subject. The result is that this small work is even more quotable than are the conscious maxims of *Some Fruits of Solitude*. As an example, consider Penn's reference to the early Quakers when he says, "They were changed men themselves before they went about to change others." When Fox died, in January, 1691, the first enthusiasm of the Quaker Movement was spent, and actual persecution was well-nigh over. It was, accordingly, a time for *careful* assessment and restatement. Penn called Fox "the instrumental author of the movement" and depicted his character with rare urbanity of style. "He was a man that God endued with a clear and wonderful depth; a discerner of others' spirits, and very much a master of his own." "He had an extraordinary gift in opening the Scriptures." "But above all he excelled in prayer . . . the most awful, living, reverent form I ever felt or beheld, I must say, was his in prayer." "For in all things he acquitted himself like a man, yea, a strong man, a new and heavenly minded man, a divine and naturalist, and all of God Almighty's making." Penn ended with a bold flourish, "To conclude, behold the testimony and doctrine of the people called

[7] *Some Fruits of Solitude in Reflections and Maxims*, 1693, Pt. 1, No. 67.

Quakers! Behold their practice and discipline! And behold the blessed men and women (at least many of them) that were sent of God in this excellent service!"

Robert Barclay, whose life and background had many similarities to those of Penn, entered the Quaker Movement at about the same time, though he was four and a half years younger. Barclay was born, in 1648, in the great house at Gordonstown, on the north coast of Scotland, which is now the scene of a school formerly attended by the heir apparent to the British throne. He was the son of Colonel David Barclay, who served with distinction in the Covenanting Army, sat in two of Cromwell's Parliaments, and was one of the trustees for the forfeited lands in Scotland. On his mother's side, that of the Gordons, Robert Barclay was related to the House of Stuart. The Barclays owned a great estate, Ury, about sixteen miles south of Aberdeen, near Stonehaven.

The boy was brought up at first as a strict Calvinist, but, curiously, was sent, in his early teens, to Paris to study in the Scots Theological College, a Roman Catholic foundation. The only reason for his being sent there seems to have been the fact that he could there be under the direction of another Robert Barclay, his uncle for whom he was named. Because it was his mother's dying request that the boy be brought home to Scotland, he returned, after her death, in 1663. Though hardly fifteen, the precocious boy was already well grounded in Latin and French. Two years later, Colonel Barclay, caught in the general confusion of the time, was imprisoned in Edinburgh Castle where he met a fellow prisoner, John Swinton, already a Quaker. The younger Barclay visited his father in prison, fell under the influence of the Quaker prisoner, and himself became a Quaker in 1666. The addition of William Penn and Robert Barclay to the Quaker Movement in the darkest days of fierce persecution, when the group seemed almost overwhelmed, was an event of importance and eventually a means of survival.

Robert Barclay, having no financial necessity, settled at Ury in 1667 and began a life of private scholarship which continued throughout his short life. He died, at the age of forty-two, just a few weeks before the death of Fox, in October, 1690. In 1670, Barclay married a devoted young woman, Christian Molleson, who shared his interests and hardships and who continued much of his work after his death. They were destined to become the ancestors of many influential people in both Britain and America, including the Barclays of the famous banking firm and the Gurneys of Earlham. The courtship and marriage of Robert and Christian set a Quaker style, the letter proposing marriage having become something of a classic:

> The love of thy converse, the desire of thy friendship, the sympathy of thy way and meekness of thy spirit has often, as thou mayst have observed, occasioned me to take frequent opportunity to have the benefit of thy company, in which I can truly say I have often been refreshed, and the life in me touched with a sweet unity. . . . Many things, in the natural will, concur to strengthen and encourage my affection towards thee and make thee acceptable unto me; but that which is before all and beyond all is that I can say in the fear of the Lord that I have received a charge from Him to love thee, and for that I know His love is much towards thee, and His blessing and goodness is and shall be unto thee, so long as thou abidest in a true sense of it.[8]

The marriage caused a scandal because it was not conducted by a clergyman. The young Quakers merely stood together, before their fellow Quakers, in a mood of reverent worship, and declared their vows to one another. This conception of marriage, once bitterly contested and denounced, is now widely accepted, at least in the English-speaking world.

Like Penn, Barclay began writing very early and engaged in vigorous literary controversy as long as he lived. These Quaker aristocrats, whatever else they were, could not honestly be called

[8] The letter, written March 28, 1669, is in the *Diary of Alexander Jaffray*, p. 295.

mild. Very soon the young scholar dedicated his life to the intellectual formulation and defense of the Quaker faith. To him, more than to any other man, during three centuries of effort, we owe the most systematic presentation of a faith that can appeal to the head as well as to the heart. He began by publishing fifteen propositions which he called *Theses Theologicae*, addressed to learned divines everywhere. This was a preview of what he intended to defend. The *Apology*, appearing in Latin in 1676, when he was only twenty-seven years old, was, in spite of his youth, Barclay's most ambitious work. Two years later, in 1678, there appeared Barclay's own English translation of the same work. In the last three centuries there have been numerous editions, this having been the most widely accepted account of the truth as Quakers have seen it, of any book ever written. The full title is *An Apology for the True Christian Divinity, being an Explanation and Vindication of the Principles and Doctrines of the People called Quakers*. Perhaps it is necessary to say at this date that Apology, as Barclay uses the word, means intellectual defense and has none of its present derogatory overtones.

Since Barclay's major book, written at an age and with a precocity similar to that of John Calvin, to whose position he was partly responding, will be mentioned in later chapters, little more need be said of it here. He went on writing, suffered severe imprisonment at Aberdeen, particularly in the winter of 1677, traveled in Europe as a Quaker preacher, and shared in the Quaker colonial enterprise in New Jersey. When he was appointed Governor of East Jersey, the appointment being made because he added moral stature to the adventure, he decided that he could best help the colony by recruiting colonists at home, the work in East Jersey being done by a deputy. Though Barclay was given Plainfield as an estate, he never occupied it.

The visit of the Quaker team to Holland and Germany in July, 1677, was a memorable event in Barclay's life. The four ablest living Quakers were on the team, Fox, Penn, Barclay, and George

Keith, a Scot who had been helpful to Barclay in writing the Latin edition of the *Apology*. Barclay was already known in Holland, since his book had been published in Amsterdam during the previous year. His greatest satisfaction evidently came in his opportunity to become well acquainted with the famous Elizabeth, Princess Palatine of the Rhine, the friend of Descartes. Both before going to Germany, and after his return to Scotland, Barclay kept up a lively correspondence with this learned and devout lady.

When Barclay died, Friends brought out a magnificent one-volume edition of his works, called *Truth Triumphant*. One of the most attractive of the smaller works is his *Treatise on Universal Love*, written in the dreadful Tolbooth, of Aberdeen. Because part of this building is still standing, the modern observer can see how Barclay and the other Quakers were confined in the cold winter of 1677. His courage in the face of persecution and his good spirit, even in fierce controversy, led to glowing accounts of his character. His kinsman, Patrick Livingstone, said, "I never knew him at any time to be in passion or anger; he was a man of a sweet, pleasant and cheerful temper, and above many for evenness of spirit." It is no surprise, therefore, that he wrote, from Aberdeen prison, "we doubt not but God would out of our ashes raise witnesses who should outlive all the violence and cruelty of man."

What is really most surprising about the Quaker aristocrats is that they never sought peculiar power or authority for themselves. They never seemed to feel superior to the rude men from the north of England who, in spite of their lesser opportunities, were their major teachers. But they did something which the rude men were unable to do. They influenced governments; they thought systematically; they wrote brilliantly. Without these four men, Penington, Ellwood, Penn and Barclay, it is doubtful if the Movement would have survived, or that the People Called Quakers would be generally known today.

ARISTOCRATS

that got the Ball rolling

Political minded

4 / The Heart of the Quaker Faith

I directed them to their Teacher, Christ.

GEORGE FOX

It is widely known that Quakers have stressed the Inner Light in all men, but it is not equally well known that Quakers have stressed, at the same time, the identity of this Light with Christ Himself. No recent Quaker thinker expressed this more clearly than did Neave Brayshaw when he wrote:

Fox and the early Friends identified this principle—the Light, as they called it—with Jesus Christ. . . . It was not for them an impersonal abstraction, a substitute for God or Christ; for them it was *Christ*, manifesting Himself in the hearts of men; it was He whom the heathen, obedient to the Light, were obeying, even though they had not heard of His earthly existence, a more eminent manifestation of Himself than any other. This is the Logos doctrine of the gospel of John.[1]

The Quaker faith, in the minds of its major interpreters, has always been "Christianity writ plain." Though Quakers are not the only ones who have declared this noble intention, there are very few others who have taken it more seriously. William Penn made it abundantly clear when he wrote a pamphlet entitled *Quakerism, a New Nickname for old Christianity.* In his *No Cross No Crown,* the word "Quaker" does not even appear, the Preface of 1682

[1] *The Quakers: Their Story and Message* (London: George Allen and Unwin, 1953), p. 46.

63

being signed, not "Thy Quaker Friend," but "Thy fervent Christian Friend." In the course of the work, Penn spoke of Jesus Christ as the one "in whose mouth there was found no guile, sent from God with a testimony of love to mankind, and who laid down his life for their salvation; whom God hath raised by his mighty power to be Lord of all."[2]

In this effort to make clear the ideal of Basic Christianity, i.e., Christianity without frills, Penn coined the phrase "Primitive Christianity Revived." By this he did not mean that anyone who seeks to follow the Quaker Way must be primitive in the ridiculous sense that he will not employ anything, whether it be steam heat or a hymn book, which was not known to the first Christians. Being a highly intelligent man, he understood, naturally, that there is always the possibility of development, but it must, he insisted, be authentic development in a direction consistent with the original convictions and experiences.

What is necessary, if our starting point is the faith emanating from the direct acquaintance with Christ, which is what made New Testament Christianity possible, is to try to distinguish between what is essential and what is nonessential. Though there is no infallible way in which this can be done, it is our duty to do our best. At least we have the enormous advantage of access to the Gospels, which is something which many of the early Christians, including the Apostle Paul, did not have. By patient study and scholarship, we can see the difference between what is central and what is peripheral, between the intrinsic and the incidental. A good example of the essential is Christ's picture of God and what He requires of creatures like ourselves. It was with such distinctions in mind that Joseph John Gurney (1788–1847) defined Quakerism. It is, he said, "the religion of our Lord and Savior Jesus Christ, without diminution, without addition, and without compromise."[3]

2 *No Cross No Crown*, 2nd ed., Chap. XX, 1.
3 "Brief Remarks on Impartiality in the Interpretation of Scripture," p. 16.

Quakers have never had a creed as something to be repeated or as a standard of admission to membership. This deliberate omission is not to be understood as an indication of the judgment that convictions are unimportant. The deepest difficulty with a fixed creed is that it inevitably becomes formal, and, consequently, can be repeated *without* conviction. Even with the best of intentions, the formula is artificial and external, and therefore something for which the sincere Christian dare not settle. George Fox believed in God with all his heart and, what is equally important, he believed that the God of all the world is like Jesus Christ. This has always been true of Quakers in the mainstream of Quaker history. God, Quakers believe, is real. He is not a figment of our imagination or a psychological projection of our hopes. God is *personal*, as truly a Person as Christ was a Person. This means that there can be a genuine "I-Thou" relationship between the finite human individual and the Living God. He is not a mere Ground of Being who does not and cannot know each finite person as an individual who is valuable in his own right. If God is not fully Person, i.e., if He cannot be rightly addressed as "Thou," then Christ was mistaken, for Christ so addressed the Father, and we do not believe that Christ was deluded in His deepest experience. By person, we do not mean a being who is bodily or material, but rather one who *knows*, who *responds*, and who *cares*. The Father, Christ said, cares even for each single bird; how much more, therefore, does He care for every individual made in His image.

The heart of the ancient faith which Fox did not invent, but which he did so much to *uncover*, involves the continual effort to avoid the loss of the reality in its seemingly inevitable formalization. In each generation, the crust begins to form and then it is necessary, unless death is to set in, for someone to break the crust. This is what Fox and the early Quakers did. Because they were themselves shaken, they shook the lifeless forms around them. They were not attacking the evangelical faith of the New Testament; they were attacking its distortion.

There is no better way in which to reach an understanding of the basic Quaker faith than to follow that remarkable woman, Margaret Fell, in her account of what occurred at Ulverston, near Swarthmore, on a memorable summer day in 1652. It was a fast day, with a lecture at the church building, and Fox was there, though he did not come in until the people were gathered.

I and my children had been a long time there before. And when they were singing before the sermon, he came in; and when they had done singing, he stood up upon a seat or form, and desired that he might have liberty to speak; and he that was in the pulpit said he might. And the first words that he spoke were as followeth: "He is not a Jew that is one outward; neither is that circumcision which is outward; but he is a Jew that is one inward; and that is circumcision which is of the heart." And so he went on, and said, how that Christ was the Light of the world, and lighteth every man that cometh into the world; and that by this light they might be gathered to God, &c. I stood up in my pew and wondered at this doctrine; for I had never heard such before. And then he went on, and opened the Scriptures, and said, "the Scriptures were the prophets' words, and Christ's and the apostles' words, and what, as they spoke, they enjoyed and possessed, and had it from the Lord": and said, "then what had any to do with the Scriptures, but as they came to the Spirit that gave them forth? You will say, *Christ saith this, and the apostles say this; but what canst thou say?* Art thou a child of Light, and has thou walked in the Light, and what thou speakest, is it inwardly from God?" &c. This opened me so, that it cut me to the heart; and then I saw clearly we were all wrong. So I sat down in my pew again, and cried bitterly: and I cried in my spirit, to the Lord, "We are all thieves; we are all thieves; we have taken the Scriptures in words, and know nothing of them in ourselves." So that served me, that I cannot well tell what he spoke afterwards; but he went on in declaring against the false prophets, and priests, and deceivers of the people.[4]

What seemed so fresh to Margaret Fell, and may seem equally fresh to many today, is the idea that the truth about God and Christ and man is not something merely for a theology book, but

[4] "The Testimony of Margaret Fox concerning her late husband," in *Journal of George Fox*, 1694, Vol. 1, p. ii. See also Isabel Ross, *Margaret Fell, Mother of Quakerism* (London: Longmans, Green & Company, 1949), pp. 11, 12.

something, rather, which can be known inwardly and intimately by anyone who will open his heart. The truth is not merely ancient, but endlessly contemporary; it is not at all a matter of outward observances, which may or may not be helpful, but of what takes place inside. We do not need to refer merely to what occurred long ago in Palestine, important as the historical record may be, because the same experience is possible here and now, because the Light which shone then continues to shine. The Spirit of God, which inspired the men who wrote the Scriptures, is still at work, in each human heart, and will be known by all who respond. Worship, therefore, is not the performance of a dead ritual, but genuine waiting on the Lord to hear His voice and to know His power at firsthand. Because rituals and creeds, though once meaningful, tend to become mummified, there must be continuous reformation.

Any uniqueness in Quaker religious thought is not to be found in its novelty, but rather in its recovery of something which is easily lost, the idea that true religion must be genuinely *experiential*. The God who is like Jesus Christ can indeed be inferred by argument, but that is never sufficient. It is experience, and especially the experience of the changed life, that is the true verification. This is another way of saying that Quakers have placed strong emphasis on the doctrine of the Holy Spirit. Though Quakers have not made much use of the Trinitarian formula, often pointing out that "Trinity" is a word which is not found in the Bible, the experiential basis of the doctrine has usually been recognized. By this is meant the observation that God, who is, in one sense, One, has been revealed in a variety of ways. He is seen *in creation* and in the order of nature; He is seen *historically* in the life, death, and resurrection of Jesus Christ; He is seen *experientially*, as the Holy Spirit, reaching directly into the human heart, giving guidance and strength on life's darkest as well as life's brightest ways.

Every person, with any degree of theological sophistication, recognizes that, in dealing with matters of depth and moment, we are forced to employ metaphors. Because there is no other way of speaking, the person who objects to figurative language is clearly inept. The only rational alternative to the use of metaphor is, unfortunately, no language at all. When we speak of God as Father, as Christ did, we know very well that we are using a figure of speech, which, because it is a figure, is inappropriate when overpressed or literalized. We certainly do not mean that God has the limitations of human fathers or that He begets children as human fathers do. All that we mean is that fatherhood is the least inaccurate conception which is available. No thoughtful individual supposes that divine personality is identical with human personality, but that is no reason for denying divine personality, because the alternative is *impersonality*, which is manifestly *less* satisfactory. Indeed, it is probable that we are only feebly and partially personal, whereas God is *wholly* personal.

The Quaker version of Basic Christianity has employed a great variety of metaphors in order to give vivid expression to what is nearly ineffable, but not entirely so. Nowhere is this more evident than in the writing of Robert Barclay. He uses "seed" because a seed if given help can grow; he uses "light" because light can penetrate at a distance; he uses "word" because he is highly conscious of the Logos idea in Greek philosophy and in the prologue to the Fourth Gospel. At the heart of the *Apology* (Propositions V and VI, 13) appears an important passage in which the metaphors are combined:

By this seed, grace, and word of God, and light wherewith we say every one is enlightened and hath a measure of it, which strives with him in order to save him, and which may, by the stubbornness and wickedness of man's will, be quenched, bruised, wounded, pressed down, slain and crucified, we understand not the proper essence and nature of God precisely taken, which is not divisible into parts and measures as being a most pure, simple being, void of all composition or division, and therefore can neither be resisted, hurt, wounded, crucified or slain by all the efforts and strength of men; but we understand one spiritual, heavenly, and invisible principle, in which God, as Father, Son, and Spirit, dwells; a measure of which divine and glorious life is in all men as a seed, which of its own nature, draws, invites, and inclines to God.

In this vivid statement we find a conception which, if it had been known and accepted, would have made the sorrowful controversy between Trinitarians and Unitarians unnecessary. Barclay is talking about the divine, but, in doing so, he is trying to stay close to experience. The experience which he knew at firsthand, and which was reported to him by people whom he had reason to trust, was the sense of being reached and striven with. So far as he could see, he was not different from other men, whatever their race, culture, condition, or age. Therefore he concluded, reasonably, that the central experience is universal. The theology is really secondary and exists only as an intellectual structure, which men employ in order to make sense out of the experience. The structure erected by Barclay, and which he attributed to all Quakers rather than to his own idiosyncrasy, is sufficiently orthodox for any Trinitarian, but the point to make is that it is more than merely orthodox. It is orthodox, not in order to be conventional, but because this is the way the truth looks, providing we try to stay close to reality as experienced.

Our discussion has brought us to the famous doctrine of the Light, which is popularly supposed to be the major theological contribution of Quakers to total Christianity. The Light is sometimes denominated "The Light Within," or "The Inner Light," but most often it is called "The Light of Christ Within." Such was the common practice of the leading Quaker intellectuals of the seventeenth century, because they wanted to maintain the identity with the Christ of history. There were sound reasons for this decision. If they had decided otherwise, Quakerism might easily have become separated from its Christian roots and have ended as something similar to theosophy. In that event, it would certainly have lacked the power which it demonstrated, and in all probability, would not even have survived. As it was, Quakers were able to stress immediate experience without in any way denying or minimizing the Biblical faith. The Light which strives to reach every man is not some vague general light, but the present continuation of the Light which shone in Jesus as He called men by the Sea of Galilee. Here the Logos Doctrine served admirably, so that the prologue to the Fourth Gospel became more precious to Quakers than almost any other single passage of the Bible. John 1:9, in the Authorized translation, which the first Quakers knew, was used so much and so often that it came to be known as "the Quakers' text."

Over and over, when Quakers have been asked to distinguish between the Christ of History and the Christ of Experience, they have refused to accept the distinction, maintaining, instead, that it is the very identity which is the central point. This is why Fox was able to claim Christ as present Teacher. What Christ said long ago and what He says now must be consistent and coherent. The ancient words are supported today, as we enter into the continuing fellowship of verification, while present leadings are unreliable if they are inconsistent with what He said when He walked on earth. In short, Quakers take the resurrection seriously and therefore do not suppose that they must mention Christ merely in the past tense.

It is not surprising that an idea as powerful as that of the "Indwelling Light of Christ" was full of danger. Just as other Christians sometimes put all of the emphasis upon the Christ of History, Friends have often had a severe temptation to put all of the stress upon the Christ of Experience. In the eighteenth century, and even in the first half of the nineteenth century, many Friends almost forgot the Biblical roots of their faith or, in any case, they neglected them sorely. It was always a temptation to make such an excessive stress on the "Inward Teacher" that the major deterrent to spiritual anarchy was removed. Some encouraged what John William Graham called a "lazy mysticism,"[5]

[5] *The Faith of a Quaker*, p. 404.

which made the careful and disciplined encounter with Christ in the Gospels supposedly unnecessary.

It was because Joseph John Gurney recognized this serious danger that, in 1816, he arranged what was a novelty at that time, the presentation of a copy of the Bible to every boy and girl in Ackworth School, with strong encouragement for its use. The result was a marked increase of Scripture knowledge, but the modern reader learns, to his amazement, that Gurney's generous act was harshly criticized by some of his contemporaries. When John Barclay visited the school, in 1819, he expressed his uneasiness at what was going on, giving it as his opinion that regular, systematic teaching of Scripture doctrine was incompatible with Quakerism.[6] This is one of the evidences to show that the evangelical revival among Quakers, largely initiated by Gurney, was a necessity, if the original balance between the Historic and Inward Christ was to be maintained and cherished.

One major danger inherent in the idea of the Light was that of a sterile humanism. It was always possible to suppose that Quakers were talking merely about human reason or even about the natural goodness of men, after the fashion later popularized in the French Enlightenment. If this interpretation had been permitted to stand, or had become general, the whole idea would have lost its power, since every emphasis on natural human goodness seems to lead inevitably to sentimentality. The truth about man is intrinsically complex and, though good human acts are possible and sometimes are demonstrated, there is a seed of evil in all men. If we did not know this before, we surely know it in the latter half of the twentieth century, after the wanton cruelty which has been experienced in two World Wars, in concentration camps, and in countless other ways. Man, alone, doesn't do very well, and assuredly needs all of the help that he can get. It is truly said today that the doctrine of original or chronic sin is the most certain of all

[6] For the letter written by John Barclay, see David E. Swift, *Joseph John Gurney, Banker, Reformer and Quaker* (Middletown, Conn.: Wesleyan University Press, 1962), pp. 59, 60.

Christian doctrines, because it is known empirically. One cure for addiction to a belief in natural human goodness is the simple one of becoming a parent.

Much of the wisdom of the original Quaker view of man lies in the fact that it rejected the twin evils of optimism and pessimism. In modern terms, the first Quakers did not believe that Romanticism and Calvinism exhausted the possibilities. There was, they believed, a third way and the Quaker intellectuals sought to define what that third way was. On the one hand, they rejected the pessimism of "total depravity" as a dogma inconsistent with the idea that man is made in God's image. On the other hand, they rejected the high opinion of man as a being fundamentally akin to God, who is a very nice creature if only left alone. The spirit of man may be the candle of the Lord, but it is a candle which often sputters.

The judgment of Barclay, in trying to outline carefully a third way, involved the insistence that the Light, which reaches out toward every human being, is a divine and not a human light. In short, it is not "natural." Characteristic Quaker writers at the beginning of our century criticized Barclay for this and tended to deplore what they called his "dualism." As the century has advanced, however, the climate of Quaker opinion has changed markedly, the leading thinkers now tending to be in fundamental agreement with Barclay, though they may not employ all of his slightly stilted seventeenth-century language.[7]

The charge of dualism now seems a curious charge, especially if dualism is assumed without argument to be something indefensible. After all, dualism, both in its epistemological and psychophysical form, has been the main tradition of Western philosophy, as the late Professor Lovejoy so convincingly showed in *The Revolt Against Dualism*. His conclusion was that the effort to avoid or to transcend dualism has failed. Nearly all contemporary theologians, in so far as they have listened, even slightly, to Karl

---

[7] See, for example, Howard Brinton, *Friends for 300 Years* (Pendle Hill Paperback, 1964), p. ix.

Barth, have come to a similar conclusion. Man can, indeed, have an encounter with the Living God, but this fact need not require the conclusion that man is partially divine.

We need to maintain the same dualism between ourselves and Christ. He was indeed a person of flesh and blood, tempted as we are tempted and wounded as we are wounded, but He was, at the same time, the very Image of the Living God. God was in Christ reconciling the world to Himself, as He is *not* in us. The experience of almost every thoughtful person who seeks to confront the Christ of the Gospels, with any seriousness, includes the recognition that, in Him, we find something different from anything which we find in ourselves. He is different in kind and not merely different in degree. In spite of the almost pathetic desire for some version of philosophical monism, it is important to say that any genuinely Biblical faith will always have a strong element of dualism in it. We are far from the truth when we forget that His thoughts are not our thoughts nor His ways our ways.

In the twentieth century, Quakers have rediscovered and have given wide application to a phrase used by Fox, which was largely neglected for the two preceding centuries. This is the phrase, already mentioned, "that of God in every one." While there is no known instance of its being used during the days of the evangelical revival, it began to be widely used when interpreters of Quaker thought placed more emphasis upon mysticism, and also when Quakers began to be more conscious of the undoubted values in religions other than Christianity. The result is that the phrase has been greatly overused in the latter part of the twentieth century, and has become a cliché. Indeed, it has not been uncommon for the phrase to provide a definition of Quakerism. To the question, "What do Quakers believe?" the frequent answer is, "Quakers believe in that of God in every man." One welcome reaction to this manifestly false use, or overuse, is the suggestion of Dr. Henry J. Cadbury that we declare a moratorium on the expression.[8]

The overuse of the expression "that of God in every man" is a

[8] "Then and Now," in *The Friends Journal*, Sept. 15, 1956.

further indication of the humanist danger inherent in all reference to the "Inner Light." In somber fact, the tendency is really one which borders upon a disguised or not frankly declared atheism. When men have ceased to believe in God unapologetically, and therefore hesitate to refer simply to God in the fully objective sense, the reference to "that of God" appears to some to be a respectable escape from the predicament. The divination of man is cherished as a substitute for theistic faith. Since Fox's phrase is highly ambiguous, it is important to be careful in our use of language at this point and to try to see what it is that we really mean. Undoubtedly, the purpose of Fox was to indicate the universality of God's grace as He reaches out to every kind and condition of person, but it is possible, by contrast, to interpret Fox as holding that each man has a piece of God in him. Some go so far, in this direction, as to claim that the divine in men is all of the divine there is, thus denying the transcendence of God altogether. It cannot be too strongly pointed out that such an immanentist conception is wholly at variance with the mainstream of Quaker thought, as represented by the brilliant men who became Fox's exponents in the learned world. With a concerted voice, they held that the saving Light is not a human light, that it is wholly divine, and that it comes to men who do not deserve it.

One of the marks of intellectual and spiritual vitality among Quakers of the present generation has been the reconsideration of the entire issue involved in the use of the expression which we are considering. It has even been the topic of a recent Swarthmore Lecture.[9] What is seen, though belatedly by some, is that to accept the expression as a substitute for a creed is very dangerous. The deepest danger is that of pride in the thought of the latent divinity and consequent glorification of man. A characteristic warning is that of a letter to The Friend, which says in part, "We are not divine. The image of God in us is as much like the infinite reality as a portrait is of the sitter—imperfect and incomplete. It is

[9] L. Hugh Doncaster, God in Every Man (London: George Allen and Unwin, 1963).

surely not even true that the spark of God within us is all that we can hope to know of God, although it may be an essential point for our adventure of discovery."[10]

The purpose of Barclay and other scholarly Quakers, in emphasizing the universality of the Light of Christ, was that of making credible the divine justice. We must remember that the climate of opinion, in mid-seventeenth-century England, was strongly Calvinistic. The average Puritan kept asking "What must I do to be saved?" but, as some began to see the logical consequences of Calvinism, the question was altered to "How can I know *whether* I am saved?" This was because, according to Calvin, the outcome was already determined. We do not understand Quakerism unless we see it as a deliberately open-ended conception, involving a total rejection of Calvin's double election, according to which God has determined, in advance, that some will be saved and some will be damned. Every Quaker saw this idea as a horrid blasphemy, because it meant that God was playing favorites.

One reason why original Quakers could not accept the notion of divine favoritism was that they were so familiar with the New Testament. On page after page, they read there what seemed to them to be both a denial of Calvinism and an affirmation of a potential universalism. They could not miss the glorious phrases of Revelation 3:20, "Behold, I stand at the door and knock: if any man hear my voice, and open the door, I will come in to him." This emphasis on "any" is hard to square with the doctrine of arbitrary elimination from divine communion of the majority of mankind. Barclay's strong insistence is that Christ died for all. Those, he says, who deny that, by the death of Christ, salvation is made possible to all men, "do most blasphemously make God mock the world, in giving his servants a commission to preach the gospel of salvation to all, while he hath before decreed that 'it shall not be possible for them to receive it.' "[11]

It is unreasonable to suppose that the character of God is

---

[10] William K. Robinson, in *The Friend* (London), Sept. 10, 1965, p. 1094.
[11] *Apology*, Propositions V and VI, vi.

internally inconsistent. Since He does not require of any man that which is impossible, it is never a man's duty to do what he cannot perform. The call to universal repentance, therefore, necessarily implies the possibility of universal salvation. That this is the clear message of Scripture, Barclay did not doubt, and he even went so far as to say "there is not one scripture, that I know of, which affirmeth Christ not to die for all." If God has determined, in advance, that some men will not be saved, we cannot avoid the shocking conclusion that God is not at all like Christ, for Christ sought to seek and to save, to the uttermost. But if God is not like Christ, the whole point of the Christian revelation is thereby denied.

What Barclay and others had in mind was the vast company of human beings who lived before the coming of Christ in the flesh, as well as those, in more recent times, who have had no direct knowledge of the Christ of history. Are all these inevitably and cruelly denied God's grace? To answer "yes" to this has seemed to every Quaker to be blasphemous. But how *can* men be saved, i.e., brought into genuine communion with the Father, if they have never known the Gospel? Did not Jesus Himself say, "No one comes to the Father, but by me" (John 14:6)? If Christ is the *only* Way, and if most men have not had the opportunity to know that Way, we seem to be involved in a damaging dilemma. Either we have to say that most men are condemned without a chance, or we must conclude that Christ was wrong when He asserted that His way was the only way.

The Quaker faith is best understood as an attempted solution of this dilemma. The central answer is that Christ is, indeed, the only Way, but that, as the divine Logos, He has revealed Himself to millions who have never had an opportunity to know Him or even know *of* Him, in the flesh. Not only did Christ say "I am the Way"; He also said "I have come as light into the world, that whoever believes in me may not remain in darkness" (John 12:46). Christ said He came to save the *world*, not merely the minority who have lived since His time, and who have been fortunate enough to hear His message.

The emphasis, not merely on the historical Jesus, but also upon the Universal Saving Light of Christ, is the most nearly original Quaker contribution to religious thought. If there is any other solution to the cruel dilemma, we do not know what it is. Unless some such conception is valid, we are forced to conclude that Socrates is in hell! After all, the famous Athenian, who sought so carefully to listen to the divine voice, had no chance whatever to know Christ, even in prophecy, because he lived four centuries before the Christian era and had no known connection with the Hebrew heritage. But if Christ is truly the universal light, operating in all stages of human history, then the Light of Christ was already reaching out to Socrates, as to millions more in the ancient world.

Here is an honest answer to the problem of apparent divine injustice. It is no wonder that the original Quakers set such store by the early verses of the Fourth Gospel. They valued John's Prologue because the idea of the Eternal Word gave them an answer to what was otherwise an intolerable problem. The central solution, as stated by Barclay, was as follows:

That God, who out of his infinite love sent his Son, the Lord Jesus Christ, into the world, who tasted death for every man, hath given to every man, whether Jew or Gentile, Turk or Scythian, Indian or Barbarian, of whatsoever nation, country, or place, a certain day or time of visitation; during which day or time it is possible for them to be saved, and to partake of the fruit of Christ's death.[12]

The Quaker faith is not that of universalism in the claim that all men will, eventually, be saved, for that outcome is beyond our knowledge. It is rather the conviction that, if God is like Christ, the *possibility* of salvation is universal. Otherwise, preaching would be ridiculous. We pray for all men, but it would be absurd to pray for that which is known in advance to be impossible. How

12 *Ibid.*, Propositions V and VI, xi.

can Christ say, "Come unto me, all ye that labor and are heavy laden," if He means only the fortunate few? Anything else than a potential universalism is injurious to the character of God, to the work of Christ, and to the welfare of men. We simply do not believe it to be true that God has predestined to eternal damnation, without opportunity, the far greater part of mankind.

The idea of Christ as reaching out, as does Light, to all men, is particularly relevant today when we are highly conscious of the coexistence of many world religions. We are forced to re-examine the relationship of Christianity to Buddhism, to Hinduism, to Islam, etc. Such a re-examination makes us reconsider the whole reason for missionary activity. To claim that all non-Christian religions are intrinsically evil is to deny the obvious truth, for each of the major religions contains elements of undoubted spiritual strength. One cannot observe the discipline of a Buddhist monastery without recognizing this. But does such a recognition undermine missions? Not if the Quaker conception of the Eternal Light of Christ is taken seriously. This means that the Eternal Christ has already been reaching into Buddhist hearts, and would do so without any help from us. Nevertheless we can help one another. The flame is there, but it can be made brighter by human instrumentality.

Christ is, indeed, the Way, but men of different faiths can teach one another what they have learned of the Way, and those who know of the historic Christ have a special responsibility. The humble yet truly dedicated Christian missionary goes to others as a learner as well as a teacher. We are not so rich in spiritual resources that we can afford to neglect any.[13] It is a striking fact that, when John Woolman, in the eighteenth century, went as a missionary to the American Indians, he told them that he had done so in order to learn something from them.

[13] I have made a detailed study of the relationship between Christianity and the World Religions in *The Philosophy of Religion* (Harper & Row, 1957), Chap. XVI.

The consequences of emphasis on the Light of Christ are many. One is that we are saved from the temptation to idolize the Bible. Quakers cannot, logically, claim that the Bible is their fundamental basis of faith, because this would be tantamount to making the Scriptures more important than Christ. This is why Quakers do not speak of the Bible as the "Word of God," as is often done by others. It is Christ, and Christ alone, who is the Word. With characteristic clarity, Barclay, while acknowledging the Scriptures "to be very heavenly and divine writing" and "the use of them to be very comfortable and necessary to the Church of Christ," goes on to say "yet we may not call them the principal fountain of all truth and knowledge, nor yet the first adequate rule of faith and manners."[14] The words of the Bible are good words, but they are not superior to the Eternal Word, from which they came. The best way to use the Scriptures is to employ them as a means by which we are led into the same spirit which impelled those who first gave them forth.

Such a view of the Bible avoids an irreverent neglect, on the one hand, and the bondage of literalism, on the other. There is no harm at all in seeing that the various parts of the Bible are vastly unequal. Otherwise we could see no distinction between the law and the gospel. We are not bound to believe that God is bloodthirsty and vindictive simply because some of the ancient Israelites thought that He was, or that marriage is a less noble state than celibacy, because that happened to be the view of the Apostle Paul (I Cor. 7:7, 8). Fortunately, we need not be limited to the alternatives of neglect and idolatry. It is possible to be deeply appreciative of the Scriptures without being bound by them. We arrive at this point when we see clearly that they are valuable, though not primary. What is primary is Christ as the Present Teacher.

No person can go very far in trying to have a thoughtful view of the world without a consideration of the fact of error. We can be more sure of error than of anything else, partly because, when

[14] *Apology*, Proposition IV, ii.

people hold contradictory views, *somebody* is wrong. The greatest intellectual weakness of the earliest Quaker thinkers came at this point. They realized that the authors of the Bible could be mistaken, and that the infallibility of the Church or Pope could not be given an adequate intellectual defense, but they were not equally alert to the possibility of error in reference to the leading of the Spirit, on which they depended. Barclay argued that the direct leading of the Spirit ought not to be subjected to reason or anything else as a more sure touchstone, because that would mean testing the greater by the lesser. "We then trust to and confide in this Spirit, because we know and certainly believe that it can only lead us aright, and never mislead us."[15]

What Barclay failed to see, along with most of the early Friends, was the inevitable subjectivity of all human judgment. Though it is reasonable to suppose that God will never mislead us and that His truth is infallible, it does not follow that we, as finite creatures, will ever have a perfect understanding of what that truth is. Even though it might be conceivable that another man's judgment is infallible, I could not know that this is the case unless I, also, were infallible in my own judgment. The truth is objective, but judgment about it is necessarily subjective. That is why we need each other and why, even when we agree, we are not absolutely sure that we are right. Barclay was on the track of this analysis when he said, of the man who cannot smell the flowers, that "the fault is in the organ, and not in the object," but he did not follow up this fruitful lead with sufficient care.

When men believe that their individual spiritual experience provides them with an infallible guide to conduct, they are bound to be open to all kinds of extravagant actions, such as that of Nayler in his pathetic "triumphal entry" into Bristol. The truth is that there is no infallibility! Though the Spirit does not deceive, *men* can be deceived. Finite men can never distinguish, with absolute certainty, between what God is saying and what they

15 *Ibid.*, Proposition II, xv.

think that they hear. All of the crude aberrations in Quaker history have arisen from the failure to give full assent to this fundamental fact about the human situation. Shameful as it is to record, the supposed direct leading caused some of the early Quakers to walk naked through the streets. This practice, undertaken as a prophetic sign of the nakedness of the prevailing culture, was more frequent in the early days than has been commonly recognized. It is not wholly surprising, however, when we realize that the vigorous new Movement naturally drew to itself some of the lunatic fringe, but it must be kept in mind as evidence of how easily sincere people may be misguided, even when they suppose that they are divinely led.[16] That the late Rufus M. Jones understood well the possibility of delusion is shown by the following words:

It seems impossible, in this world of conflicting views, to have any movement for the illumination and spiritual enlargement of men which is not more or less blocked and hampered by the blunders, the littleness, and the selfishness of persons who are one-sided, and who push some one aspect of the "truth" out of balance until it turns out to be misleading "error."[17]

The cornerstone of Quaker conviction is that God, as revealed in Christ, can, and indeed does, reach out to communicate with each of the spirits whom He has made, and that He never leaves Himself without a witness in any heart. But next to this cornerstone must stand a constant reminder of the pervasiveness of human ineptitude and sin. Though there is a tendency to think of the Light Within in a flattering or optimistic sense, such an opinion is partly erroneous. Actually the Light, as interpreted by Fox, was almost as negative as was the voice which Socrates heard, and which told him what *not* to do. More than any other Quaker scholar, Professor Hugh Barbour has pointed out the fact that the

16 For a fair and impartial treatment of the practice of nakedness as a sign, see William C. Braithwaite, *The Beginnings of Quakerism* (Cambridge: Cambridge University Press, 1955), pp. 148–51.

17 Rufus M. Jones, *Quakers in the American Colonies*, p. 275.

Light, as early Friends understood it, was at first more a source of terror than of hope. "The essence of pain was to know one's sins and self-will, but the source of the pain was the Light, itself."[18] Our difficulty is that we have read back our essential optimism into what was a more strenuous time. The words of Margaret Fell make the point abundantly clear. "Now, Friends, deal plainly with yourselves, and let the Eternal Light search you. . . . for this will deal plainly with you; it will rip you up, and lay you open . . . naked and bare before the Lord God, from whom you can not hide yourselves. . . . Therefore give over deceiving of your Souls; for . . . all Sin and Uncleanness the Light condemns."[19]

Christ taught us to pray for forgiveness of sins. This presented a genuine problem to the earliest Quakers, especially George Fox. Fox was deeply aware of human sin, but, being essentially simple-minded, he held that men should expect to be made perfect, if they would take God's power and leading seriously. "If your faith be true," he said to those who argued with him, "it will give you victory over sin and the devil and purify your hearts and consciences." Fox held that those who denied the possibility of Christian perfection were "pleading for sin." It is foolish, Fox thought, to ask God for a pure heart, if you know in advance that this is impossible.

This emphasis upon perfection has appeared in various chapters of the Quaker story, especially in the development of what was called the Holiness Movement in the late nineteenth century. In this Movement, led by such strong men as John Henry Douglas and David Updegraff, there was an effort to be loyal to Fox's doctrine of perfection, by stressing the possibility of "sanctification" as a second definite experience, different from, and subsequent to, conversion. Though the main power of this particular Movement is now gone, it is important to realize that it made a valid point. This is essentially the point, which many are making

[18] *The Quakers in Puritan England*, p. 98.
[19] Margaret Fell, *Works*, pp. 95, 136.

today in the current stress on commitment, to the effect that there is a radical difference between nominal Christianity and full commitment to the Cause of Christ.

The mood of our time has made any doctrine of literal perfectionism hard to defend. Partly because of the brilliant reasoning of Reinhold Niebuhr, in his Gifford Lectures, *The Nature and Destiny of Man*, literate Christians are acutely conscious of the pervasive quality of human sin. Perhaps the best thing to say about perfection is the paradox that *it is wrong to claim it,* and that *it is equally wrong to deny its possibility.* To claim it is to be guilty of self-delusion, and also the sin of pride, while to deny its possibility is to limit God's power.[20]

The doctrine of the universal light of Christ is a great intellectual contribution to human thought because it solves an intolerable dilemma, which is as old as Christianity, but which is felt with especial keenness by contemporary man. But it is a serious mistake to see the central Quaker message in purely intellectual terms, however clarifying they may be. It was reserved for John Hunt, a simple Quaker of the late eighteenth century, to state the central point with a clarity which modern man has not surpassed. "Perfection," wrote Hunt, "does not consist in teaching truth, but in doing it."[21] The experience of the Light is never genuine unless it leads to power. This is the point of William Penn's memorable statement, in referring to the early Quakers, that they became changed men themselves, "before they went about to change others."[22] The central experience is that of the direct contact with Christ as the immediate and present Teacher, and the chief verification of the genuineness of this contact is not mere illumination, but the consequent power of a new life.

The enduring value of the brand of perfectionism preached by

[20] For a contemporary Quaker attempt to deal with this thorny question, see the Pendle Hill Pamphlet, by Cecil E. Hinshaw, *Apology for Perfection* (Pamphlet 138, 1964).

[21] *Journal of John Hunt, Friends Miscellanies,* Vol. X, p. 250.

[22] *Rise and Progress,* p. 38.

George Fox is its insistence that the primary Christian experience is that of power and specifically, power over sin. There is no doubt that Fox was sometimes naïve, but there is also no doubt that he was fundamentally on the right track. If the grace of God does not, in fact, give power to overcome sin, it is really an empty phrase. As the logic of the Quaker understanding of the Gospel develops, it moves, by its essential character, from emphasis on *light* to emphasis on *power*, for the fundamental justification of the Quaker faith consists not in new doctrines, but in new lives. Quakerism rests its case upon experience, rather than upon speculation, but the fundamental experience is not ecstatic union with God. It is the more practical experience of watching for light on the pathway, and being given power to follow it.

5 / Reality in Worship

> I do not feel that ours is the only lawful manner of
> worship. But I do believe it to be the purest conceivable.
>
> CAROLINE STEPHEN

In August, 1948, when the formative Assembly of the World
Council of Churches was held in Amsterdam, a bold and novel
plan of worship was inaugurated. The committee charged with
arrangements fastened upon the happy idea of asking each of the
major groups to conduct one period of worship to which all
attenders should be welcomed, and carried on according to the
purest or most characteristic pattern familiar to the sponsoring
group. Thus there was, one morning, a Lutheran service, on
another morning the Anglican *Morning Prayer*, and so on. One
gathering was sponsored by Quakers and was attended by more
than six hundred people, most of whom had never attended a
Quaker meeting before.

The result of the total experiment was highly satisfactory and a
tribute to the wisdom of the committee in charge. These men
might have been expected to plan the same service daily, presenting a least common denominator of Protestant practice in public
worship, but such a conventional procedure would not have been
nearly as good as was the richness of variety actually displayed.
Unity we undoubtedly had, but it was not the unity of sameness;
it was the unity of variety. Our practice of worship had the
richness of a patchwork quilt, including many contrasting colors,
rather than the drabness of a single neutral shade. In this total
undertaking there was provided a glimpse of what true ecumenicity might eventually become.

Since all of the other groups expected to follow a printed liturgy of some kind, Quakers were asked to prepare something to place, in advance, in the pews of the great church where the worship was conducted each day. Because the building is many-sided, most of the people could see one another, which was ideal for the Quaker purpose. The high pulpit was not even entered. A few Quakers sat together on one of the sides, one of them calling attention to the cards in the pews and explaining, in the beginning, that the meeting would be ended by his shaking hands with the man next to him. He asked all present to shake hands, similarly, at the close of worship, and to walk out of the building without feeling the necessity of routine conversation. The response to this suggestion turned out to be complete compliance, in that there was no conversation until the worshipers were again in the open air. The text of the card, which appeared in three languages, German, French, and English, was as follows:

WORSHIP, according to the ancient practice of the Religious Society of Friends, is entirely without any human direction or supervision. A group of devout persons come together and sit down quietly with no prearrangement, each seeking to have an immediate sense of divine leading and to know at first hand the presence of the Living Christ. It is not wholly accurate to say that such a Meeting is held on the basis of Silence; it is more accurate to say that it is held on the basis of "Holy Obedience." Those who enter such a Meeting can harm it in two specific ways: first, by an advance determination to speak; and second, by advance determination to keep silent. The only way in which a worshipper can help such a Meeting is by an advance determination to try to be responsive in listening to the still small voice and doing whatever may be commanded. Such a Meeting is always a high venture of Faith and it is to this venture we invite you this hour.

The time of worship at Amsterdam turned out to be so extremely creative that it has often been mentioned in the subsequent years. All present appreciated the healing silence, which came as a boon after so much talk in the sessions of the Assembly.

Attenders likewise appreciated the prayers in German, in French, and in English, as well as three spoken messages, all given in English. Though no one item had been prearranged, all parts fitted together beautifully. Of those who gave messages, one was an Episcopal bishop, one was an official of the World Council in Geneva, and one was an American Quaker. The chairman gave no message at all. One happy feature was that the prayers, in three languages, were not translated, and no one seemed to feel any necessity of translation. All present seemed to be brought, by means of words, to a place deeper than words.

The way of worship which was shared at Amsterdam is not, at the present time, employed by all Quakers, and perhaps is not employed by the majority, but all Quakers recognize it as a standard of comparison and as the original contribution which Quakers have been able to make to the whole theory and practice of Christian worship. Even in the many Quaker groups in which, because of various community developments and needs, the completely open-ended form of worship is not regularly practiced, there is a constant hope of its recovery. Sometimes, today, Quakers hold meetings in harmony with the Amsterdam ideal at one time of the week, while they hold another and more prearranged meeting at another time. Thus contemporary Quakers often recognize the value of the patchwork-quilt approach, even within their own religious communities. The same people may, with no hint of inconsistency or compromise, worship at times on the basis of immediate guidance, while they worship at other times in a manner which includes the prearranged reading of Scripture, the use of hymns and anthems and prepared preaching. The fact that we see no inconsistency in employing a variety of ways of worship is a distinct gain. It is good to know that things can be different without being better or worse.

The Quaker discovery in worship, which occurred in the middle of the seventeenth century, was really a very remarkable one, and, like many great things, extremely simple when once recognized.

The whole idea was that Christians, or anybody else for that matter, can come together with the double freedom to engage in words or to be released from the necessity of uttering words. The reverent people, whom we have called Seekers, and whom Fox reached so effectively in the summer of 1652, had already, before they knew Fox, begun to gather in some such simple way. They were not dependent upon a priest or his blessing; they were not bound to any form of words; they were not bound to silence. They simply *gathered, listened, waited,* and sought to be *obedient.*

Sometimes, in the past, this simple way of worship has been called "worship on the basis of silence," but it is now widely recognized that this is an unfortunate and fundamentally inaccurate use of language. We need to indicate something more affirmative than the mere absence of words, and this is provided by the happy suggestion of the late Thomas Kelly when we say that we meet "on the basis of Holy Obedience."[1] To be obedient is to be deeply engaged and consequently responsive. The person who is determined to say nothing and who thinks of himself merely as "audience" has not begun to understand what the significance of obedience is.

It is important to make clear the naturalness of the unique Quaker worship. Distinctive Quaker worship is not queer in any way, though it is widely regarded as such. Is there anything queer or strange in listening together for God's voice? What would be really *strange* would be a conversation in which one did all of the talking. Probably no interpreter of worship has been more successful than was Caroline Stephen in showing the naturalness of the way of worship to which we have already alluded. Caroline Stephen, sister of Sir Leslie Stephen, was a member of a brilliant nineteenth-century English family, distinguished by intellectual restlessness as well as gifts in expression. After much searching, this lady found herself, in 1872, within reach of a Friends Meeting

[1] See Thomas Kelly, A *Testament of Devotion,* chapter on "Holy Obedience" (Harper & Row, 1942).

and, in a time of need, attended it. Her account is still rewarding and still contemporary.

> When lo, on one never-to-be-forgotten Sunday morning, I found myself one of a small company of silent worshippers, who were content to sit down together without words, that each might feel after and draw near to the Divine Presence, unhindered at least, if not helped, by any human utterance. Utterance I knew was free, should the words be given; and before the meeting was over, a sentence or two were uttered in great simplicity by an old and apparently untaught man, rising in his place amongst the rest of us. I did not pay much attention to the words he spoke, and I have no recollection of their purport. My whole soul was filled with the unutterable peace of the undisturbed opportunity for communion with God—with the sense that at last I had found a place where I might, without the faintest suspicion of insincerity, join with others in simply seeking His presence.[2]

Caroline Stephen was attracted to what she found in 1872, not because it was strange or bizarre, but because it seemed as natural as breathing. "Our manner of worship," she wrote later, "is the natural (as it seems to me even the inevitable) result of the full recognition of the reality of Divine inspiration—of the actual living present sufficient fulness of intercourse between the human spirit and Him who is the Father of spirits."[3] This gifted woman did not pretend to feel, as some have fatuously done, that prearrangement is itself unlawful or sinful. If one really believes in the reality of the Divine encounter, he can hardly fail to see that this can occur as truly on Tuesday as it can on Sunday. It is wholly reasonable, therefore, for a devout person to be led, early in the week, concerning what he ought to say on Sunday, and to deny this is to make an illicit discrimination between days. Having recognized this fact, Caroline Stephen went on to affirm that the experience which had brought her, she said, to the very gates of heaven, represented the highest known spiritual ideal. Having admitted that other ways are helpful, she again referred to the

[2] *Quaker Strongholds* (London: Headley Brothers, 1911), p. 3.
[3] *Ibid.*, p. 42.

Quaker Way and said, "I yet must avow my own conviction that that ideal of public worship is the purest which has ever been recognized, and also that it is practically identical with that which seems to have been recognized in the days of the Apostles."[4]

This last point is an important one, requiring some elaboration. It is slightly shocking to some contemporary Christians, accustomed as they are to their liturgies, whether of the mass or some other, to realize that the New Testament includes not even one order of service. The early Christians, many of whom had had a background of synagogue worship, from which they had consciously departed, seem to have gathered in the simplest possible way, and with the complete absence of any prearranged pattern. That there was great spontaneity and general participation in original spoken messages is the clear implication of the well-known passage in Colossians 3:16, "Let the word of Christ dwell in you richly, as you teach and admonish one another in all wisdom, and as you sing psalms and hymns and spiritual songs with thankfulness in your hearts to God." There is not even a suggestion that there is one officiant in charge or that participation is limited to a special ecclesiastical order. In a revealing passage in Paul's First Letter to the Corinthians, one of the early books of the New Testament, there is abundant evidence that the worship practices of early Christians had not yet hardened into a mold. Paul described to the Corinthian Christians what their practice was, and thus provided later generations with the best evidence available of what the actual character of the earliest Christian worship was. Far from being a one-man affair, each worshiper was supposed to be a member of the team and therefore obedient to Christ's leading. "When you come together," says Paul, "each one has a hymn, a lesson, a revelation, a tongue, or an interpretation" (I Cor. 14:26). The problem was not that of too little general participation, as ours is, but rather that of too much. Therefore the writer had to admonish the Corinthian Christians to wait for

[4] *Ibid.*, p. 44.

one another. "Let two or three prophets speak, and let the others weigh what is said" (I Cor. 14:29).

The more we contemplate the evidence which is available concerning the practice of the early church, the more we see that William Penn's title, *Primitive Christianity Revived*, is not an idle boast. Great beauty came into the Roman Church with the development of a liturgy, but, at the same time, something of power and wonder was consequently lost. There is always a loss when religious expressions become the monopoly of a professional caste. Early Christianity, whatever else it was, was certainly a tumultuous affair, with all involved in the act and without any limiting stereotype. In so far as Quakerism has tried to recover this vitality, and this participation, it has represented a universally valid ideal, rather than the peculiarity of a particular sect.

It is generally recognized by those who know Barclay's *Apology* that his chapter on worship is one of his finest and most enduring. He tells clearly, for example, why it is necessary for people to meet together. Obviously it is possible for individuals to pray alone, and we are commanded by Christ to do so (Matt. 6:6), but the experience of being together is wholly a different one, and equally necessary. "To meet together," wrote Barclay, "we think necessary for the people of God; because, so long as we are clothed with this outward tabernacle, there is a necessity to the entertaining of a joint and visible fellowship, and bearing of an outward testimony for God, and seeing of the faces of one another."[5] If we were angels, this might not be necessary, but we do not happen to be angels. Consequently, we need the strength that comes from one another, as God reaches the entire company. The finest figure of speech which we ever employ to explain the need we have of one another is that of the burning logs or coals. When people gather for genuine worship, said Penington, "they are like a heap of fresh and burning coals warning one another, as a great strength, freshness and vigor of life flows into all." As almost anyone knows,

[5] *Apology*, Proposition XI, iii.

it is hard to have much of a fire with only one log, whereas several rather poor logs may make quite a conflagration.

To the person who contends that it is sufficient for Christians to pray alone, Barclay answers by employing his own clarifying figures of speech.

As iron shapeneth iron, the seeing of the faces of one of another, when both are inwardly gathered unto the life, giveth occasion for the life secretly to arise, and pass from vessel to vessel. And as many candles lighted, and put in one place do greatly augment the light, and make it more to shine forth, so when many are gathered together into the same life, there is more of the glory of God, and his power appears, to the refreshment of each individual; for that he partakes not only of the light and life raised in himself, but in all the rest.[6]

Barclay is reminded in this connection of the words of Christ, to the effect that where two or three are gathered He is in the midst (Matt. 18:20). The fellowship, far from being something added to the Christian way of life, is intrinsic to it. There is one thing impossible for a Christian, and that is to be Christian alone. The deep recognition of this fact has made Quakers among the most insistent on the reality and necessity of group life. Even the sense of being led to undertake a journey in the ministry is not normally looked upon as a merely individual affair, but something which requires a group decision.

Barclay's great essay on worship is abundantly quotable. He preceded Caroline Stephen by pointing out that a wholly simple form of worship is in no way an oddity. "And though," he said, "this worship be indeed very different from the divers established invented worships among Christians, and may therefore seem strange to many, yet hath it been testified of, commended and practised, by the most pious of all sorts, in all ages, as by many evident testimonies might be proved."[7] Barclay anticipated the emphasis of Thomas Kelly by referring to the central experience as

[6] *Ibid.*, Proposition XI, xvii.
[7] *Ibid.*, Proposition XI, xvi.

"holy dependence." "The great work of one and all," he said, "ought to be to wait upon God; and returning out of their own thoughts and imagination, to feel the Lord's presence."[8] Over and over, he insisted that this is a matter of experience, rather than mere speculation. The noblest passage of all is clearly autobiographical.

> Yet many and great are the advantages, which my soul, with many others, hath tasted of hereby, and which could be found of all such as would seriously apply themselves hereunto: for, when people are gathered thus together, not merely to hear men, nor depend upon them, but all are inwardly taught to stay their minds upon the Lord, and wait for his appearance in their hearts; thereby the forward working of the spirit of man is stayed and hindered from mixing itself with the worship of God; and the form of this worship is so naked and void of all outward and worldly splendor, that all occasion for man's wisdom to be exercised in that superstition and idolatry hath no lodging here; and so there being also an inward quietness and retiredness of mind, the witness of God ariseth, whereby the soul cometh to see its own condition. And there being many joined together in this same work, there is an inward travail and wrestling; and also, as the measure of grace is abode in, and overcoming of the power and spirit of darkness; and thus we are often greatly strengthened and renewed in the spirits of our minds without a word.[9]

If there is anything which the world looks upon as original with Quakers it is the practice of group silence, such as that to which Barclay refers. It is, indeed, a fact that, though individual silence is common, group silence is extremely rare. In most human gatherings, because silence is embarrassing, frantic efforts are made to keep up a stream of words even when they are inane. That Quakers have made a contribution to the world, providing a slight antidote to an overvocal culture, there is no doubt. There is great merit in keeping still when one does not have something valuable to say. Sometimes, especially when men are distraught, silence can be healing. The very discipline of getting one's body still and one's

---

[8] *Ibid.*, Proposition XI, vi.
[9] *Ibid.*, Proposition XI, xvi.

mind still, dismissing the multitude of worries and concerns, is often highly beneficent, and the best of it is that such a process does not require any special talent or aptitude. The whole of the Quaker experience gives abundant evidence that it can be learned by all kinds and conditions of men, including those of low degrees of learning.

Barclay was insistent that it is not sufficient, for creative silence, merely to abstain from *words*. We must also, he emphasized, abstain at times from all of our own thoughts, imaginations, and desires. The result can be "a flood of refreshment." There is a sense in which those who seek are likely to find, but there is another, and equally important sense, in which those who seek, especially if they seek frantically, are hindered from finding. Most of us know that the poorest method we can employ in trying to recall a forgotten name is to cudgel the brain. Frequently, if we only stop trying, taking our attention off the problem, the name will suddenly appear in consciousness. In a similar fashion, the encounter with the Living God often comes best when we cease to try and are simply willing to wait. It is surely foolish for us to dominate the conversation by continued silent talking, when what we really need is the willingness to listen and thus to learn. The relevance of this is contemporary. The silence which modern man needs, especially in view of the cacophony of radio and television, is not the mere outward silence of the lips, but a deep silence of mind and heart.

Quakers have never, as some suppose, practiced enforced silence, but instead have encouraged an open silence, with the recognized possibility and usually the expectation that the silence will lead to vocal messages, prayer, or even song. It is sometimes maintained, by critics, that those Quakers who engage in singing, now constituting the majority in the world, have somehow shown themselves disloyal to the original pattern. Two important answers need to be given to this frequently voiced harsh judgment. The first is that there is nothing wrong with development, and the one thing to avoid is slavish adherence to a fixed pattern. If we are led to sing, when some of our ancestors were not so led, this need not indicate a decline and will not automatically be seen as such, except by those who have allowed their adherence to the unprogrammed meeting to become a new idolatry. If there are some who believe more in an unprogrammed form of worship than they believe in God's leading, this is a disease which can be cured by wider experience and by more honest thinking.

The second thing to say is that the Quakers of the first period, before the age of deadly quietism had set in, most certainly did sing and shout. Contrary to popular opinion, they were, much of the time, very far from silent. Fox, in his *Journal*, tells how he sang in prison. In 1656, a visitor to Swarthmore Hall reported that, in the meeting there, he heard many speakers and prayers and singing such as he had not heard before. In the account of a visit to Ireland, shortly prior to the American visit, Fox reported that at Cork "the power of the Lord was so great that Friends, in the power and spirit of the Lord, broke out into singing many together with an audible voice, making melody in their hearts."[10]

The singing which the earliest Quakers did, and which was nearly absent in the eighteenth century, was not congregational singing, as we understand it. Indeed, modern congregational singing, even among the Baptists, did not become a common practice until 1690. The original singing was spontaneous, as it apparently was with first-century Christians. The earliest Quakers, who made Apostolic Christian practice their model, saw no reason why they should resist a tendency which is so normal in joyous hearts, and which receives such a strong support from the words of the Psalms, particularly Psalm 100:2, "Serve the Lord with gladness; come before his presence with singing." Quite naturally the nineteenth-century Quakers, who introduced congregational singing, made much of the New Testament record, in this particular regard, including that of Ephesians 5:19.

10 *Journal*, 1670.

It is only honest to admit that it is difficult, and probably impossible, to bring together in one pattern all of the features which are potent means of worship to all people. Though the unique Quaker practice of trying to avoid all human arrangements has immense merit, as Caroline Stephen and many others have so strongly attested, it is also a fact that great numbers of people are helped, in finding reality in worship, by experiences which are not possible *unless* they are arranged in advance. While there is a manifest difference between real worship, which is the direct contact of a group with the Living God, and any particular pattern of words or actions, whether in responses, kneeling, or chanting, honesty compels us to say that there are words and actions which are helpful and which many people seem to need as instruments to bring them to the sense of communion with God.

Good as the practice of extreme simplicity in worship may be, it is not the only practice that is good. There is little doubt, for example, that many are helped to achieve a sense of reality in worship by the singing of a really good choir. Since this is clearly something which cannot be achieved without a great deal of prearrangement, it is obvious that it will not fit into the pattern in which the mark of uniqueness is the rejection of all prearrangement. Choral music requires the advance work of a composer, of a conductor, and of many trained voices. This is potentially very good, but its goodness is not the kind that is compatible with the rejection of prearrangement.

What is a reasonable solution of the apparent conflict in ideals of worship? As soon as we think seriously about the matter we sense that the solution comes from the recognition of a multiplicity of values. The fact that the singing of the cathedral choir and the worship of God on the basis of Holy Obedience are radically different does not indicate that we need to reject either one. We have many *different* human needs; there is more than one way of being brought to the very gates of heaven. Herein lies the major secret of true ecumenicity. There are many who have learned the joy of spending one hour in a gathered meeting in which people are glad to be free from all ritual whether of rising and kneeling or of verbal response, so that they can be still and know, and later or earlier in the same day, spending another hour sharing in a liturgy which has been developed and beautified by the centuries. What we need to affirm, with all of the clarity which we can command, is the central ecumenical fact that *the appreciation of the one does not entail the rejection of the other.* It is not only true that different individuals have different spiritual needs; it is also true that the same individual may have radically different needs at different times.

If this analysis is correct, the responsibility of the People called Quakers is clear. As we seek to preserve and purify a way of worship which, in its totality, is unique and which can be extremely creative, we are not required to decry other ways. Our responsibility is to make available this way, hoping that it will be widely adopted in many denominations and not looked upon as a possession which Quakers hug to themselves.[11]

Though we tend to speak of worship as formal or formless, the distinction is not wholly valid. As a matter of fact, any experience of worship is necessarily formal, because the alternative is anarchy which would not permit worship at all. Even the original Quaker pattern of worship, spontaneous as it was, included the formality of gathering in a given place at a given time, as well as that of ending the meeting when two people, appointed for the purpose, shook hands. Handshaking is a symbol and a good one, but to claim that this involves no form is to be the victim of self-deceit. There were certain Quakers of the seventeenth century, particularly John Perrot, an Irish Quaker from Waterford, who claimed that Fox and the majority of Quakers were being unspiritual in employing any forms at all. Perrot shared in a bold but foolish Quaker venture in Italy, in which his closest companion was

[11] The writer has shared in a Methodist congregation which sponsored a Quaker meeting at 9 A.M. and a more formal service with choir at 11 A.M.

hanged in the Inquisition, after an audience with the Pope, and Perrot himself was placed in the madhouse in Rome for three years.

After returning to London, in 1661, John Perrot began a crusade against even the simplest of forms in public worship. He objected to the removal of the hat in prayer and to the shaking of hands at the close of meeting. This extreme view, involving even the rejection of a set hour of worship, appealed to some because it seemed to represent the extreme degree of spirituality. Perrot's influence did harm for a while, even in the colonies, Quakerism in eastern Virginia being weakened by this emphasis. Because extreme spirituality makes public worship no longer possible, George Fox felt forced to oppose Perrot's supposed "revelation." The Christian ideal is not that of the elimination of forms, for, since we are not angels, we require some forms. The ideal, rather, is to know the difference between the forms and the reality, to be ever aware of the danger of allowing the forms to take the place of reality, and to employ only those forms which lead to reality. The mainstream of Quaker life has always rejected mere spirituality as a heresy, because it has been widely recognized that we have bodily as well as spiritual needs. Many Quakers were delighted with the famous comment of the late Archbishop William Temple, to the effect that Christianity is the most materialist of all of the world religions. Spirits inhabiting bodies cannot meet unless they have a time and place in which to do so.

Though there is great value in gathering for any kind of worship, with open and expectant minds, listening for divine guidance, this is not the same as appearing empty. There is deep wisdom in an early form of the Hebrew law of worship, in which God is represented as saying, "None shall appear before me empty" (Exod. 23:15). We are far more likely to come into a deep sense of God's presence if we have engaged in some preparation of mind and heart before we gather with our fellows. The Spirit of God enlightens men, but usually it does not do so until men are ready. Light comes, sometimes in a burst, but the normal experience is that it comes to those who have already followed the light already seen. Many of the most revolutionary of scientific hypotheses have come to their originators, notably Newton and Darwin, in a brilliant flash of insight, but the flash comes, either in science or in religion, only to those who are ready or even expectant. This fact was so well understood by Rufus M. Jones that he made it the cornerstone of his understanding of worship. He made no secret of the fact that he regularly prepared his mind for every experience of public worship. The operation was already in progress when he joined the gathering of his fellow worshipers. One of his vigorous expressions of this idea was as follows:

The Quaker group silence, the cooperative team work of the entire assembly, the expectant hush, the sense of divine presence, the faith that God and man can come into mutual and reciprocal correspondence, tend to heighten the spiritual quality of the person who rises in that kind of atmosphere to speak. But that group situation, important as it is, will not work the miracle of producing a message for the hour in a person who is sterile and has nothing to say.[12]

One of the ablest of English interpreters of Quakerism, the late John William Graham, was even more explicit in reference to his own practice of preparation. "I think," he wrote, "one may rightly begin one's meeting before meeting begins—that is, on Saturday or Sunday morning, may in a time of quietness lie open to ideas. I spend some time Saturday evening, when it is free, recalling the thoughts that have struck me during the week; very often with no result but a gathered spirit."[13]

Theoretically it is possible to engage in worship anywhere. No thoughtful person supposes that it is necessary to have a particular kind of building or even to have any building at all. Christ and the inner group of Apostles surely had no kind of physical structure when they worshiped on the Mountain of Transfiguration. But,

[12] The Trail of Life in the Middle Years (New York, 1934), p. 45.
[13] The Quaker Ministry (London: Allen and Unwin, 1925), p. 85.

once this point is made abundantly clear, we must go on to say that some settings are more congenial to the achievement of reality in worship than are others. The ideal seems to be that of a building in which, with a minimum of distraction, the worshipers can be conscious of one another. After all, it is more in human faces than in brick or stone that the Living Christ is likely to be revealed. This is why the auditorium type of building is a mistake. The newer and more creative types of Quaker architecture tend, for this reason, to make it possible for the company of worshipers to arrange themselves in a hollow square. Then most people can see the faces of others, if they choose to do so, rather than their backs. As we look at each other's faces we can more easily enter deeply into one another's joys, sorrows, and needs.

The early Quaker meetinghouses, when they were first built, tended to be plain structures, with no intended symbols, and with clear glass in the windows. Frequently there were raised seats in the front, where it was expected that those most likely to speak, as well as those appointed to end the gathering by shaking hands, would be seated. These seats, comprising one, two, or even three rows, as might be required, were variously termed the "facing seats" and the "minister's gallery." It is generally agreed today that this arrangement was a mistake because it made too great a difference between the ordinary members and the ministers, thus denying, in part, the very idea which Quakers arose to promote. As Quakers became more formalized in the eighteenth century, it was a matter of importance whether a person were seated on one row or another. In short, there was, without intention, the development of what can only be called a hierarchy. Indeed, as younger men and women advanced in acceptability in speaking, it was understood that they would be invited to "come up higher." The top seat of the minister's gallery was supposed to be the best.

It is a mark of the intrinsic vitality of Quakers today that we are clearly moving away both from the employment of the minister's gallery and also from the auditorium type, which some Quakers adopted in revulsion against the old forms. The ideal building seems to be one which is beautiful in the sense that it has pleasing proportions, clean lines, and an absence of distractions. Just as the best glass is that which we cannot see, and accordingly lets all the light come in, so the best architecture is that which does not attract attention to itself. It is in this sense that some of the colonial meetinghouses are extremely satisfactory. The stone meetinghouse at Abington, Pennsylvania, is a good example of such a pure style. Fortunately, it is possible to copy the fundamental honesty and the golden proportions of such a building, and yet adapt it to modern needs by making a more flexible arrangement of benches.

The worship which most often comes to our minds is that of Sunday morning, but we are well aware that real worship need not be limited to such occasions. Barclay pointed out that "all days are alike holy in the sight of God," yet held that there are at least four reasons why worship on the First Day of the week is a valuable experience, worthy of being maintained. First, it is necessary that there be *some time* set aside to meet together, second, it is good to have a time set free from outward affairs, third, our helpers and even our animals need some cessation from continual labor, and fourth, "it appears that the apostles and primitive Christians did use the first day of the week for these purposes." Though Barclay's reasons are, for the most part, convincing ones, and though the general mentality which encourages such a use of Sunday is an asset in our culture, of which we are foolish not to take advantage, there is considerable doubt about Barclay's fourth reason. Many were shocked when William Law pointed out that the New Testament does not include one single command to engage in worship on Sunday, but what he wrote two hundred years ago was undoubtedly true. What is valuable in this connection is not the particular sacredness of any one day, but the general practice of the rhythm of the week. Tuesday would, of course, do as well as Sunday, but, unless *some* day is set aside, something of great cultural and spiritual value is undoubtedly lost. While we stress the virtue in gathering on special days, we must likewise stress, at the same time, the wisdom of gathering on other days, as the earliest Christians seem to have done.

The Quaker effort to reach reality in worship is especially successful in connection with life's high moments, such as marriage and death. These times are important, partly because people are unusually open on such occasions. The characteristic Quaker wedding is a thing of simple beauty. The philosophy is that, since the parties engaging in marriage are entering into a deeply sacred commitment, which involves others as well as themselves, private marriage is always a contradiction in terms. The occasion is public, open to anybody, and is carried on in a gathering in the mood of worship. In this gathering there may be, and often is, a considerable amount of unplanned vocal participation, including prayer, message, and sometimes song. At some point in this period of worship, the couple to be married rise, take each other by the hand, and declare their commitment to each other, "before God and this company." Because the theory is that it is God who makes them man and wife, there is no need of the words of a clergyman or other officiant to produce, by his words, a change of status. The nature of the public commitment is such that nothing else is required. Often a certificate of record is signed, during the gathering, and read immediately by someone appointed for this task. Sometimes every person present signs the certificate, thereby providing the married persons with visible evidence of the participation of numerous fellow worshipers in their own great experience. Such a marriage is legal today in most of the American states, with no signature from an ordained clergyman or a justice of the peace required.

At first blush, this Quaker way of marriage, without benefit of clergy, seems very different from the usual marriage practices in which, normally, the clergyman says the vows first, after which they are repeated. On deeper thought, however, we realize that the difference is slight. Both in the ordinary Christian marriage and in the Quaker Way, it is clearly understood that it is the entire worshiping fellowship which witnesses the sacred undertaking and which gives its blessing. The clergyman operates, not as an individual, but as the legal representative of the group whose servant or minister he is. The only important difference, in the Quaker marriage, is that the support of the group is expressed directly, rather than through a representative.

When the pastoral system among Quakers began nearly a century ago, it soon became possible for recognized Quaker ministers to operate, in regard to marriage, as clergymen, and thus to abandon, if they chose to do so, the beautiful and meaningful practice of Quaker marriage which had meant so much for two hundred years. Though a strong intellectual defense can be made and is being made increasingly today for the introduction of a pastoral system, it is only honest to admit that it was a serious mistake for many Quakers to abandon a practice as rich in significance as was the historic Quaker way of marriage. Since, however, we can change again, the adoption of a clerical pattern need not be continued and, as we move forward in the recovery of vitality, it seems likely that the Quaker pastors may be the ones to insist upon the employment of a practice which is too precious to be lost. One evidence of a Quaker pastor's integrity is his insistence on developing a procedure in which his own ceremonial service is not required. Often the best men are those who seek, not to magnify their office, but to make themselves unnecessary.

Though the Quaker way of worship is valuable and relevant in a great variety of situations, it comes into its own most fully in a memorial service. Indeed, it would be hard to exaggerate the value of a meeting for worship in which, with a deep sense of reverence, Quakers gather to honor the one who has died and to reaffirm the corporate faith in the Life Everlasting. It is wonderfully satisfying to observe real freedom of expression, whether in message or vocal prayer, which often appears when people are deeply saddened by their loss, yet, at the same time, visibly lifted by their vital faith. Sometimes there will be eight or ten spontaneous tributes, not necessarily in fulsome praise, but in the mood of gratitude and consequent dedication of life. Some may tell, reverently, of experiences involving the departed Friend, and of unrecorded acts of love, which otherwise would not have been a matter of general knowledge.

Though in some Quaker meetings for worship, which involve unplanned speaking, the general level of speaking is poor and thin, the high emotion engendered by the loss of a loved one usually cures this malady. Indeed, the level of speaking in such a memorial service is often very high. A person has to be unusually insensitive to indulge in insipid clichés on such a moving occasion. Frequently, as we are lifted by listening to expressions marked by integrity or even by eloquence, we are very glad that it is not necessary to go through a stereotyped ritual. There is much to be said for the funeral service of the *Book of Common Prayer*, and certainly it is vastly superior to a ritual made up by any one man, yet it cannot equal the glow of life when there is the sense of reality with no ritual at all. The ritual is good, but, just as there is something better about fresh food than about the best of tinned food, so there is something better than the best ritual ever composed.

One of the fine developments of our time is the increasing tendency to bring into a memorial service the mood of a joyous victory. Contemporary Quakers, like many others, are in open revolt against the pagan atmosphere, which still marks funerals. The pagan element is indicated both by the pressure to engage in ostentatious expense, on caskets, flowers, and tombstones, and by the mood of unrelieved sorrow. Whenever Christianity understands itself, the mood inevitably becomes one of victory and even of rejoicing. The early Moravians who blew a trumpet, on the occasion of death, to announce the arrival of another into the direct communion with the Father, were demonstrating a deep understanding of their faith. This is why there is an increasing tendency, on the part of really thoughtful Christians, to employ hymns of victory in their funerals and to minimize the carnal loss, as represented by the open casket. In some Quaker memorial services today, there is no casket evident at all.

Another development, in line with the more truly Christian response to death, is that of insistence upon simple burial.[14] Among some Quakers today there is a planned movement designed to help people to face the decisions involved in the death of loved ones, before the crises come. This includes legal advice to help people who want to spend their hard-earned money for projects among the living rather than in ostentatious display. Here is an area in which Quakers can give leadership to their fellows and in which such leadership is a matter of solemn responsibility.

In all of the Quaker emphasis on worship it must be understood that there is, at the same time, a far *greater* emphasis upon common life in the world. Worship is important, but it is not all-important. It is best envisaged, not as the end to which our religious efforts point, but rather as the beginning, from which our service in the world arises. We come in, chiefly in order to go out! This is the meaning of one of the best of all humorous stories which Quakers love to tell. The story is that a stranger, unaccustomed to Quaker ways, wandered into a meeting for worship and, when he arrived, found that there was absolute silence. Being perplexed by what he saw about him, the stranger assumed that the occasion had not yet started. Consequently he whispered to the man next to him and asked, "When does the service begin?" To this came the classic reply from his neighboring Quaker, "The service begins when the meeting ends." This is the point, stated perfectly, but the understanding of it is by no means limited to Quakers. There are a good many congregations, of different de-

[14] In the burial of the only Quaker President of the United States, Herbert Hoover, there was, apparently for the first time in history, no gun salute, and the person who conducted the service wore a plain business suit.

nominations, which now print, at the bottom of their Sunday
bulletins

The End of Worship;
The Beginning of Service.

As we face the future, we can be very glad that we need not be
bound by any stereotype, even the best. If we truly believe in
guidance, we are bound to conclude that God is still leading His
children and that new and more valuable ways than any which we
have ever known may appear.

6 / A Practical Alternative
to Clergy and Laity

To equip God's people for work in his service.
EPHESIANS 4:12 (New English Bible)

Of all the mistaken notions about Quakers, the most extreme is
the supposition that they have no ministers. The misunderstanding on this important point is so widespread that it is actually
grotesque. In the beginning of the Movement the fact that a large
proportion of the members, of both sexes, were clearly engaged in
the ministry, was perhaps, from the point of view of the outside
observer, the most striking single feature of Quaker life. Not only
were the rank and file of the members ministers in the sense that
they performed humble services to their fellow men in daily life;
many of them were also ministers in the sense that they preached
wherever and whenever they could.[1]

In the tumultuous sixth decade of the seventeenth century, men
of the character of Edward Burrough hardly missed a chance to
preach, even when under arrest. A characteristic experience came
in Ireland, about 1653, when, according to the *Journal of the Life
of William Edmundson*, Burrough and his friend Francis Howgill,

[1] The importance of the ministry among early Quakers is attested by the
official title of the *Journal* of George Fox (Ellwood edition, 1694). The full
title is as follows: A *Journal* or Historical Account of the Life, Travels,
Sufferings, Christian Experiences and Labour of Love in the Work of the
Ministry of that ancient, eminent and faithful Servant of Jesus Christ, George
Fox, who departed this Life in great Peace with the Lord, the 13th of the
11th Month 1690.

though banished from Ireland, nevertheless used their banishment as an opportunity for their vocal ministry.

The priests and professors in the south of Ireland were so envious against truth, that they got an order from Henry Cromwell, then lord deputy of Ireland, to banish Edward Burrough and Francis Howgill out of the nation, and a guard of soldiers were ordered to conduct them from place to place, till they were shipped off. But the guards were loving to them and suffered them to have meetings where they came; so that several received the truth, and small meetings were settled in divers places, particularly in Dublin.

Edmundson, himself, used all opportunities to preach the truth as he saw it. He wrote in his *Journal:*

The next day, I came to Londonderry; it was market day, and there were stage players and rope-dancers in the market place, and abundance of people gathered. The Lord's spirit filled my heart, his power struck at them, and his word was sharp. So I stood in the market-place and proclaimed the day of the Lord among them, and warned them all to repent.

Later, he says, feeling a burden lifted because of what he had done, he walked along the street where the people flocked about him. Since this was a new opportunity, he spoke again. "I stood still," he wrote, "and declared truth to them directing them to the light of Christ in their own hearts."

Such a *Journal* entry, which can be matched by many others, gives a vivid impression of the abundance, the urgency, and the fundamental message of the public ministry of the numerous Quaker preachers of the first generation. The late William W. Comfort, President of Haverford College, summarized the original situation in a succinct manner when he wrote: "For the first fifty years of their existence, Friends were a zealous crusading and proselytizing body of Christians."[2] The strategic instrument of this crusade was the Quaker ministry.

It would be a mistake to suppose that an extreme emphasis on

2 *The Quaker Way of Life,* p. 3.

the ministry ended with the death of Barclay and of Fox or even of William Penn. As a matter of fact, though there have been periods of relative lethargy, when the fire has merely smoldered, there has not been one generation, during more than three hundred years, which has not witnessed outstanding Quaker ministry. A number of brilliant Quaker preachers have been widely recognized in the twentieth century, the most obvious examples being H. G. Wood, Professor of Theology at the University of Birmingham, in England, and Rufus M. Jones and Elbert Russell, in America. Elbert Russell finished his influential career as Dean of the Divinity School and also Dean of the Chapel at Duke University. A number of contemporary Quakers have had large opportunities to influence theological education, the most distinguished examples being those of Henry J. Cadbury, formerly Hollis Professor of Divinity at Harvard University, and Alexander C. Purdy, long Dean of Hartford Theological Seminary, in Connecticut.

Though, as we have suggested, a great many of the earliest Quakers were looked upon as ministers, it was soon recognized that some were more truly in the ministry than were others. This was the chief reason for providing a "ministers' gallery" in the early meetinghouses. Some of the earliest general gatherings of Quakers in England were confined to "Friends in the Ministry," and there was a distinct difference between what went on in such a meeting and what went on in a general meeting concerned with business matters, such as the collection of funds and the relief of suffering occasioned by imprisonment and other forms of persecution.

It must not be supposed, however, that, in the first generation, there was any hard and fast distinction between ministers and other Quakers. A sharp distinction would have been difficult to make, inasmuch as there was no ordination and no distinction of dress or ceremonial duties. Nevertheless, the distinction between the types of ministry was well understood. Some messages from

Fox were addressed to all of his followers, but others were addressed specifically to those who were understood to be ministers. The admonition to "walk cheerfully over the world," which was produced during the imprisonment in Cornwall in 1656, was addressed, not to the entire public and not to Quakers in general, but to "Friends in the Ministry." Under date of 1658, Fox said in his *Journal*, "I was moved to declare and open many things to those Friends who had received a part of the ministry, concerning the exercise of their spiritual gifts in the church."

The thoughtful reader is likely to wonder how anyone knew who a Quaker minister was, since there was nothing in the nature of an ordination ceremony. The answer is that Friends watched in order to see. A minister was simply one who ministered. If a man or a woman began to speak well and effectively, everyone knew it and that was the end of the matter. What is important to understand is that the Quaker Movement would never have continued or even have begun apart from a powerful ministry, and this George Fox understood very well. While objecting to preaching as an end in itself, he valued it highly as a means to the development of new life. In insisting on the importance of the ministry, he said, "It is a mighty thing to be in the work of the ministry of the Lord God and to go forth in that; for it is not as a customary preaching, but to bring people to the end of all preaching." The Quaker minister is one who seeks, not to glorify himself, but to make himself unnecessary. The purpose of the preaching is to help to produce something more valuable than preaching.

William Charles Braithwaite, in both of his great historical volumes, *The Beginnings of Quakerism* and *The Second Period of Quakerism*, was meticulous in tracing the growth of the idea of the ministry in Quaker experience. He put emphasis upon this because he recognized, he said, that "the spiritual leaders were the chief factor in the organized Society of Friends, as they had been in the earlier stages of the movement."[3] When Braithwaite tried to indicate the distinctive character of the Quaker ministry, he realized that the task was a very difficult one.

It is not easy to define the position of the Quaker minister: his authority was great, but it was not derived from human appointment; it depended from meeting to meeting upon the call of the Lord and upon the message which He might give raising up the witness to its truth in the hearts of Friends.

Difficult as it may be to distinguish, in theory, between Quaker ministers and other Friends, there is no doubt that, in the early generations of the Movement, the spiritual government of Friends was almost entirely in the ministers' hands. "Only slowly, and almost imperceptibly," says Braithwaite, "did the spiritual government of the Church pass to the main body of Friends."[4]

The chief instrument by which the recognized ministers kept some order in the potentially chaotic movement came to be called The Morning Meeting. Most of them were of course traveling ministers, with nothing resembling settled pastorates. Naturally the travelers tried, when possible, to keep in close touch with one another. Without any official arrangement at first, they collected at the home of Gerrard Roberts in London, which became a kind of headquarters. Thus the Quaker preachers maintained a close fellowship with one another, while inquirers soon learned where to find them if they wanted to ask any questions.

At least as early as 1670, the ministers were in the practice of meeting at the home of Roberts early on Sunday mornings, in order to tell one another where they felt moved to attend. Thus they became a sort of planning and distributing society, so far as the spoken word was concerned. Soon it was realized that, since the written word was more enduring and more far-reaching than

[3] *The Second Period of Quakerism* (London: Macmillan and Company, 1919), p. 278.
[4] *Ibid.*, p. 543.

the spoken one, they also had some responsibility in deciding what could be printed with official Quaker approval. Otherwise, it was obvious that there was no check on the effusions of the lunatic fringe.

When in London, after his return from America, in 1673, Fox set up what came to be known as the "Second-day's Morning Meeting," building consciously on the experience of the almost unplanned gatherings at the home of Gerrard Roberts. This new organization, meeting every Monday morning, was made up exclusively of men ministers, and was charged chiefly with the double duty of supervising the publication of books and the distribution of the spoken ministry in the London area. This gathering soon became, in fact, an executive body. It even prohibited ministers, charged with moral lapses, from preaching until they had cleared themselves.

It is from this body and its deliberations that there arose the practice of recognizing a gift in the ministry which is the basis of the present practice in the great majority of Quaker bodies today. This is variously called "recording" or "recognizing" and differs from ordination, in that it only claims to record a *fact* which can already be observed, rather than conferring a *status* not previously enjoyed. Such recognition of the ministry is one of the chief grounds of the pastoral system and is honored by all of the Yearly Meetings of what is now known as Friends United Meeting.

At first the only objective means of knowing who was accepted as a minister was to look at the book in the home of Gerrard Roberts, where visiting ministers signed their names. Later it became necessary to inaugurate more formal and careful methods of deciding which ones should be recognized and which ones should not. Today, in the minutes of most of the Yearly Meetings, there can be found lists of recognized ministers, some of whom are appointed as pastors and some of whom are engaged in secular employment. For example, Professor Rufus Jones, though never a pastor, was listed, through many years, as a minister by New England Yearly Meeting.

Even though British Friends officially abandoned the practice of recording gifts in the ministry in 1924, the Quakers of Great Britain continue to set great store by the spoken word. No one has made this more clear than that strong leader of English Quaker life and thought, Neave Brayshaw. "We must understand," wrote Brayshaw, "that it is not the only way of the spirit to speak to us in the stillness. He has another and equally important way of speaking, namely, through one another. And one of the ways of this communication (I am not saying the only way or the most important), but certainly one of the ways is by the spoken word, and any ruling of it out, any refusal to use one of the means put at our disposal, leads to weakness."[5]

The really difficult point for the reader to understand is how it is logically possible for Quakers to stress the ministry so greatly and yet to reject the distinction between clergy and laity. Since the point is as important as it is difficult, it is one which justifies careful exposition. The original basis of the rejection of the distinction between clergy and laity was the effort to be faithful to the New Testament conception, with which the earliest Quaker spokesmen were almost universally familiar. Rude and unlettered as these men were, they could discern that first-century Christianity had no counterpart of what the modern world means by a clergyman. The young William Penn, writing as a prisoner in the Tower of London, reported that the clergy of his day had become so puffed up with pride and spiritual position that the words of Jesus to His disciples sounded like heresy. The unreasonable and antiquated instructions, he said sarcastically, were, "Be ready to teach: answer with meekness: if anything be revealed to him that sits by, let the first hold his peace: be not lords over God's heritage, but meek and lowly; washing the feet of the people, as

[5] In *The Friend* (Philadelphia), June 19, 1930, p. 601.

Jesus did those of his poor disciples." The deepest mistake of the clergy, Penn held, is that they no longer heed the words of Christ, "Whosoever will be chief among you, let him be your servant" (Matt. 20:27). The very idea of the clergy as people of prestige, Penn held, is fundamentally inconsistent with the New Testament pattern.

For by this time, their pride has made them the Church and the people but the porch at best; a cipher that signifies nothing, unless they clap their figure before it: forgetting that if they were as good as they should be, they could be but ministers, stewards, and under-shepherds; that is, servants to the church, family, flock, and heritage of God: and not that they are that Church, family, flock and heritage, which they are only servants unto.[6]

It is obvious that men like Penn and Barclay did not object to preaching, since they did a great deal of it themselves. What they objected to, in the most strenuous manner, was not the ministry, but the *perversion* of the ministry which made it into a trade or a profession, which a man might enter without any sense of spiritual urgency, but chiefly because it provided a way of becoming a gentleman, with a considerable degree of prestige and honor in any ordinary community. The pattern was already developing in the seventeenth century, according to which the parson and the squire normally joined forces as the chief community leaders. Men could succeed in this business without any real fire in their souls, since the main skill involved was that of reciting the liturgy, which could be learned quickly by a wholly irreverent man.

At one of the high points in the *Apology* Barclay explained, with his customary clarity, exactly what is rejected. "That which we oppose," he wrote, "is the distinction of laity and clergy, which in the scripture is not to be found."[7] Being a scholar, Barclay knew, of course, that the words *laos* and *kleros* are found in the New Testament, but he also knew that they meant, originally,

---

[6] *No Cross No Crown*, 2nd ed., Chap. XII, Section 9.
[7] Proposition X, xxvi.

something very different from what they have finally come to mean in their English translation. Because Barclay was keenly aware of the fact that the ministry of the early Christian Church was a matter of function rather than of status, he was saddened when he observed the alteration which had come about in sixteen centuries. Once ministers of Christ had been indistinguishable outwardly from other Christians, but now a clergyman "must also be distinguished from the rest by the colour of his clothes; for he must only wear black."

It would be a great mistake to suppose that Quakers, in following the lead of Barclay and Penn in this important matter, were merely anticlerical or objecting to only one side of the familiar dichotomy. The idea of the lay Christian is, indeed, as objectionable as is the idea of the clerical Christian. For this reason the Quaker must always fight on two fronts simultaneously. To use a Biblical analogy, he must "beware of the leaven of the Pharisees and the leaven of Herod" (Mark 8:15). It is wrong to be a layman, if by layman is meant, as it popularly is, a person who is primarily a supporter of the work which the clergy do, rather than a vital member of the Christian team. In contemporary parlance, because of its use in connection with the law and with medicine, the word layman means a person who does not or cannot *practice*. It ought to be obvious to all that there is no rightful place in the Christian cause for anyone whose function can be so described. For this reason, the practical Quaker purpose is sometimes described as that of "the abolition of the laity." There is, in any case, no justification for the role of the mere observer. Christianity, when it truly understands itself, can never be a spectator sport.

As the Quaker, of any generation, fights his unrelenting battle on both fronts at once, it is necessary to try to be fair to that which is being rejected. It must be freely admitted that great numbers, among those who are called clergy today, adopt for themselves the same humble pattern as that outlined by Penn, in reference to the New Testament model. It must be understood that early Quakers were staking out their own position, not in reference to men who took seriously the acted parable of washing the feet of the Apostles, but rather in reference to those who were already beginning, in some places, to illustrate the pattern of later generations which was so brilliantly caricatured by Lytton Strachey.[8]

For many generations the Church of England had slept the sleep of the . . . comfortable. The sullen murmurings of dissent, the loud battle-cry of Revolution, had hardly disturbed her slumbers. Portly divines subscribed with a sigh or a smile to the Thirty-nine Articles, sank quietly into easy livings, rode gaily to hounds of a morning as gentlemen should, and, as gentlemen should, carried their two bottles of an evening. To be in the Church was in fact simply to pursue one of those professions which Nature and Society had decided were proper to gentlemen and gentlemen alone. The fervours of piety, the zeal of Apostolic charity, the enthusiasm of self-renunciation—these things were all very well in their way—and in their place; but their place was certainly not the Church of England. Gentlemen were neither fervid nor zealous, and above all they were not enthusiastic.

If there is confusion in the public mind about the Quaker ministry, there are good reasons for that confusion. One reason for it is that contemporary Quakers are not entirely agreed about the subject, but a far deeper reason is that the entire subject of the ministry is involved in essential paradox. When once we try to take the Christian religion seriously, as Quakers have always claimed to do, this paradox is faced. On the one hand, it might easily be supposed that there would have to be an entire rejection of the ministry because of opposition to the professionalized clergy. One does not go very far into the Gospels before he discovers that some of Christ's most adamant enemies were the men in the priesthood. They desired His destruction, partly because what He said and did seemed to undermine their entire position. It would have not been surprising, therefore, if Chris-

8 *Eminent Victorians* (New York: Garden City Publishing Co.), pp. 11, 12.

tianity had become a completely lay religion. The paradox is that the very movement, which had rejected the official priesthood, advanced by producing, as the price of survival, its own kind of spiritual leadership.

The early Quaker Movement repeated much of the first-century pattern. Beginning with fierce opposition, both to and from the professionalized clergy, Quakers soon developed their own strong ministry. The practical paradox of Quakerism is that of an exceptionally able ministry arising in opposition to the ministry. How can this be explained?

The solution of the paradox comes when we think deeply enough about the ministry to realize that, if it is to be effective, it must be both universal and specialized. The universal ministry is based on the idea that there is a sense in which every follower of Christ is and must be a minister. In short, he must be a servant of Christ and of his fellow men, and the church must actually be a "servant people." In Colombo, Ceylon, there is a Presbyterian congregation, made up largely of burghers, who have taken the attractive name, "The Church of the Servant Lord." If such a term is truly meaningful, it is obvious that every member, both male and female, must be in the ministry. In short, a Christian society which understands its own essence will not only affirm, but also practice, the glorious doctrine of the priesthood of all believers.

The priesthood of all believers, to which millions give lip service, may be understood in more than one way. Sometimes it appears to carry the ridiculously negative meaning that no man needs a priest. The full and important meaning, however, is the affirmative one that each person *can be* and *should be* a priest to somebody. Each person has a relationship to others which is truly unique and, therefore, each has unique opportunities for reaching other minds and hearts. Sometimes the sincere yet uneducated man is a better priest to *someone* than is the educated theologian. It is only when we stress facts of this order that we understand one side of the paradox, that of a truly universal ministry. This is what we mean when we say that it is necessary to abolish the laity.

One might suppose that the emphasis on the universal ministry would be the end of the matter, but it is not. The practical question remains, of how the universal ministry is to be changed from a slogan into a practical reality. How is the idea to achieve embodiment? How, in sober practice, is the priesthood of every believer to be actualized? Certainly it does not come to pass by means of an announcement. The task of actualization is really a difficult one and success is only approximated at best. It will not do itself; it will not be done unless there are people who are willing and able to work at it relentlessly and patiently.

This is where the other side of the paradox comes in. We must have a specialized ministry, which is dedicated to the realization and actualization of the universal ministry. The two conceptions which, on the surface, appear to be incompatible and, therefore, in necessary conflict, can be seen, on deeper analysis, to be mutually necessary to one another. There will always be, in practice, some tension between the two conceptions of the ministry, but both are deeply entrenched in Quaker history and both operate best when they operate in tension. It is easy, of course, to relax the tension. Then we settle for a mere lay religion, on the one hand, or for a predominantly clerical religion, on the other, but whenever we do so, and the tension is consequently eliminated, decay inevitably sets in. In a mere lay religion the ministry tends to become scrappy or even trivial, while, in a mere clerical religion, though sermons may be eloquent or even deep, the members tend to become audience-minded. Death comes equally in both situations.

In the light of what has just been said, the title of this chapter is probably now understandable to the thoughtful reader. Much of the inner genius of Quakerism, helping to account for its influence so disproportionate to its numbers, lies in the effort to achieve a third way. Quakers simply do not believe that the classifications of clergy and laity together exhaust the possibilities. There is a third class, which is truly an alternative to either that of layman or that of clergyman. It is made up of persons who claim neither clerical status nor special privilege, and who certainly are not marked by any distinctive garb or addressed by any special titles, but who, nevertheless, are deeply involved in the ministry because they are seeking to equip others for *their own* ministry. This conception of the ministry, which is now receiving a degree of attention which it has not enjoyed for years, has been brilliantly depicted by Thomas J. Mullen, a Quaker pastor, who has been successful in applying the central Quaker insight to the Church in general.[9]

The further paradox is that the Religious Society of Friends, the very body which is popularly supposed to reject the ministry, may prove in the end to give the world, as its most valuable single practical gift, its conception of what the ministry means and can mean. When the Quaker pastoral system began, almost a hundred years ago, there were people, both inside and outside the Society of Friends, who supposed, without much examination, that the employment of pastors represented a complete break with the Quaker heritage. But more mature thought can easily show that this judgment was not justified. Though, when pastors were appointed, there were naturally some who were totally ignorant of the tension already mentioned, and who, therefore, became clergymen in fact, if not in name, this was by no means the universal experience. There were others, and they were the characteristic ones, who were as far from being clergy as they were from being laity. Some of these people are still alive and represent in their own careers the central Christian witness, according to which a minister is fundamentally a servant, drawing out the powers of others and never calling attention to himself.

The recognition of the fact that some men were gifted by nature to be pastors was an almost inevitable one, if people were to take the New Testament seriously. How can one claim to accept, as a

[9] *The Renewal of the Ministry* (New York and Nashville: Abingdon Press, 1963).

standard, the original New Testament model and yet not see the great variety of gifts in the ministry that the early Christians noted? On the one hand, we must recognize the ministry of plumbers and carpenters and housewives, but, on the other hand, we are blind indeed if we fail to recognize the ministry of those who are especially able to teach and to develop the powers of these other members. Following the classic usage of Ephesians 4:12, we speak of such men as those engaged in the equipping ministry. It is wholly right that they should speak more often than do many others, because their witness is desperately needed. Such a man, in the modern Quaker Movement, was Rufus M. Jones. Whether such a man is called a pastor or not is a trivial matter. He was in fact a pastor and teacher, in the sense of the passage in Ephesians.[10]

The equipping minister is a necessity, because, without his work, the fire tends to burn low and sometimes becomes extinguished altogether. It is not very important whether the man who tends the fire arises spontaneously or is appointed. If the first alternative fails to occur, the second must, providing death is not acceptable. That George Fox understood this very well is shown by his decision to build up the "Second Day Morning Meetings," to which reference has already been made. Fox determined to make a deliberate effort to distribute the ministry and not to rely on chance or the whims of individuals. The modern pastoral system, when it has been most conscious of its heritage, and has resisted acceptance of a conventional clerical pattern, has been essentially a logical development of what Fox instituted so effectively in 1673.

The problem of support is one which must be faced, if we are trying seriously to do something to equip the universal ministry. Though some men are no doubt right in seeking to serve as equippers and, at the same time, earn their daily bread in a secular occupation, there are others who are so valuable in their unique

10 As a matter of record, I never attended a meeting for worship, with Rufus Jones present, when he did not speak.

capacity that they ought to be liberated from the necessity of secular earning. From the very beginning Quakers understood this practical necessity and, accordingly, raised funds to liberate men of the character of Edward Burrough and George Fox. So far as we know, Fox never, after he became a traveling preacher, worked with any regularity at his trade of shoemaker, to which he had first been apprenticed. His associates quickly saw that he was needed for other tasks, and this did not involve any tendency to downgrade the cutting of leather.

As we study the records of the powerful burst of life in the early Quaker community, we soon realize that the most important business which necessitated some organizational structure was that of collecting funds. These funds were used to support traveling ministers and to relieve those who were suffering from imprisonment or in other ways. It is sometimes supposed that the strong condemnation of "hireling priests" is incompatible with payment of those who serve in the ministry, but this is a patently superficial judgment. When Fox and others condemned the hireling priesthood, what they had in mind was, primarily, the avarice of men who looked upon the ministry as analogous to a secular profession, with its own peculiar opportunities for advancement and prestige. Men of the clerical profession were called "hirelings," not chiefly because they were supported financially, but because they seemed to make the ministry more of a job than a calling.

Most Quaker pastors today receive salaries, but these are, for the most part, in such modest amounts that only an unreasonable critic would suppose that such payment makes the Quaker ministry something which is undertaken for the sake of financial gain. Payment simply represents "liberation," in the sense that a person is set free from the financial struggle of the market place in order to do all that he can to *arouse*, to *incite*, to *teach*, and to *equip*. Far from being paid to preach, the Quaker minister often affirms that he earns his living through the week, by his organizing and teaching labors, and then gives his vocal ministry on Sundays.

When a person, for one reason or another, already has adequate
financial support, as was clearly true of wealthy men like Barclay
and Penn, no collections for support are needed, and none will be
arranged. The whole idea is that, in a Christian society, the
members help one another to enter into the kind of life to which
it appears that God has called them. This is a far cry from the
system in which, by dependence upon legal tithes, the appointment to a parish was sometimes looked upon as a financial
bonanza. There is nothing in Quakerism even faintly resembling
such a system.

It is important for the reader to understand the reasons why,
more than eighty years ago, Quakers for the first time recognized
the need for pastoral leadership.[11] The truth is that in many
communities, including the one in which I was born, the case was
desperate. Because the reliance on a mere lay ministry had finally
proved delusive, the only remaining alternatives were either the
development of a new kind of ministry or slow extinction. Some
congregations, out of blind conservatism, refused to change, and
consequently died. Nearly all of the meetings of Indiana, the
center of the Quaker population in America, in which innovations
were rejected, have since ceased to be. Something clearly had to be
done, but what? In England, the answer came, in part, by the
exciting work of John Wilhelm Rowntree and his associates, in
establishing summer schools and eventually Woodbrooke, on the
edge of Birmingham, dedicated to the deepening of Biblical and
other knowledge.[12] One of the results of this conscious effort at
renewal was the inauguration, in 1908, of the annual Swarthmore
Lectureship. In one sense the Swarthmore Lectures provide really

[11] My mother, who is now ninety-eight, was a young woman at the time
and has been able to give me a first hand account of the stirring events which
occurred. For a fair and sympathetic, yet critical account of the rise of the
pastoral system see Rufus M. Jones, *The Later Periods of Quakerism* (London: Macmillan and Company, 1921), Vol. II, pp. 917–922.

[12] For an understanding of what occurred in Britain it is suggested that
the reader see *The Quakers, Their Story and Message*, by Brayshaw, pp.
320–23. The passage includes a general letter on the ministry, emanating from
London in 1919.

good preaching, and have come to be the closest approximation which we have to an authoritative Quaker literature in the twentieth century.

In New England, in North Carolina, and in the Middle West the alternative to decay turned out to be a pastoral system. This was never instituted in the areas dominated by Philadelphia and Baltimore, partly because the better financial position of the leading members was itself a means of liberation to permit the operation of a truly equipping ministry. In Baltimore, for example, there happened to be wealthy and cultured Quaker families, several members of which were highly effective in the ministry, in the specialized and not merely the universal sense of the word. A brilliant example was that of Anna Braithwaite Thomas. Though never called a pastor, Mrs. Thomas performed highly effective pastoral work for many decades.

In all frankness, we must admit that some serious mistakes were made when the pastoral system was inaugurated. At first the development came in such natural steps that no intellectual examination of the change seemed to be required. Consequently, there was no effective barrier against the return, in some places, to practices similar to those which Quakerism had arisen to oppose. The mistake was that, too often, a fundamentally alien system was taken over, almost intact, so that the basic Quaker witness tended to be minimized or even forgotten. It was easy for the members, delighting in a new leadership, with sermons so much more appealing than were the poor ones to which they had become accustomed, to leave too much responsibility to the new order of men that was arising. Soon some of these men were addressed as "Reverend," and a good many of the pastors began to conduct weddings and funerals, exactly after the fashion of the neighboring clergy. It was an easy step to the public acceptance of the Quaker Movement as merely another denomination, fulfilling the same function as sister denominations, rather than representing the radical spiritual revolution which had been originally intended.

The most hopeful fact about the Quaker ministry today is that there is in it an agonizing reassessment of its role. More and more the new pastors, especially those who are truly conscious of history, are increasingly unwilling to be cast into the conventional mold. This sense of ferment is associated with the new searching which is going on throughout Protestantism and which is fundamentally a hopeful phenomenon.

The hope of our day, so far as the People Called Quakers are concerned, lies not in a rejection of the gains which the pastoral system of the last century has brought, but in a creative reappraisal from which may emerge something better than we have ever known before. In this, as in so many other avenues, the Quaker genius consists in finding or in creating a "third way," rejecting both of the undesirable alternatives which are uncritically supposed to exhaust the possibilities. It is not good enough to accept the pastoral system as it is; it is not good enough to reject the pastoral system; the only hope lies in its reconstruction, which cannot be accomplished without a more careful attention to the philosophy upon which it or indeed any ministry must be based.

In pointing out, as we must, the mistakes of the pastoral system, it is likewise necessary to point out the equally glaring mistakes of the nonpastoral system. However exciting the possibilities of a wholly unprofessional ministry may sound, in the pages of Caroline Stephen or other expositors of the system, the actual practice is often dismal. It is by no means uncommon for a Quaker Meeting, in which there is no specialized ministry, to gather in a fundamentally sleepy fashion and for the vocal ministry, when it arises out of the silence, to be almost wholly insipid. Frequently it is obvious that the shallow ideas which are expressed have been thought up on the spur of the moment, with little or no preparation, while the mode of expression may easily be little more than a string of clichés. Because there are many such meetings in which there is never any Biblical preaching, the output is correspondingly weak.

Where there is nothing but lay ministry, the speaking tends to be superficial because it does not arise from any serious and sustained effort. However good a "silent meeting" may be at its best, it is seldom at its best, and certainly the system involves no inherent magic. It is not able to bring living water out of shallow wells. At worst, such a meeting can decline in spiritual power so that it includes almost no vocal prayer and sometimes becomes little more than a political forum, in which people answer one another or merely voice their opinions. It is, indeed, hard to say which is worse, the conventional pastoral meeting in which the members merely listen to their preacher or the conventional nonpastoral meeting in which they listen to nobody and many sleep.

There is no hope for a brilliant future in the Quaker story without a conscious, deliberate, and sustained effort to enlist and to train a ministry related to the peculiar needs of our time and therefore different from any of the stereotypes with which we have been familiar in the recent past.[13] This will not be accomplished unless the fire gets much hotter than it now is.

The encouraging fact is that Quakers have, inherent in their total philosophy, a conception of the ministry which may be precisely that for which the modern world is looking. One of the reasons why attendance at theological seminaries is reduced today is the widespread rejection, especially on the part of idealistic young men, of the clerical image as they have observed it. They can easily see that clergymen are almost forced, by the pressures of the lay members of the churches, into utterly false positions. They are expected to be officially religious men, always praying at banquets, always giving the address of welcome, and being accorded an ambiguous honor in return. They are called "men of the cloth," with the consequence that conversation tends to take on a different tone and character when they appear in any social

---

[13] The Earlham Graduate School of Religion, the only Quaker Seminary, is dedicated to this task. Enrollment is not limited to Quakers, but is open to any who are trying to get ready for a truly creative ministry.

group. In short, they become the official holy men of the community unless they make almost superhuman efforts to reject such a role.

The Quaker ideas of the ministry may come as a breath of new life to men who now reject the only pattern of which they have been aware. This radical idea is that the *function* of the ministry can be disassociated from its *status*. Unless there is a public ministry, Christianity will surely die, for nothing ever does itself. No fires burn unless someone gathers the sticks and does the enkindling, as well as the replenishing. But the persons who perform this necessary function in this incendiary fellowship can be those who are personally humble men. They can look upon themselves, not as those who have a monopoly on the ministry, but rather as men who, in one sense, share a ministry with all Christians. The pastor, in the New Testament sense of the word, is not *the* minister, but one of many ministers, whose joy it is to liberate and to nurture the powers of his fellow ministers.

The pattern of the ministry which so many are seeking today is not something to be created as a novelty, because the thinking has already been done. It was, in fact, carefully expressed nearly three hundred years ago by Robert Barclay. Barclay, with a maturity hard to understand in one so young, saw with great clarity that there is no contradiction in a pattern which includes both a generalized and a specialized ministry. After having insisted upon the priesthood of every member, holding that every follower of Christ is free "to speak or prophesy by the Spirit," Barclay went on to insist that a more intense kind of ministry is also valid and is, indeed, *required*. It is clear that this man thought of himself as one who was called to the ministry in this second sense. He would not claim that it was higher, but simply held that it was, in fact, *different*. The crucial passage, which rewards careful study, is as follows:

We do believe and affirm that some are more particularly called to the work of the ministry, and therefore are fitted of the Lord for that purpose; whose work is more constantly and particularly to instruct, exhort, admonish, oversee, and watch over their brethren; and that . . . there is something more incumbent upon them in that respect than upon every common believer.[14]

Here is a conception of such intrinsic nobility that, if it is rightly presented, it cannot but appeal to those of outstanding gifts who are seeking, today, to live lives of genuine dedication. The new ministry which, may be, as we have already said, Quakerism's most original single contribution to practical Christianity, is not, and dare not be, the private possession of those who happen to be called Quakers. It must eventually belong to all, because it is basic to the total Christian ideal, which was etched by Christ Himself when He girded Himself with a towel and said, "I have given you an example."

[14] *Apology*, Proposition X, xxvi.

7 / A Sacramental World

> For surely there are not merely two or seven sacraments,
> but seventy times seven.
>
> T. EDMUND HARVEY

Sometimes when people who have only a little knowledge of Quakers are asked how Quakers are distinguished, it is answered that they are the peculiar Christians who do not observe the sacraments. Because this answer is so profoundly erroneous, some clear explanation is required. Whatever the truth about the observance of sacraments may be, a description of the Quaker practice in negative terms is grossly inadequate and misleading. It would be nearer to the truth to say that Quakers are distinguished by the intensity with which they accept the idea that ours is a sacramental universe.

One of the major evidences that Lord Macaulay, in his famous history, was grotesquely unable to understand George Fox is shown by his treatment of the sacramental issue. With heavy sarcasm he wrote that Fox took literally commands of Christ which nearly all other Christians had taken figuratively, while he allegorized those which others interpreted literally. Though Macaulay was incapable of appreciating a man of the originality of Fox, he was right in his report that the majority of Christians have supposed that it is clear and obvious that, according to the Gospel account, Christ made explicit and unambiguous commands to engage in at least two ceremonial practices, baptism by water, and Holy Communion. The conclusion is that those who do not observe these practices are simply disobedient to the expressed will of their Lord. This is precisely what Quakers deny.

At the time of the Reformation there was a general consensus, among Reformed Churches, that five of the medieval sacraments, not having New Testament authority, failed to meet the test of true sacraments, whereas two, baptism and the Supper, were retained and emphasized.[1] Why, the thoughtful reader naturally asks, did Fox and his earliest associates break with the main Protestant tradition on this issue? There is probably less public understanding of this than of other items of Quaker uniqueness.

By a sacrament we usually mean a liturgical act in which a physical entity achieves spiritual significance. That this should be possible seems in no way surprising, providing we take seriously the conviction that the entire world is God's world. In such a conception water or milk or any other physical reality, being ultimately an object of divine creation, might reasonably be used by God for a spiritual purpose. With this conviction Quakers do not now have, and never have had, any argument. The point at issue is the question of what Christ was trying to institute as a genuinely new departure in the world. Though Christ obviously recognized some continuity with His Jewish heritage, there was also, and more importantly, an element of radical discontinuity in the new revelation. This is exemplified by the rejection of the strict Sabbath laws, when they collided with human need, by the slight attention given to the existing priesthood, and by the obvious transcendence of the entire religious system centering in the Temple. Like a brilliant landmark, there stands out Christ's statement to the censorious Pharisees, "I tell you, something greater than the temple is here" (Matt. 12:6).

At first the closest followers of Christ had enormous difficulty in knowing that He was trying to start something really new. Even after all of the teaching and healing, as well as the crucifixion and the resurrection, the intimate followers asked the profoundly mistaken question, "Lord, will you at this time restore the king-

[1] See "Articles of Religion" as printed in any edition of *The Book of Common Prayer*. The articles relevant to the Sacraments are XV–XXXI.

dom to Israel?" (Acts 1:6). Only by a series of slow steps the
members of the early Christian community realized that a religion
based upon the ceremonial requirements, which most of them had
once considered necessary, was something to be left behind as pre-
Christian. Only by a tremendous emotional upheaval could Peter,
in his relationship with Cornelius, come to see that dietary laws
and restrictions have nothing to do with true religion or with the
love of God and man. Whatever value the ancient emphasis once
had upon clean and unclean foods, which was akin to the sacramental idea, it no longer retained any value at all for those whose
communion was with the Living Christ.

Another big break was that which concerned the sacramental
act of circumcision. Because men of the character of Simon Peter
had considered circumcision as *really* important, the recognition
that it was not significant was a step of enormous proportions. The
genuineness of the emancipation of the early Christians is shown
by the fact that they did not proceed from refusal to require
circumcision to the claim that the act of circumcision was, in itself,
evil. There was, they said, no intrinsic merit in accepting it and
there was no intrinsic merit in abstaining from it. This represents a
step of genuine spiritual maturity. "For neither circumcision
counts for anything, nor uncircumcision, but a new creation"
(Gal. 6:15). Here was already stated the position which Fox and
the early Quakers were later to make pivotal. All that Quakers did
was to extend the logic to other sacramental acts. If we have the
new creation, nothing else is required; if we do not have the new
creation, nothing else will suffice.

It is the Quaker contention that the break which Christ inaugurated is greater than is ordinarily supposed. Certainly it is greater
than is envisioned by those who think that Christ's novelty of
approach was to substitute new ceremonial acts for old ones. But if
it is true that Christ meant to say that a man cannot be a follower
of His unless he is baptized with water, whether by immersion or
by sprinkling, then the break with the past was essentially trivial.

What is the difference in kind between requiring circumcision of the flesh and requiring immersion in a tank of water? Both are purely physical acts, which may or may not have moral and spiritual concomitants. It is obvious that either operation can be performed without a real change of heart, while, on the other hand, a man may have a genuine change of heart with no outward ceremony at all. This is the clear point of Christ's words to the thief on the cross, who became a follower without any outward sign. The words of Christ to this penitent and therefore changed man are a challenge to all upholders of the necessity of particular sacramental acts: "Truly, I say to you, today you will be with me in Paradise" (Luke 23:43).

In all discussion of these matters it is important to make clear that the question is that of *necessity*. A full understanding of the newness of the Gospel does not mean that outward ceremonial acts are to be disdained. If they are helpful, we can only thank God that this is so. The crucial issue arises, however, whenever it is claimed, as it sometimes is, that particular acts are required. It is not unknown, for example, for a Quaker to be told that he is not a Christian at all because he has never been baptized with water. Whenever this statement is made it reveals more about the critic than it does the one who is being criticized, for it shows that the critic is still fundamentally pre-Christian. It indicates a fundamental misunderstanding of what it is with which Christianity is concerned. After all, external acts are *easy*; the new creation, by contrast, is difficult, and is never wholly accomplished.

Christ's clearest statement of the nature of the demands of the new order came when He contrasted what goes on outside a man, with what goes on in his inner consciousness. His words referred specifically to foods, but can be applied, by logical extension, to all external religious requirements. The only thing that is important, He taught, is what comes "out of the heart of man" (Mark 7:21). Here is a religious revolution of the highest order, but it is by no means surprising that the recognition of its significance appeared only by slow and painful degrees. In the untutored yet clear mind of young George Fox there came the recognition that this revolution was to be taken seriously. Since the new creation is everything, all else is secondary; therefore no particular acts, not even the historically honored ones of water baptism and the bread and wine, can be requirements. This was his first fundamental insight. Whatever else it was, it was not trivial.

The Quaker attitude toward baptism is completely affirmative. The notion that Quakers are distinguished from other Christians in that others believe in baptism while Quakers do not, is erroneous. The question at issue is what baptism means. Almost every thoughtful Quaker, if he is asked whether he is a baptized Christian, will say that he, indeed, is. By this he means that the baptism of the spirit, being all that counts, has, he humbly trusts, occurred in his life. Some, who have studied deeply, will reply that real baptism is tantamount to ordination into the priesthood of all believers.

The fact that Christianity has something to do with baptism is clearly indicated in many parts of the New Testament, but the question of what baptism means is not so easily answered by a scholar or by anyone else. Perhaps the best approach is to note what Christian baptism is *not*. It is not, for example, any analogue of Christ's baptism by John in the Jordan River. Sometimes those who are arguing for the necessity of immersion fall back on reference to the Jordan experience, claiming that the entire issue is a simple matter of obedience. Christ, they say, was immersed and we are commanded to follow His entire example. Only a little examination shows how extremely unsound this specious argument is. If we were required to do everything that Christ did we should become sacerdotalists of the deepest dye. It is obvious that we are not required to remain single, just because Christ was unmarried, or that Christian men are required to be circumcised because He was circumcised. We do not need to dress as He dressed or to eat as He ate. That would be slavish and therefore pre-Christian.

Accordingly, the baptism in the Jordan places upon the contemporary follower of Christ no requirement of any kind. The ceremony was, indeed, pre-Christian, and was performed by a man who never became a Christian, though he was undoubtedly a good and important preliminary figure. One of the most fantastic evidences of the misunderstanding of what Christianity is about is the practice of bottling the muddy water of the Jordan River and using it to sprinkle babies or converts. It is really difficult to know what the people who engage in this practice have in mind. Even if they have some vague notion of magical efficacy, they are certainly confused, since the water thus bottled can, by no stretch of the imagination, be exactly the same water which flowed from the Sea of Galilee to the Dead Sea nearly two thousand years ago. Their action is surely one for which Christ Himself would have had fine scorn. It is precisely by emphasis on such irrelevant externals that the deeper demands of the Gospel are likely to be neglected.

That Christ, when He mentioned His baptism, was not referring to the physical or ceremonial experience at the Jordan is shown by His use of the future tense. If He had referred to the act of immersion in water, He would, necessarily, have used the past tense. "I have," He said, "a baptism to be baptized with; and how I am constrained until it is accomplished!" (Luke 12:50).

The probability is that some of Christ's followers insisted upon a ceremonial act of physical baptism, as a sign of entrance into the new movement, but that Christ Himself did not do so. Quakers, accordingly, have been more concerned to follow Christ than to follow His followers, since the latter were so slow to understand and were so often mistaken. Quakers have placed strong emphasis upon the record of the Fourth Gospel, which explicitly states the essential contrast between the actions of Christ and the actions of the disciples. The Fourth Gospel, after saying (John 3:22) that Christ baptized in Judea, goes on (John 4:2) to clarify the point by saying explicitly that what is meant is that "Jesus himself did not baptize, but only his disciples."

The clarification made in John 4:2 was evidently necessary because of the fundamental ambiguity of the word "baptize." To some it meant a physical act; to others it meant the start of a new life; to all it meant introduction to the Christian community. That some early Christians supposed that the word involved an intrinsic physical reference is shown by the words of the Ethiopian to Philip. As they went along the road this new convert said, "See, here is water! What is to prevent my being baptized?" Both Philip and the Ethiopian, we are told, went down into the water, where Philip baptized the new convert (Acts 8: 36, 38). But while the word had, for some, this necessary ceremonial significance, it did not mean the same to all. The continuing ambiguity in our generation is shown in the fact that some contemporary Christians insist on full immersion, some are satisfied with sprinkling, some demand the use of running water, etc. If there is one valid physical demand, they cannot all be right!

The more we ponder the early Christian use of the word baptism the more we conclude that it was a valuable and profound figure of speech. When the writer of Ephesians spoke of one Lord, one faith, one baptism, it is absurd to suppose that he was taking sides in any minute controversy about how a particular external ceremony must be performed. Clearly he was talking about the new creation in union with Christ. His interest, as the context shows, was not in sacerdotal acts, but rather in *new men*. To be baptized, then, means, fundamentally, to enter into an experience of great significance. The obviously figurative use is demonstrated by Paul in I Corinthians 10:1-4, where the experience of ancient Israelites, in being freed from Egypt, and guided in the wilderness, is referred to as their "baptism." Baptism means the immersion of a person's whole being in the love of Christ. It is in this sense that Quakers, when they have understood their own position, have always maintained that their attitude to baptism is a wholly affirmative one. Quakers believe in baptism with all their hearts. They believe in baptism so much that they refuse to be sidetracked by argument about the right way to perform an ecclesiastical or priestly function.

Since the physical ceremony is neither necessary nor sufficient, it is not something to be denounced, and, if it is helpful for any to dramatize their faith, this certainly does no harm. All that is harmful is a magical conception or efficacy. There are, unfortunately, still a number of alleged Christians who contend that a soul is lost eternally if physical baptism is not administered. The evidence that they think in this fashion is shown by the extremes to which they will go in order to see to it that a newborn baby is baptized, when the life of the child is threatened. Though the people who engage in frantic efforts, on such occasions, probably have not bothered to think through their position, it is impossible to avoid the conclusion that the theology implicit in their act is monstrous. It means, they must claim, that the Living God is so lacking in compassion that He will reject an unconscious baby for lack of a ceremonial performance. If God is like that, it follows that He is not even remotely like Jesus Christ and the whole Christian position is thereby undermined. If salvation is of such a nature that it can be determined by anything as trivial as a few drops of water, then the entire revelation of Christ has been in vain. Furthermore, it follows that Christ was mistaken when He spoke to the thief on the cross. It is absurdities of this kind that Quakers feel bound to reject. They are convinced that, in doing so, they are not merely maintaining a sectarian oddity, as Macaulay supposed, but rather are helping to preserve something sacred for the whole of Christendom. Whatever else the Quaker insistence on the reality rather than the externals of baptism may involve, it is not a little thing.

The Biblical literalist often says that a Christian must be baptized with water because Christ commanded it. Such a literalist, when he takes this particular stance, is usually referring to the words attributed to the risen Christ, "Go therefore and make disciples of all nations, baptizing them in the name of the Father and of the Son and of the Holy Spirit" (Matt. 28:19). But the literalist, when he does this, is in a highly vulnerable position. If he says that he takes the words straight, without any metaphor, he is bound, in consistency, to do the same with other commands, many of which are equally explicit. What, for example, is he going to do with baptism by fire? He cannot, in view of his attention to John at the Jordan, be unaware of John's prediction that his divine Successor would, in contrast, baptize "with fire" (Luke 3:16). Of course no person, no matter how much of a literalist he is in theory, will take this reference as anything but a metaphor. Moreover, everyone interprets figuratively the experience referred to as that of heaping burning coals of fire on a person's head (Rom. 12:20).

The logical question, which faces the literalist, is the question of why he arbitrarily insists on the nonfigurative character of commands having to do with the conventional sacraments, while he admits that other commands have metaphorical significance. The Quaker claim is that there is no justification for making such arbitrary distinctions. The problem is not so much theological as moral. It is immoral to make demands upon others which we do not apply to ourselves. Furthermore, it is not adequate to take one text out of context, in order to put the whole weight of the argument upon it. If we are trying to understand the full teaching of Christ, and of the early Church, it is incumbent upon us to see the record in its entirety. For example, we shall not merely call attention, when we read the Book of Acts, to Philip and the Ethiopian. We shall also note the vivid contrast between the pre-Christian John and Jesus, as made by Peter in his address at Antioch. "And I remembered the word of the Lord, how he said, 'John baptized with water, but you shall be baptized with the Holy Spirit'" (Acts 11:16). Peter's reference seems to be to the words of the risen Christ in Acts 1:4, 5. The prominence of the word "but" in these passages has seemed to Quakers very significant. Whatever Christ stressed, He did not stress water.

Of all the difficulties encountered by any who criticize the Quaker position on literalist grounds, the greatest difficulty which they face is that concerning the washing of the feet of the disciples. So important is this incident, in the Fourth Gospel, that it is practically the only feature of the Last Supper that is recorded. What is the sacramental literalist to do with this incident? If he is looking for specific commands, there is no doubt that he has one in this incident. "I have given you an example, that you also should do as I have done to you" (John 13:15). Here is a commandment far more explicit than anything, in all of the four Gospels, about physical baptism or Holy Communion. The person who accepts the latter, on the claim of specific command, while he rejects the former, is simply dishonest. Why pick and choose?

It is heartening to realize that some Christian groups, particularly the Brethren, have actually made foot-washing a sacramental act. The author has shared in a Brethren Love Feast, with the washing of one another's feet, and has found it deeply meaningful and reverent. The only mystery is that so many Christians, who think of their religion as a matter of specific commandments, have been able to find a pretext to avoid such a practice. Quakers avoid it because they try to make foot-washing, which is looked upon as an acted parable, a metaphor of humble service to one another in the ordinary life of the world. It is because of the Quaker effort to be consistent that the same understanding applies to baptism and to the Lord's Supper.

The Gospel abounds in metaphorical references. The fellowship of Christ's followers is *salt*, and *light* and *leaven*. We are concerned with the *water* of life, with the *door*. The entire Church is referred to as those of the Way (Acts 9:2). We wholly misunderstand the Gospel if we do not recognize that these *are* metaphors. The full recognition of this point leads, not to a denial of sacraments, but rather to a vast enlargement of the entire sacramental idea. Ours, says the Christian, is a sacramental universe. Bodies are important, just as truly as minds and spirits are important. This is why Quakers, like other Christians, feed the hungry; it is why they seek to heal broken bodies. Quakers do not intend, and have never intended, to establish a merely spiritual religion. Quakers take so seriously the idea that ours is a sacramental universe that they cannot limit the notion to a particular ceremony of initiation. The water which washes children's clothing is as holy as water that is called "holy water" when it has been blessed by a priest. How many sacraments are there? There are seventy times seven.

There is no doubt of the importance of Holy Communion in the totality of Christian experience. In one form or another, it is celebrated daily all over the world, bringing to many Christians their deepest sense of fellowship with one another and with their Living Lord. It is a misfortune, then, that the ceremony which might be expected to be the most unifying of any among Christians has often, in fact, been divisive. Though there are some celebrations in which all who love the Lord are invited to participate, there are others in which the invitation is pointedly selective. In some sections of Christendom people are not expected "to communicate" if they have not previously engaged in the experience of the confessional.

The ways in which Holy Communion is actually administered are numerous and surprisingly varied. Among Roman Catholics the two elements, bread and wine, are taken by the officiating clergy, but only the bread is taken by the ordinary communicant. In the Anglican, Lutheran, and Methodist Churches, the people come, in a series of small detachments, to the altar rail, where they take both elements. Among many others, including the Presbyterians and the Disciples, the people ordinarily remain seated in their pews while the elements are brought to them by elders or by others who are designated for this particular task. There are still other fellowships in which the communicants sit, several at a time, at actual tables. This was done at Amsterdam at the time of the formation of the World Council of Churches, in 1948.

In all of the above instances, the food is merely symbolic, the elements being a tiny piece of bread or wafer, on the one hand, and a sip of wine or grape juice, on the other. The liquid is taken either from a tiny separate container or from a common cup. In contrast to such practices, there are others, such as the Brethren, who partake of genuine food, the communion then being called the "love feast." Usually the food is boiled beef, covered with bread, soaked with the beef broth. This is done in the desire to operate in a fashion more like that of the original Lord's Supper, as well as more like the practice of the early Church. Accordingly, in this case, the celebration is carried on in the evening. If one is trying to copy, as nearly as possible, the original experience, it is clear that the timing employed by Brethren is correct. In fact, it is something of an anomaly that the "supper" is so often memorialized early in the morning.

In each of these practices there is a conscious effort to establish some sort of continuity with the experience of Christ and His inner circle in His last fellowship with them. Among many Christians it is freely recognized that the physical elements are merely symbols and that they, accordingly, have no intrinsic merit. The effect sought is frankly a psychological one, in that a common physical act enables those who are together to feel a deeper sense of oneness. By contrast, there are some Christians who attribute a kind of magical efficacy to elements, once they are blessed. Then a problem arises concerning what is to be done with the elements which have been blessed, but not consumed. Here we find a development which can be given no rational justification and which is undoubtedly alien to the original conception.

Each of the canonical Gospels describes the Supper, though they do not agree on the details. As already mentioned, John puts an almost total emphasis upon the washing of the feet, as a demonstration of humble service, and as a standing rebuke to all struggles for prestige and power in the Christian community. The Synoptic Gospels all indicate that Christ employed the supper as an opportunity to instruct His followers. Because the disciples were so slow to understand, and because the idea at stake was intrinsically difficult, a vivid teaching effort was required. The notion that Christ would actually be killed, in pursuance of the Messianic pattern, was one which Peter had already rejected as soon as he had received the great insight concerning who Jesus was. He had, no doubt, spoken for all when he blurted out "This shall never happen to you" (Matt. 16:22). How could Christ make these dull men understand? Perhaps an acted parable would make the point clear when words did not suffice.

The parable which Christ acted was one with which everyone is familiar, whenever he eats and drinks. In one sense, the food is destroyed, but, in another sense it is not. The life of the animal or plant is certainly lost when it becomes food for another, yet it is not fully or irretrievably lost, because new life emerges as a result of the sacrifice.

To suppose that, because Christ said "This is my body," he meant to say that the piece of bread and His body were substantially identical is to fall into the trap of all literalism. In fact, it was a trap against which Jesus had already warned, when he emphasized His figurative use of language and asked, impatiently, "How is it that you fail to perceive that I did not speak about bread?" (Matt. 16:11). Immediately after this pointed question, He went on to speak of "leaven" in a metaphorical sense. To speak of a piece of Passover bread as actually the body of Christ, and, by extension, to claim that every piece of bread used in a communion service is also Christ's actual body, is to be the victim of naïveté about the meaning of the word "is." It is a commonplace of modern, as well as ancient, logic that the word "is" is extremely ambiguous. It may mean *identity*, it may mean *equality*, it may mean class *inclusion*, it may mean *existence*, etc. Only by the context can we tell, in any language, what the exact meaning may be, but we must always beware of the fallacy of simplification. When Christ says "I am the door" He certainly does not mean that He is made of wood. If the ambiguity of the verb "to be" had been more clearly recognized, many of the fierce and profitless theological debates of the past could have been avoided.

The theological sophistication of George Fox and his closest associates is something which is really quite surprising. While setting great store by the story of the Last Supper, and while making communion with Christ the very center of their religious experience, the early Quakers were absolutely convinced that Christ did not mean to institute a ceremony which it would be necessary for subsequent followers to perform ritualistically. Fox was so sure that Christ had come to end all ceremonies, so far as religion is concerned, that he could not believe it when supposed religious experts told him that Christ had commanded a perpetual memorial. How could this be if Christ had come to liberate men from external performances and to direct them to His presence in their hearts?

Now, as a result of modern Biblical scholarship, we have something of a vindication of Fox's bold insight. If we pay attention to the best and oldest of available Gospel manuscripts, the striking fact is that not one of the four Gospels even suggests the setting up of a continued practice, based on the Last Supper. We have long seen that there is not one word about a ceremonial establishment in either Mark or Matthew. The entire reference, instead, is to the particular time. Christ is not, in these passages, telling His disciples what to do in the future, but is explaining His contemporary action in terms other than those of absolute defeat. The only Gospel support for the necessity of a continuing memorial, within the context of previous Christian scholarship, was that found in Luke, where, according to the Authorized Version, Christ was reported to have said, "This do in remembrance of me" (Luke 22:19). Now, however, we have a striking reversal, in that the oldest manuscripts do not include these words at all. This is why they do not appear in the text of *The New English Bible* or of The Revised Standard Version. We are forced to the conclusion that, so far as the Gospels are concerned, the unforgettable experience of the bread and wine was an attempt at explanation of the present problem and nothing more.

Quakers do not deny and never have denied that some kind of memorial of the Last Supper soon became part of the experience of the early Church. Indeed, since there is no valid evidence for its establishment in the Gospels, the only evidence is in the Epistles, particularly Paul's First Letter to the Corinthians. There the Apostle, who, since he never saw Christ in the flesh, was only a secondhand witness, gave a report to the effect that Christ had commanded a memorial act, saying "Do this, as often as you drink it, in remembrance of me" (I Cor. 11:25). Paul gives instructions for the right conduct of the ceremony, which indicates that he is dealing with something already practiced.

What Quakers claim is not that early Christians did not have such a practice but, rather, that such a practice cannot rightly be looked upon as a necessity for the Christian life. If the teaching of Christ Himself, as recorded in the Gospels, is taken seriously, the requirements must always be moral and spiritual, never ritual. The Gospel is seen, then, as, in one sense, a totally new emergent in the religious life and, in another sense, the logical conclusion of the prophetic development. The prophetic development is always a movement from the stress upon the outer to stress upon the inner. From "Bring no more vain oblations" (Isa. 1:13, AV) we move to a climax with, "He hath shewed thee, O man, what is good; and what doth the Lord require of thee, but to do justly, and to love mercy, and to walk humbly with thy God?" (Mic. 6:8, AV). To claim that the divine requirement includes the necessity of taking bread and wine in a particular ceremonial context is not merely to retrogress into becoming pre-Christian; it is to become pre-prophetic.

We owe to Robert Barclay, in regard to communion, as in regard to so much else, the clearest statement of the basic Quaker position. The thirteenth of his *Theses Theologicae* is as follows:

The communion of the body and blood of Christ is inward and spiritual, which is the participation of his flesh and blood, by which the inward man is daily nourished in the hearts of those in whom Christ dwells. Of which things the breaking of bread by Christ with his disciples was a figure, which even they who had received the substance used in the church for a time, for the sake of the weak; even as abstaining from things strangled, and from blood, the washing of one another's feet, and the anointing of the sick with oil; all which are commanded with no less authority and solemnity than the former; yet seeing they are but shadows of better things, they cease in such as have obtained the substance.

Barclay was deeply conscious of what we might reasonably call the evolution of religious ideas and practices. Circumcision served a purpose, but eventually became outmoded. There is even something to be said for the ancient Jewish attitude of exclusiveness, with its attendant unwillingness to compromise. If the primitive Israelites had not been so strict in their monotheism they might not have survived at all and, if they had not been meticulous about the rejection of graven images, their own austerity of worship would have deteriorated. But the time finally came when such attitudes had to be transcended. Peter's personal revelation is a vivid example of a development, the time for which has come. "You yourselves," he said, "know how unlawful it is for a Jew to associate with or to visit any one of another nation; but God has shown me that I should not call any man common or unclean" (Acts 10:28). It is in this sense that we rightly speak of the revelation of the Bible as progressive revelation. There is progress, not only as between the Old Testament and the New, but also within the New Testament itself. It is not surprising, therefore, that Quakers have normally held to the conviction that there can be progress, as between the time of the New Testament and our own day. The proposition that revelation ceased, once and for all, nearly two thousand years ago, is far from self-evident and, in fact, has nothing to commend it. The fact that the Church at Corinth used the physical elements of bread and wine to dramatize their relation to the Living Christ does not mean that contemporary Christians must necessarily do the same. There may, indeed, be new ways of sensing Christ's presence, of which we are as yet wholly unaware, and which will be later revealed to our children or to our children's children. There are backward-looking religions, but Christianity is not one of them. It is intrinsically developmental.

The person who is trying to understand the full nature of the Quaker experiment in radical Christianity would make a mistake if he were to suppose that Quakers think of the physical participation in a communion service as something to be ridiculed or even avoided. Though there are some differences in practice, a great many contemporary Quakers, when they are invited to participate in the Eucharist, now do so. At an unusually attractive communion service, on the island of Iona, in the chancel of the Cathedral of the Isles, three Quakers were present with Dr. George MacLeod as the officiant. Each of the three Quakers represented a different geographical background, yet each of the three, without any advance decision in common, took the bread and the wine. Afterward, at lunch in the common room, what remained of the big Scottish loaf, from which all had broken pieces, was on the table as ordinary sustenance, thus symbolizing the continuity of religious and secular experience. Each Quaker participated, because the experience was a lovely one and because, furthermore, refusal to participate would have seemed both schismatic and censorious. If it had been claimed, as it was not, that such participation was a necessity for the obedient Christian, that would have been another story altogether.

The Quaker attitude toward the celebration of the Eucharist, in whatever form, is today one of complete freedom. Anything that will help to deepen or to sweeten human life is to be encouraged. All that Quakers insist upon is that they not be counted out of the Church of Christ because of what they believe to be an unusual effort to accept Christ's words and actions in the way in which they appear to have been meant. It can be said that, whereas most Protestants employ *two* physical elements, while Roman Catholics, so far as the ordinary worshipers are concerned, employ *one* element, Quakers employ *no* element. In a number of areas today the "silent meeting" is termed "communion after the manner of Friends."

The degree to which Quaker toleration can go in the matter of Holy Communion is indicated by the established practice of the Quakers in what is called "Ohio Yearly Meeting," centered at Damascus. This includes some Friends outside the State of Ohio, particularly those of southern Michigan. In this body of Quakers, freedom has reached the ultimate limit, in that the Discipline permits the physical celebration of the Lord's Supper on occasion, if the local congregation desires this experience. In short, they have gone the whole way in that they have both "freedom from" and "freedom to." Though Ohio Friends have sometimes been criticized for this departure from former Quaker practice, the criticism is clearly not justified. The whole idea is that of freedom from *any* ceremonial requirements, after which other freedoms are possible.

It is important to emphasize that the characteristic Quaker attitude toward communion, like that toward baptism, is meant to be a wholly affirmative one. The truth is that Holy Communion is that in which Quakers do most intensely believe! One evidence of this is found in the fact that the best loved of all Quaker paintings is "The Presence in the Midst" by Doyle Penrose. The painting is loved because the central Quaker conviction is that of "The Real Presence." The Presence in the Midst shows a group of Friends, in plain garb, seated quietly in the Jordans Meetinghouse, mentioned in Chapter 3. High above the heads of the worshipers the artist has painted what he conceives to be the face of Christ.

The argument about the nature of the mass is one which Quaker thought proposes to transcend. Whether Christ is actually present, in the bread and wine on the altar, becomes an idle question when once we understand that He is found *wherever* His followers are truly members one of another, because they are ingrafted into Him. That such presence is not limited to times when people partake of physical bread and wine is obvious. Christ's presence may be as vivid in the consumption of rude fare in a humble cottage, where a man and a woman toil to feed their children, as it is at any altar consecrated by any priest. The notion that Christ is especially identified with bread and wine, simply because these were the staples of Palestinian diet centuries ago, has no rational basis at all. It is agreed that the sharing of food and drink is something which facilitates a deepening of fellowship, but the drink need not be wine; it might just as well be coffee.

It is a fortunate fact that the ceremony of the recognition of Christ's presence, which is what Holy Communion really is, became connected with such common things as bread and wine. This is a vivid way of saying that Christ is connected with common life, whatever the period and whatever the geographical location. He is to be found, not in some Holy of Holies, access to which is limited on the basis of ecclesiastical status, but wherever and whenever men and women truly open their hearts to Him. The Quaker criticism of Holy Communion, as usually understood, is not that it says too much, but that it says too little. The ideal which seems a high one, but may not be too high, is that every home should become a Christian society and every common meal a sacramental experience.

It is surely a good thing that would-be followers of Christ should, whenever they eat and drink, remember Him. We are glad that our Lord was of flesh like ours, and that He needed to sustain His body, as we need to sustain ours. We are glad that He was not merely "spiritual." The constant significance of the Last Supper, says Barclay, in one of his finest passages, was "that being the last time that Christ did eat with his disciples, he desired them, that in their eating and drinking they might have regard to him, and by the remembering of that opportunity, be the more stirred up to follow him diligently through sufferings and death."[2] It is a fact, as the original disciples learned after the resurrection, on the road to Emmaus, that Christ can be known in the breaking of the bread (Luke 24:35). The Quaker insistence is that the miracle of the recognized presence can occur in connection with common bread and in the midst of common life.

[2] *Apology*, Proposition XIII, **vi.**

8 / The Genius of John Woolman

Get the writings of John Woolman by heart.

CHARLES LAMB

Eighteenth-century Quakers are easy to caricature. On the whole, Quakers of the eighteenth century appeared to their contemporary neighbors as inoffensive, industrious, frugal, and conscientious people. The city which they had founded became the most influential and prosperous of all of the cities of the English colonies, yet not one Quaker signed the Declaration of Independence or sat in the Constitutional Convention. Quakers on both sides of the Atlantic were increasingly content, in this long aftermath of violent persecution, to tend to their own affairs, to prosper in their businesses, and quietly to establish the climate which was conducive to social change, especially in connection with the enormous evil of human slavery.

We learn a great deal about the Quakers of this interesting period, so different from the first period, by references in secular literature. So far as English literature is concerned, the characteristic reference, as illustrated in Boswell's *Life of Johnson*, is to those whose chief mark is that of prosperous rectitude. Dr. Johnson's own closest Quaker connection was with one such, a Barclay descendant of the Apologist. Because Hester Thrale liked to have Johnson available at her ambitious dinner parties, she encouraged the great Cham of literature to occupy, whenever it pleased him, a room in the Thrale mansion. Her husband was the owner of the thriving brewery on the south bank of the Thames, not far from Southwark Cathedral. When Henry Thrale died, Dr. Johnson being a more or less permanent house guest, the widow asked the great man to act as the executor of his friend's estate. Johnson, instead of being the incompetent businessman, which others expected a writer to be, turned out to be a very sharp administrator and asked what appeared to be an unusually high price for the brewery property.

Not many men in London could afford to buy anything as expensive as Thrale's brewery, but the Barclays were among those who could. Accordingly, the property was sold to David Barclay, great-grandson of the Apologist, and his associate John Perkins. Thus the famous establishment operated as Barclay and Perkins for the greater part of two centuries.[1] When the astute Quaker investor objected to the stiff price, the still more astute executor did not budge. His famous remark was that he was not merely selling a parcel of boilers and vats, "but the potentiality of growing rich beyond the dreams of avarice." Thus, in an eighteenth-century Quaker purchase, we have one of the first statements of the economic principle of the capitalization of prospective income.

It will be noted that the Apologist's Quaker descendant had not the slightest moral objection to owning and managing a brewery. Most Quakers of his period drank ale. It is something of a surprise to the modern reader, who associates Quakers with strictness in regard to indulgence, to realize that there was very little objection to either alcohol or tobacco in the first century and a half of Quaker history. The bookkeeping accounts of Swarthmore Hall even list expenditures for tobacco pipes for George Fox.

The earliest known Quaker suggestion of the evil of rum is found in the *Journal* of Joshua Evans, an American contemporary of John Woolman, as follows:

[1] The contemporary visitor to London may, if he wishes to do so, visit the Board Room of the brewery, which includes, in its furnishings, Dr. Johnson's desk and study chair, as well as the deed, signed by Samuel Johnson as executor.

I received a plain, gentle intimation, as in a silent language inwardly spoken on this wise:

Use no more rum; it is a great evil in the country; and thou shalt have peace in declining it.

This seemed to try me closely. It had been a custom long practiced, and was become deeply rooted. It was also generally believed to be of great service to drink rum as thereby men were supposed to be supported under the fatigue of hard labor in time of hay-making, harvest, etc. I had been of the same opinion myself and had heretofore used it pretty liberally; for some entertained a notion that men's health was in danger without the use of it; and I had heard of some who were said to have died instantly when they had drunk cold water, for want of rum in it.[2]

The date of the above *Journal* entry is 1757 and it clearly represented at that time a minority view. Such fresh and unconventional ideas were almost universally looked upon by eighteenth-century Quakers as direct messages from their Heavenly Father. It was to those who were habitually expectant that these "openings" came. Joshua Evans was one who also had a leading to give up, as early as 1761, the use of any articles which appeared to be the fruit of slave toil and thus to avoid the hypocrisy of profiting by a system which he denounced.

The French and Indian War presented a crisis to Quakers, particularly to those in Pennsylvania where Quakers had had a majority in the colonial legislature. The real crisis came when the Quaker legislators were faced with the decision, as they saw it, of prosecuting the war against the French and their Indian allies, or of abandoning political power. We know that they chose the latter. Whether this was a wise moral decision no one knows.

The difficulty of the decision arose partly from the fact that white settlers were being murdered on the western frontier. In 1756, Philadelphia Quakers established what was called, after the London model, a "Meeting for Sufferings," a body set up in order to care for Quaker interests in the long periods between the actual

2 Evans' *Journal, Friends Miscellany,* Vol. 10, p. 34.

sessions of the Yearly Meeting. In the first session, September, 1756, John Woolman, being one of the first to be appointed to this new body, signed a minute having to do with raising additional funds in order to aid Friends "in their distressed state on the frontier settlements." Just as, in the early days, there were "Sufferings" because of imprisonment, now there were other sufferings. The interest in those who suffered was by no means limited to Quakers and soon included the suffering slaves. All of the interests of Quakers at home and abroad were finally involved.

After the death of General Braddock, the Earl of Loudon arrived in 1757, as General of the forces, and popular feeling rose. In spite of the fact that Quakers had an official position condemning participation in military service, a large number of patriotic young Quakers joined the troops. But, characteristically, the major Quaker concern was for the enemy, particularly for the Indians, because there was always the recognition that these primitive people had not been fairly treated. Penn had, indeed, tried to make a genuine treaty with the Indian chiefs and some payment was actually made for land, but there was no doubt that the more worldly-wise white man had received the better end of the bargain. When we have the temptation to become sentimental about treatment of the Indians, as though it was always noble, we do well to remind ourselves of the Walking Purchase of 1737.[3] An arrangement was made in which it was agreed that land would be ceded by the Indians to the white men, measured by the distance a man could walk in a day and a half. The Indians assumed that the man would go at a normal rate, stopping for rest occasionally, but the walkers, being athletes trained for the purpose, and following the letter rather than the spirit of the bargain, walked with prodigious speed and persistence. They walked sixteen miles and then slanted the line to the Delaware. This added to the legend

[3] For a fuller account of this disgraceful episode, see Rufus M. Jones, Quakers in the American Colonies (London: Macmillan and Company, 1911), pp. 501, 502.

that the Quaker businessman is honest, but crafty, and possibly a bit devious, even though the responsible parties were not actually Quakers.

At the end of 1756, the minutes of the Philadelphia Meeting for Sufferings contain an epistle to the corresponding body in London. This shows how Quakers on both sides of the Atlantic were attempting, in spite of the geographical barrier, to share interests and to maintain a certain unity of outlook. It also shows how keen was the desire to be fair to the Indians whom the white settlers had displaced. The most interesting part of the letter is as follows:

Some of the Indians in the Interest of the French having committed Hostilities on the Frontiers, . . . the Consideration of the Circumstances of those Indians who had been our old Friends and Neighbours, led some of us to think whether we, as a Society in Particular, & this Government in General, had fully discharged our Duty towards them? A little Reflection was Sufficient to convince us that there had been a Deficiency, & incited to a Concern to give them some fresh Testimony of our regard, which some of us in our private Stations were willing to Manifest, & Others by their Endeavours to engage the Government to do it in Such Manner as would be more immediately Effectual.

A careful consideration of the moral sensitivity represented by such an epistle produced in the midst of a military struggle provides an ideal intellectual background for the understanding of John Woolman. The importance of Woolman, for our present study, is that, by contemplating his life and character and writings, we get a better understanding of the Quaker Way of Life than can be had in any other fashion. To tell the truth about Woolman it is necessary to stress two important truths at once. In the first place, he was so clearly superior to his neighbors in both his integrity and in his moral sensitivity, as well as in purity of life, that it is wrong to present him as a characteristic or representative Quaker of the eighteenth or any other century. The second, and equally important truth, is that the superiority of Woolman rests squarely on a Quaker base. Though he was clearly superior to the surrounding

Quakers, his peculiar excellence is unthinkable apart from the Quaker cultural setting. He was extremely different from the stormy George Fox or from the courtly Penn, yet all of his major insights arose in a moral and spiritual atmosphere which men like Fox and Penn had made possible. Woolman was a universal saint, as so many kinds of people have been quick to recognize, but his saintliness was Quaker before it was universal. In the character of Woolman we do not learn what every Quaker is, but we do learn something of the richness of the Quaker potential. In studying such an individual we arrive at glimpses of the truth which the study of doctrine can never provide, and which detailed history can never demonstrate.

John Woolman was born October 19, 1720, in the little New Jersey village which we now call Rancocas. It is for this reason that the standard edition of his *Journal* and other writings, edited by Amelia Mott Gummere, is called the Rancocas Edition. The Northhampton section in which Woolman was born was made up almost entirely of English Quakers. It was in marked contrast to similar communities in what was known as East Jersey, where there were many Dutch and Scottish settlers. In the entire Burlington area much of the culture of the early Yorkshire Quakers was continued in an unbroken line. Accordingly, the setting of Woolman's life was marked by the combination of four major elements, *reverence, simplicity, frugality,* and *toil.*

Woolman's *Journal,* called by Mrs. Gummere "the most impersonal autobiography ever written," records the necessary facts with an amazing economy of language. "I was born," he wrote, "in Northhampton, in Burlington County, in West Jersey, in the year of our Lord, 1720, and before I was seven years old, I began to be acquainted with the operations of Divine Love." As we read these lucid words we begin to see why Woolman has seemed to so many to provide a standard in the purity of his prose style. The pictures of his childhood are brief, but adequate for the purpose, which is that of a careful account of the growth of his religious consciousness. "My parents having a large family of children, used frequently on first-days after meeting, to put us to read in the Holy Scriptures, or some religious books, one after another, the rest sitting by without much conversation, which I have since often thought was a good practice." The picture which he gives of the reaction of a sensitive Quaker boy to reproof is moving in its very simplicity.

About the twelfth year of my age, my Father being abroad, my Mother reproved me for some misconduct to which I made an Undutiful reply & the next first-day, as I was with my Father returning from Meeting, He told me he understood I had behaved amiss to my Mother, and Advised me to be more carefull in the future. I knew myself blamable and in shame and confusion remained silent. Being thus awakened to a sense of my Wickedness, I felt remorse in my mind, and getting home, I retired and prayed to the Lord to forgive me; and I do not remember that I ever after that, spoke unhandsomely to either of my Parents, however foolish in some other things.

When he was about twenty-one years old, "having had schooling pretty well for a planter," Woolman hired out to a man who owned a shop in Mt. Holly, five miles distant from his father's house. Being now away from home, he began to think of himself as an adult and even spoke briefly in the Meeting. As the *Journal* says, "I said a few words in meeting in which I found peace." Speaking was difficult for the shy young man, but he tried courageously to follow his leading. Like Fox at the same age, he had "openings," and these were a foretaste of his later sensitivity to all suffering everywhere. "About the twenty-third year of my age I had many fresh and heavenly openings, in respect to the care and providence of the Almighty over his creation in general, and over man as the most noble amongst those which are visible."

Soon this keen sensitivity was severely tested. His employer owned a Negro woman slave, whom he decided to sell. The purchaser was waiting and young Woolman was commanded by his employer to write a bill of sale. Here was a genuine moral predicament. Woolman had come, alone, to the conviction that slavery was wrong, but he was under orders. Two principles were clearly in conflict, and he had little time to resolve the problem.

The thing was sudden, and though the thoughts of writing an Instrument of Slavery for one of my fellow creatures felt uneasie, yet I remembered I was hired by the year; and that it was my master who [directed] me to do it, and that it was an Elderly man, a member of our society who brought her, so through weakness I gave way, and wrote it, but at the Executing it I was so afflicted in my mind, that I said before my Master and the friend, that I believed Slavekeeping to be a practice inconsistent with the Christian Religion; this in some degree abated my uneasiness, yet as often as I reflected seriously upon it I thought I should have been clearer, if I had desired to be Excused from it, as a thing against my conscience, for such it was.

Here, as early as 1743, is the fountainhead of one of the chief tributaries of what eventually became a mighty stream of anti-slavery conviction, leading to a tragic conflict which, as Lincoln said, "no mortal could make and no mortal could stay." There was something about the Quaker way of life and worship which enabled an inconspicuous young man of Mt. Holly, New Jersey, to see an element of deep and terrible sin in a practice which others accepted uncritically. The key lies largely in the fact that Woolman saw, in a clear-eyed fashion, that the Negro woman was indeed his "fellow creature." The outcome was that the next time he was asked to write an instrument of slavery, Woolman modestly, yet firmly, refused. Something of magnitude was beginning to occur.

Desiring a certain independence, Woolman became a tailor as well as a retailer of goods, because he thought he might be able, in this manner, to "get a liveing in a plain way without the load of great business." Because the public ministry was drawing him, Woolman made the deliberate decision to enter a secular occupation which would not occupy an inordinate amount of time and attention. Later, at the age of thirty-six, when he had begun to prosper and feared that a prosperous business might occupy too much of his thought, Woolman guided prospective customers to his competitors. There was something more important in life, he thought, than the prospect of becoming rich. This decision was not entirely original with Woolman, since a similar one had been made, in the days of Charles II, by an early Quaker tailor, named Gilbert Latey, whose work Woolman read. His decisions were his own, but they were steeped in the Quaker heritage. Because Woolman's decision to avoid wealth, and the close attention which is its price, seems to us so unusual, it is good for the modern reader to be acquainted with the relevant *Journal* passage:

The increase of business became my burthen, for though my natural inclination was towards merchandize, yet I believed Truth required me to live more free from outward cumbers. There was now a strife in my mind betwixt the two, and in this exercise my prayers were put up to the Lord, who Graciously heard me, and gave me a heart resigned to his Holy will; I then lessened my outward business; and as I had opportunity told my customers of my intention that they might consider what shop to turn to: and so in a while, wholly laid down merchandize, following my trade as a Taylor, myself only, having no prentice. I also had a nursery of Apple trees, in which I spent a good deal of time, howing, grafting, trimming & Inoculating.

Woolman married, at the age of twenty-nine, "a well inclined Damsel, Sarah Ellis." Since the couple lived with simplicity and frugality, more and more of Woolman's time could be spent in the traveling ministry, to which he felt so strongly called. We are a little surprised to discover that one of his longest journeys was undertaken three years before his marriage, when he was only twenty-six years old. This was his first of two important southern journeys, and it took him as far south as the populous community north of Albermarle Sound in North Carolina. It surprises us to realize that one so young and so fundamentally humble had the courage to take this journey, which was bound to lead to a controversial encounter with slaveowners.

Woolman's companion on his first southern journey was his beloved friend Isaac Andrews. Both men found that they had "drawings" to go in the same general direction, but, unwilling to proceed in their own private judgment, they presented their plan to the Quakers of both Haddonfield, where Andrews was a member, and Burlington, where Woolman then belonged. Since all were agreed, there began the journey which led Woolman to the same Quaker settlements of lower Virginia and eastern Carolina which George Fox had visited seventy-four years earlier. The southernmost point of the journey was the Perquimans River area, then the home of many well-known Quaker families which later, partly as a reaction against the slavery system, emigrated to the Northwest Territory and established the foundations of Quakerism in Indiana. The influence of the young New Jersey tailor was greater than he knew, for he spread the ideas which led to a famous mass migration.

Whatever Woolman had sensed before about the sinfulness of human slavery was much enhanced by his experience in the Southern colonies. When he ate and drank and lodged, at no personal expense, with people who lived in luxury, because of the hard toil of the slaves, he felt increasingly uneasy. He knew that he was profiting personally from something which was wrong. Woolman's remarkable sensitivity made him have a foreboding of tragic events to come. One hundred fifteen years before the beginning of the Civil War, John Woolman saw the institution of slavery "as a dark gloominess hanging over the Land," and predicted, with terrible accuracy that "in future Consequence will be grievous to posterity."

On his return home to New Jersey Woolman used his free time to complete his first serious writing, that of a small book entitled *Some Considerations on the Keeping of Negroes.* In the subtitle the book was "Recommended to the Professors of Christianity of every Description."[4] The work remained unpublished for eight years, being available in that period only for private reading. In 1754, Part I was officially sanctioned and printed by Philadelphia

---

[4] To Woolman, as to Fox before him, a "professor" was not a teacher but anyone who made a profession of faith.

Yearly Meeting. Part II, written in 1760, was printed in 1762. When we begin to understand how bold Woolman's position seemed to his contemporaries, it is not surprising that he was unwilling to press for early publication.

The recognition of the evil of slavery follows directly, in Woolman's clear thinking, from the acceptance of the truth of the Christian revelation. Woolman proceeds to take seriously the ideas that all men are of one blood, because all are made in God's image. This leads directly to "an Idea of general Brotherhood, and a Disposition easy to be touched with a Feeling of each others Afflictions." If every man, who tries to be a Christian, must put himself in the other man's place, this includes the place of the slave. Remember, says Woolman to his white readers, that these black people did not come voluntarily to dwell among us.

To the theme of the necessary connection between the Christian religion and the necessity of freedom for all men, Woolman returned again and again, over a period of twenty-five years. Even in his last illness, as he was dying of smallpox in York and already too weak to write, he dictated to his English host a passage to be added to his *Journal*, and, as usual, his mind was dwelling on the human suffering caused by the slave trade. He mentioned the bloodshed in America, the "lives destroyed through insupportable Stench and other hardships in crossing the Sea" and that through "extreme oppression Many Slaves are brought to an untimely end." What saddened him equally, at the end, was the fact that all of this suffering was produced for the sake of financial gain.

It is true, as Whittier wrote, that Woolman's saintliness was almost entirely unconscious. He was not trying to be a saint; he believed, like a child, that God was his Father and that Christ was his present Teacher, in the sense made central a hundred years earlier by George Fox. It followed, necessarily, that all men were brothers, persons for whom Christ had died. If they were brothers, then he could not be remote from their sufferings. That this included the sufferings of Indians and Negro slaves seemed to

Woolman's clear mind entirely obvious. The brotherhood was so deep that it even bridged the barriers of language. For example, when Woolman took his famous journey along the Wyalusing Trail from Easton on the Delaware to the upper Susquehanna, he usually spoke with the help of interpreters, but he had both the wisdom and the taste to see that prayer requires no interpretation.

So we helped one another, and we Laboured along, Divine Love attending, and afterwards, feeling my mind covered with the Spirit of Prayer, I told [those who] Interpreted that I found it in my heart to pray to God, & believed if I prayed Aright he would hear me, & Expresst my willingness for them to Omit Interpreting.

Papoonal, a prominent Indian converted by the Moravian missionaries, attended this meeting at Wyalusing and spoke appreciatively to one of the interpreters, saying "I love to feel where words come from."

Woolman paid close attention to his dreams and particularly to those concerning the sufferings of his fellow men. In 1770, he had such a dream when he was ill with pleurisy and he recalled it, for insertion in his *Journal*, when he was in England two years later. Because the account of this dream, with its interpretation, belongs to the classic literature of religious experience, it can rightly be inserted here, just as Woolman wrote it in the final year of his life. All who seek to understand the total Quaker contribution should study it carefully. Many, as they ponder it, will be reminded of the well-known sermon of John Donne with its memorable sentence, "Never send to know for whom the bell tolls; it tolls for thee." Though Donne was an English clergyman and Woolman was a New Jersey tailor, they bore almost identical witness to the impossibility of their being separated from the sufferings and deaths of other men. There is, of course, no probability that Woolman had ever read Donne's now-famous sermon. The Woolman passage is:

I was brought so Near the gates of death, that I forgot my name. Being then desirous to know who I was, I saw a mass of matter of a dull gloomy collour, between the South and the East. and was informed that this mass was human beings, in as great misery as they could be, & live, and that I was mixed in with them, & henceforth I might not consider myself as a distinct or Separate being. In this state I remained several hours. I then heard a soft melodious voice, more pure and harmonious than any voice I had heard with my ears before, and I believed it was the voice of an angel who spake to the other angels. The words were *John Woolman is dead*. I soon remembered that I once was John Woolman, and being assured that I was alive in the body, I greatly wondered what that heavenly voice could mean.

I believed beyond doubting that it was the voice of an holy Angel, but as yet it was a mystery to me.

I was then carried in Spirit to the mines, where poor Oppressed people were digging rich treasures for those called Christians, and heard them blaspheme the name of Christ, at which I was grieved for his Name to me was precious.

Then I was informed that these heathen were told that those who oppressed them were the followers of Christ; and they said amongst themselves, If Christ directed them to use us in this Sort then Christ is a cruel tyrant.

All this time the song of the Angel remained a Mystery, and in the morning my dear wife and some others coming to my bedside I asked them if they knew who I was, and they telling me I was John Woolman, thought I was only light-headed, for I told them not what the Angel said, nor was I disposed to talk much to any one; but was very desirous to get so deep that I might understand this Mystery.

My tongue was often so dry that I could not speak till I had moved it about and gathered some moisture, and as I lay still for a time, at length I felt divine power prepare my mouth that I could speak, and then I said, "I am crucified with Christ, nevertheless I live yet not I, but Christ [that] liveth in me, and the life I now live in the flesh is by faith [in] the Son of God who loved me and gave himself for me."

Then the Mystery was opened and I perceived there was Joy in heaven over a Sinner who had repented, and that that language, *John Woolman is dead*, meant no more than the death of my own will.[5]

It must not be supposed that John Woolman, with all of his tenderness, was, for that reason, lacking in intellectual sharpness. He was especially sharp in seeing through the self-deceit by which

[5] *Journal*, Rancocas Edition, pp. 308–9.

men masked their real motives. As he traveled in the ministry among slaveowners, he found some who felt the need of defending slavery on moral grounds. The most common argument presented to him was to the effect that the lives of the Negroes were so wretched in their native Africa that it was a kindness to bring them to America. One man called attention to the cruelty of the tribal wars in Africa. Woolman's reply is a splendid example of the sharpness of his powers of analysis. He told the apologist for slavery that "If compassion to the Africans, in regard to their domestic troubles, were the real motives of our purchasing them, That spirit of Sympathy being Attended to, would Incite us to use them kindly, that as Strangers brought out of Affliction, their lives might be happy amongst us, And as they are Human creatures, whose Souls are as precious as ours, and who may receive the same help & Comfort from the Holy Scriptures as we do, we could not omit sutable Endeavours to instruct them therein."[6]

Being as tough-minded as he was tender, Woolman said sternly to his southern Friends, "The love of ease and gain are the motives in general of keeping Slaves, and men are wont to take hold of weak arguments to Support a cause which is unreasonable."[7] More than once Woolman saw, with stark realism, the dark time coming, if the sin of slave holding were not renounced. "I believe," he said, "that burthen will grow heavier and heavier, till times change in a way disagreeable to us."[8] This was said in 1757, one hundred four years before the attack on Fort Sumter. The slaves, he said, far from being the advantage they were generally thought to be, were really a burdensome stone to those who owned them. Believing in the objective reality of the moral law, Woolman was convinced that slavery was a sin of such great depth that it would bring sorrow and pain, even to subsequent generations. The profound insight, which seems strange in one so kind,

[6] *Ibid.*, p. 191.
[7] *Ibid.*, p. 192.
[8] *Ibid.*, p. 191.

was that "*by Terrible things in Righteousness* God may answer us in this matter."[9]

Part of the surprising toughness of Woolman is shown by his practice, on some occasions, of leaving money for his lodging when his hosts refused to give up their slaves. The visitor's reasoning was that, if he accepted free hospitality based on slavery, he was then himself profiting from this manifest evil. The desire to avoid involvement led him, in the last ten years of his life, to wear undyed clothing because he had been told that dyes were produced by slave labor.

One of the most revealing incidents, in connection with the rejection of hospitality, occurred at London Grove, Pennsylvania, on November 18, 1758, a year after Woolman's last southern journey. At this delightful rural scene, between Philadelphia and Baltimore, Woolman preached a powerful sermon against slavery and was then taken to the home of Thomas Woodward for dinner. Upon entering the house, the visitor noted some colored servants, about whose status he immediately inquired. On learning that they were slaves he, without saying anything more to anyone, quietly left the house. The Woodwards supposed Woolman would soon return, but he never did. Thus, without a word, the quiet man was able to make his witness felt. The effect on Thomas Woodward, an important man of the community, was immediate. On waking the next morning, he told his wife that he must liberate his slaves; and he carried out his decision in spite of the remonstrance of his wife who burst into tears at the thought of losing her highly prized serving woman. Thomas Woodward, it is important to note, was influenced by a demonstration, as he had not been influenced by mere words. In any case, as a man who was proud of his hospitality, he was determined not to keep a house at which those whom he honored were unwilling to be entertained.

Though Woolman did not carry on his crusade against slavery alone, his was undoubtedly the most influential single voice, and

[9] *Ibid.*, p. 217.

soon the voice was heard. Philadelphia Yearly Meeting of 1758 made a notable step on the way to ultimate emancipation, partly because the simple tailor was able, by his appeal, to move the entire body to its depths. Woolman gives a brief digest of his address in his *Journal*, under date of 1758. It was in this address that he employed the phrase already mentioned, about the *Terrible things in Righteousness*. The outcome of this crucial encounter was that, so far as Quakers were concerned, the tide was turned against both the purchase and the continued ownership of slaves. The next step in the strategy was that by which Woolman and others went directly to the slaveowners, in order to appeal to them personally, rather than to discharge propaganda artillery from a distance. The effort was so remarkably effective that the ownership of slaves was made a disciplinary matter by Philadelphia Yearly Meeting in 1776. The system itself was abolished by law in Pennsylvania in 1780, and in New Jersey in 1803. What was even more remarkable was the effect of Woolman and others in the strong Quaker communities of the south, where slavery was more deeply entrenched and where it was seemingly a necessary element in the total economy. The amazing fact is that, prior to the year 1800, more than sixty years before the Emancipation Proclamation, every Quaker of North Carolina had liberated his slaves.

The last chapter of Woolman's life was, in many ways, the best. Though seemingly too weak in body for such a big undertaking, Woolman entered on a ministerial visit to England, in 1772. He seemed to have a premonition that it was his last earthly journey, for he sent home from London the mattress that he had made for his personal use in the steerage of the ship, as though he felt that he would not need it again. Woolman decided to take passage on the ship *Mary and Elizabeth*, but to go by steerage rather than in the cabin. This decision was not taken lightly and was not an easy one for a man of Woolman's physique, who would undoubtedly have been helped by more comfort. He took passage in the steerage, not out of poverty, but as a social testimony against class distinction. As he told the owner of the ship, a fellow Quaker, of his decision, he found the experience painful. "Here my mind was turned toward Christ, the heavenly Counsellor; & I feeling at this time my own will Subjected, my heart was contrite." His reason for the refusal of better quarters was intrinsic to his entire witness against luxury. The key paragraph is as follows:

I told the owner that on the outside of that part of the Ship where the cabbin was, I observed sundry sorts of Carved work and Imagery, and that in the Cabbin I observed some superfluity of workmanship of several sorts, and that according to the way of mens reconing, the Sum of money to be paid for a passage in that Appartment bore some relation to the Expense, in furnishing the room to please the minds of such who give way to a conformity to this world; and that in this case, as in other cases, the moneys received from the passengers are calculated to answer every expense relating to their passage, and amongst the rest of the expence of these superfluities. And that in this case I felt A scruple with regard to paying my money to defray such expences.[10]

After a voyage of five weeks, Woolman landed at one of the London docks, barely in time to reach Devonshire House where London Yearly Meeting gathered for its first session of 1772. His entrance was clearly startling to the cultivated London Quakers, of the character of David Barclay and his associates. With his undyed clothing and his rumpled appearance resulting from five weeks in the steerage, Woolman made an unfavorable impression. Here, apparently, was another fanatic who would be an embarrassment and a burden. The reception was still cool after the official presentation of Woolman's certificate from Friends in America.

The problem before the proud London Quakers was how to get rid of this New Jersey rustic, who appeared to them to be a crank. Accordingly, one Quaker remarked that "perhaps the stranger Friend might feel that his dedication of himself to this apprehended service was accepted, without further labour, and that he might now feel free to return to his home." Since Woolman was

[10] *Ibid.*, p. 290.

no fool, he understood what was meant, and because he knew that these were cruel words, he was moved to tears. But what was he to do? If he were to accept the rebuff and go home to New Jersey, that would mean defeat in the pursuance of a long-cherished hope. Furthermore, and more importantly, it would mean that he was failing to follow what had become an unusually clear leading of the Living Christ. Only four hours before he died, Woolman referred to this clear leading when he used a pen for the last time and wrote painfully, with blinded eyes, "I believe my being here is in the wisdom of Christ; I know not as to life or death."

While leaving England, as was suggested, was unthinkable to Woolman, the other clear alternative, that of open conflict, was equally unthinkable. He was willing to fight for the slaves, but he would not fight for John Woolman. What is most important to realize is that Woolman recognized the existence of another alternative to both submission and fighting. In this discovery of a "third way" he was operating in the mainstream of Quaker life and thought. His decision was to *remain*, but to remain as no burden to others and with no responsibility on the part of his intended hosts. He conceived that his right method was to live among these strangers, who were so cool to his coming, in such a manner that eventually they would be glad to let him speak to them.

After sitting long in silence, his weeping ended, Woolman arose to say that he did not feel himself released from the prospect of ministerial labor in England. Nevertheless he realized that he could not rightly travel among Quakers without consent. Therefore he would stay, without any financial cost to English Quakers. He had, he said, a trade by which he could support himself if given employment. That was all. A deep silence followed, after which Woolman again arose and this time delivered a powerful sermon which convinced all present of the authenticity of his vocation. Subsequently the very man who had made the harsh suggestion arose to say that his doubts were gone, and others concurred. It was, perhaps, the greatest single victory of Woolman's entire life.[11]

Soon the American visitor started north. He wanted to see the country where the first work of Fox and his associates had taken place one hundred twenty years earlier. Because of reports of overdriving the horses and overexposure of men, connected with the stagecoaches, he walked all the way to York, by way of Westmorland County, traversing more than four hundred miles. It took him about six weeks to reach the borders of Yorkshire. In his moral scruple against personal gain from suffering and its consequent encouragement, Woolman was as strict as ever.

As my journey hath been without a horse I have had several offers of being assisted on my way in these Stage Coaches but have not been in them nor have I had freedom to send letters by these posts, in the present way of their riding, the stages being so fixed and one body dependent on another as to time, that they commonly go upward of 100 miles in 24 hours, and in the cold long winter nights, the poor boys suffer much.[12]

When Woolman reached York, he asked for a retired place and was lodged at Almery Garth, the home of Thomas Priestman, outside the city walls. There he soon showed symptoms of smallpox, the very disease which he had often mentioned and which he most feared.[13] His tenderness to all who helped him in his illness was a treasured memory among the leading Quakers of York. The good man died on October 7, 1772, and his body was buried in Bishophill graveyard. Thus the most authentic saint who has emerged in the Quaker Movement is a permanent link between America and England.

The paradox of Woolman is the paradox of Quakerism, pre-

[11] We owe to the poet, John Greenleaf Whittier, this story. It is not found in Woolman's *Journal*. Whittier had the story on good authority.

[12] *Journal*, p. 306.

[13] Woolman had good reason to dread the loathsome disease. His sister, his cousin, William Hunt, and his own daughter, all died of it. He was aware of the possibility of inoculation, but rejected this innovation.

sented in extreme form. It is the paradox of something seemingly small making a very great difference in the world. It is the paradox of "holy boldness" combined with a sensitive tenderness. His *Journal*, produced with no conscious artistry, has become a devotional classic. First presented by Charles Lloyd to Charles Lamb in 1797, it was given by Lamb an immense impetus in the estimation of the literate public. The consequence is that the story of Woolman, which is the best single introduction to the Quaker ideal, is not the sole possession of the people called Quakers, but has reached the hearts and minds of millions. All who read Woolman have a chance to realize that the best thing in the world is a really good person.

9 / The Gurneys of Earlham

A landscape or view of any kind is defective, in my
opinion, without some human figures to give it animation.

JAMES BOSWELL

It is impossible to have an adequate understanding of modern
Quakerism without considerable attention to the remarkable family which lived in Earlham Hall at the beginning of the nineteenth
century. From this beautiful home stemmed important influences,
destined to alter the stream of Quaker history and possibly to keep
it from drying up altogether. A movement depends ultimately
upon people and life in the great house was marked by interesting
human figures. One of these, Joseph John Gurney, became the
most influential Quaker of the nineteenth century, while his sister
Elizabeth, who married Joseph Fry, became the most famous of all
Quaker heroines. These help to give the Quaker landscape the
kind of animation which Boswell said was required to keep it from
being defective.

Earlham Hall is situated two miles west of the East Anglian
metropolis of Norwich, the beautiful old house being surrounded
by well-kept gardens and abundant grassland. Today the Hall is
the central building of the recently established East Anglian University, but for many decades, after 1786 when John and Catherine
Gurney moved there, it was the best-known Quaker home in
England. Indeed it became for its period something of what, in
another fashion, Swarthmore Hall had been more than a hundred
years earlier. There is a fine appropriateness in the fact that two of
the Quaker colleges of America bear the names of the two most
famous of English Quaker homes.

The Gurneys, when they moved from the city of Norwich to the splendid estate in the country, seemed the very picture of Quakers as seen by Dr. Johnson and other public men. John Gurney was already wealthy, amiable, and charitable, but too relaxed to take his religion very seriously. He used the plain language, which meant that he said "thee" and "thou" to a single person, and referred to the days of the weeks and months by number, rather than by their heathenish names. He wore "plain dress," but was not extreme about it. Plain dress, for men, involved coats which avoided the superfluity of collars and beaver hats with broad brims. His attitude toward the Christian faith was almost the opposite of that of George Fox, for his character exhibited not the slightest touch of fanaticism. He was naturally proud of his large and brilliant family.

In 1775, the Norwich wool merchant married Catherine Bell, a great beauty who was the great-granddaughter of the famous Robert Barclay of Scotland. Gainsborough painted her just before her marriage. She lived only seventeen years as Mrs. John Gurney, but in that short time she bore twelve children, seven girls and five boys. All of these except one survived infancy and the youngest, Daniel, lived until 1880. The Gurneys had eight living children when they moved to Earlham Hall, the last three, Samuel, Joseph John, and Daniel being born at the estate.

The outside observer of life at Earlham when the Gurney children were young would have predicted a steady movement in the direction of gay society and adherence to the Church of England, for he would naturally have expected all of the Quaker nonsense to wear off in time. The beautiful house was the scene of gay entertainment with many distinguished visitors. Often the Bishop of Norwich was a guest, while, in the winter of 1797, the charming teenage girls were delighted to entertain Prince William Frederick, his regiment being then stationed at Norwich.

Janet Whitney had a brilliant idea for the start of her successful book, *Elizabeth Fry, Quaker Heroine*, when she decided to picture the Gurney girls, stretched across the road west of Norwich, determined to stop the coach.[1] Seven of them, in their bright red coats, stood laughing, hand in hand, utterly unafraid of the lead horses, until, to the consternation and chagrin of the driver, and the pleasure of some of the passengers, they brought the coach to a stop. Then the charming girls gave apples to the horses, blew kisses to the driver, and went dancing up the tree-lined lane to the big brick mansion which was their home. The seven were Catherine, Rachel, Elizabeth, Richenda, Hannah, Louisa, and Priscilla. The eldest of these was only nine and a half years older than the youngest. They had a wonderful life together as children, and they stayed close together in fundamental interests throughout their lives. Hannah and Louisa became the wives of men of prominence in public life, the former marrying Sir Thomas Fowell Buxton and the latter marrying Samuel Hoare. Richenda, the most gifted of all with her brush, married an Anglican clergyman, Francis Cunningham. Elizabeth married the Quaker banker of London, Joseph Fry, and spent most of her mature life in the great city, though, like the others, she visited Earlham countless times. In fact, none of the Gurneys could stay away. Three of the girls, Catherine, Rachel, and Priscilla, never married. Samuel, like Joseph John, became a famous banker, the consequent large incomes giving credence to the well-known line of W. S. Gilbert, in *Trial by Jury*, "At length I became as rich as the Gurneys."

John Gurney was undoubtedly rich, but being well aware of the fact that his greatest wealth was his family, he treated his children well. He was sufficiently worldly to employ John Crome, later to be widely known as a member of the Norwich school of painters, to instruct his gifted children. Not only the girls, but even Joseph John Gurney, showed considerable skill in drawing.[2] The Gurneys were Quakers, all right, but their Quakerism did not make them

---

[1] Boston: Little, Brown and Company, 1936, pp. 3–5.
[2] A drawing of Earlham Hall by Joseph John Gurney has been discovered as part of the uncatalogued Bevan-Naish Collection at Woodbrooke, Selly Oak, England.

dull, nor did it shut them off from a multitude of influences. Their cultivated neighbors, with whom they conversed freely, were, of course, chiefly Anglican, but others were Roman Catholics and Unitarians. Some, like Dr. Alderson, were skeptical in religion and republican in politics, admiring the principles of the French Revolution.

The public worship conducted by the local Quakers was of the kind which might have been expected to alienate the gay young Gurneys entirely. Sunday after Sunday the family worshiped in the drab meetinghouse on Goats Lane, which the Gurney girls irreverently called "Goats."[3] Each girl kept a journal and, when the meeting for worship was dull or long or uninspiring, it was common for one of them to confide to her journal that "Goats was dis." This meant that the meeting was disgusting. It was disgusting because the ministry was, for the most part, merely traditional, with little hint of the fire demonstrated in the words of George Fox, or even of their famous ancestor, Robert Barclay. The obvious probability was that they would move, on maturity, into the more respectable Anglican communion, attend gay parties, and mingle chiefly with the aristocrats. How surprising that some of them would eventually adopt the plain garb, that Elizabeth would become famous for her prison ministry, and that Joseph John would develop into the most influential Quaker preacher on either side of the Atlantic.

One of the major causes of the surprising turn which life at Earlham took was the habit of the Gurneys of welcoming traveling Quaker ministers. From these the young people got a glimpse of what Quakerism beyond Norwich might be. Also the young people were reading Quaker books of an earlier generation, particularly

---

[3] The chief variation from worship at the Goats Lane Meetinghouse was provided by attendance at the Meetinghouse at Wymondham, a village about fourteen miles west. Attendance at Wymondham came during schooling in the vicinity. Though the Wymondham Meetinghouse is now dismantled, parts of it have been incorporated in the Stout Meetinghouse at Earlham College in Indiana.

Barclay's *Apology*. This we know from the existence today of copies annotated by the Gurney children. Though the Quakerism which they knew in Norwich, outside the walls of their own home, presented little to attract them, they had, by means of visitors and books, some contact with a faith which was more vital and consequently more exciting than their own.

Many of the Quaker visitors looked with a good deal of misgiving on the gay life of the Gurneys, with its dancing, laughter, horseback riding, and abundant contact with the "world." Though the father's coat was "plain" the cloth was exceptionally good. The dangers of prosperity were often mentioned, never better than by John Hunt. In his *Journal* this deeply committed Quaker wrote, "Not all the persecutors, open apostates and enemies we have ever had in the world, ever have done us the hurt that prosperity has done."

The most crucial of Quaker visits to the Norwich community at the end of the eighteenth century was that of William Savery. This man, of the general stamp of John Woolman, had observed slavery in its most wicked form, as the following excerpt from his *Journal* shows:

Rose in the morning, and whilst at the door musing, I heard someone begging for mercy, and also the lashes of a whip. Not knowing whence the sound came, I ran, and presently found the poor boy tied up to a post, his toes scarcely touching the ground, and a negroe whipper, with five or six hazel rods lying by him. He had already cut him in an unmerciful manner, and the blood ran to his heels. I stepped in between them and ordered him untied immediately, which with some reluctance and astonishment was done.[4]

The terrible punishment, says Savery, was administered because the young slave had, on the previous evening, fallen asleep through weariness. As Savery reached England, he was shocked, at Liverpool, to see ten vessels, outward bound, going to Guinea for slaves. It is not wholly surprising, in view of his subsequent influence on

[4] *Journal of the Life of William Savery, Friends Library*, Vol. I, p. 331.

the young people of Earlham Hall, that the great house later became one of the chief centers for the promotion of emancipation throughout the British Empire, as well as for the abolition of the slave trade.

William Savery, traveling in the ministry among English Quakers, and with many travels already behind him, arrived in Norwich on February 4, 1798, when Elizabeth was seventeen years old, and beginning to wonder what direction her life might take.[5] The visitor was an eloquent, but untrained Philadelphia Quaker who represented the beginnings of a more evangelical approach than the prevailing quietism had encouraged previously. Savery attended the meeting at Goats Lane and preached with a power which the relaxed Quakers of Norwich had seldom experienced. He did not wholly approve of what he saw, especially the sight of the gay clothing of the stunning row of Gurney daughters. His own reaction was far from favorable, as follows:

> The marks of wealth and grandeur are too obvious in several families of Friends in this place . . . ; several of the younger branches, though they are enabled, through divine grace, to see what the Truth leads to, yet it is uncertain whether, with all the alluring things of this world around them, they will choose the simple, safe path of self-denial.[6]

The Gurneys were better impressed by the American visitor than he was by them. Even Louisa, then aged thirteen, wrote, "He appears to me a truly good man, and a most upright Christian. To me he is quite different from the common run of disagreeable Quaker preachers." But the impression made on Louisa's older sister Elizabeth was really profound. The precocious young woman was ready for a big new change in her life, and Savery provided the impetus. It is fortunate that the Gurney children, and especially

[5] A full-length biography of Savery is available. See Francis R. Taylor, *The Life of William Savery, of Philadelphia* (New York: The Macmillan Company, 1925).

[6] *A Journal of the Life, Travels and Religious Labours of William Savery* (London, 1844), pp. 278 f.

Elizabeth, kept journals, because in these we have firsthand evidence of the change that was going on.[7]

That there was some public notice of Savery's ministry is indicated by the following passage in his own *Journal*, under date of 1798:

A publication appeared in one of the public papers approving of what was delivered at Norwich and Bath; but I thank my God, who has yet preserved me from being elated or much depressed, by the well or ill-done of the world. If I can but obtain the answer of a conscience void of offence to God and man, that is the great object of my concern and will be enough.

Though by no stretch of imagination could the modest American have known the extent of his influence, as a result of his visit in 1798, he did have the satisfaction of seeing that, for the moment at least, Elizabeth's life was changed and immeasurably deepened. The event provides one of the best examples of the power implicit in a dedicated itinerant ministry. Even Elizabeth's sisters took note of the change in her, admitting that her character was improved, even though they were not entirely pleased. The fifteen-year-old Richenda, destined finally to be the wife of a clergyman, wrote in her own journal about a month after Savery's visit, as follows:

I have felt extremely uncomfortable about Betsy's Quakerism, which I saw, to my sorrow, increasing every day. She no longer joined in our pleasant dances, and singing she seemed to give up, she dressed as plain as she could, and spoke still more so. We all feel about it alike, and are truly sorry that one of us seven should separate herself in principles, actions, and appearance from the rest.

But, however her six sisters felt about the change, Elizabeth was delighted. In a passage in her *Journal* with the word "felt" underlined five times, she wrote, "I wish the state of enthusiasm I am now in may last, for today I *have felt* there is a God. *I have been*

[7] The fifteen notebooks of Elizabeth's *Journal* are in Friends Reference Library, London. A microfilm version of the entire *Journal* is at Earlham College.

devotional, and my mind has been led away from the follies that it is mostly wrapt up in—I loved the man as if he was sent from heaven." She felt especially drawn to Savery because he, like herself, had once been gay and worldly and had changed. She saw that her own worldly background would be a genuine asset to her, in her intended effort to reach worldly people. "If I were to grow like him a preacher," she wrote, "I should be able to preach to the gay and disbelieving, better than to any other for I should feel more sympathy for them and know their hearts better than any others." It is the record of history that the prediction of this girl, not yet eighteen years old, was fulfilled as she saw it in the winter of 1798.

Elizabeth was true to her new-found Quaker life by combining at once her faith and service. Quickly she started to collect the poor children of the neighborhood, in order to provide instruction which otherwise they would not have had. The spacious rooms of Earlham Hall allowed her to have as many as seventy of what her disapproving sisters called "Betsy's Imps." Also the young convert began to visit the sick and the poor of Norwich in their homes.

The girl's *Journal* shows how ready she was for Savery's visit and how seriously she took the change in her life. Before February, 1798, she was certainly a Seeker. Her seeking is indicated by the fact that, on a bright summer morning in June, 1797, she wrote, "I am at this present in an odd state. I am like a ship put out to sea without a pilot. I feel my mind and heart so overburdened. I want someone to lean upon." A few days later the same theme was continued: "I am in an unsettled state. I do not know what is come, or what is coming. I'm sure my mind seems changing." The visit of the royal Prince pleased her, yet she doubted her motives. "Why do I wish so much for the prince to come? Pride is the cause. Do such feelings hurt my mind? They may not in this instance, but if once given way to they are difficult to overcome. . . . How am I to overcome them?" On July 27, 1797, she confided, "I shall either turn out a *flirting,* worldly woman or I may be a virtuous interesting woman." Clearly her mind was ready. Just before Savery's visit she wrote, "My mind is in a state of fermentation. I believe I am going to be religious or some such thing." After the visit of William Savery, Elizabeth had an important confrontation in Wales with a perceptive Quaker woman, Deborah Darby, who told her, with rare foresight, that she would be "a light to the blind, speech to the dumb and feet to the lame." Later, in her diary, the young woman wrote, "I think my feelings that night at Deborah Darby's were the most exalted I ever remember. My mind felt clothed with light as with a garment, and I felt silenced before God."

Not long after these experiences Elizabeth Gurney adopted the plain garb, stopped going to dances and made clear to all what her vocation was. Apart from the fact of marriage her acts were similar to those of women who take the veil. On August 19, 1800, at the age of twenty, the new convert became Elizabeth Fry, the name by which she is widely known, as she was joined in marriage to Joseph Fry.

With a large family of her own children and a big house in Mildred's Court, London, where visiting Quakers were graciously entertained, Elizabeth Fry settled down to the public and private life of a dedicated Christian. When her children were old enough to permit her absence without harm to them, she traveled widely in the ministry. For example, she accompanied her brother, Joseph John, on an ambitious speaking tour in Holland, Germany, and Denmark in the summer of 1841. The brother and sister had a threefold purpose. This was, first, to preach, second, to extend to the European continent Elizabeth Fry's crusade to improve the conditions of prisons, and third, to press for the limitation of the slave trade and the abolition of colonial slavery.

The most notable public service of Elizabeth Fry, that at Newgate Prison, began in 1813, when she and her husband were in straitened financial circumstances and she was the mother of eight children.[8] It seems strange to us that most people of her period, including dedicated Christians, were almost wholly undisturbed by the foul and crime-producing conditions of prisons. It is the supreme mark of Mrs. Fry's sensitivity that she became disturbed and consequently effected great changes. Her Quaker conscience made her feel the sufferings of prisoners much as that of Woolman made him feel the sufferings of slaves. It is another chapter of the same story. The essence of Mrs. Fry's approach was to treat the prisoners as persons, because she could so easily imagine herself in their place.

It is reasonably certain that the interest in prison reform was lodged in Elizabeth's mind during the momentous visit of William Savery before she was eighteen. In any case we know, from Savery's *Journal*, of his own strong interest at the time. While in London, in 1798, he wrote, "For several days past my mind has been turned to think of the poor prisoners in Newgate; four men and one woman were executed last week. It is truly an afflicting circumstance, that numbers are continually sent out of the world in that way, in this country; many for small crimes."[9] Fifteen years later Mrs. Fry's well-known work in Newgate began.

The genius of the Quaker ministry is brilliantly exhibited in the combination of influences which helped to lead Mrs. Fry to her famous work of prison reform. As had occurred before, it was trans-Atlantic influence that was particularly effective. When the seed sown by Savery had had fifteen years to mature, another American Quaker preacher appeared on the scene and made the crucial difference. This was Stephen Grellet (1773–1855), a Quaker of French origin, who was born at Limoges, of a noble Roman Catholic family, and who, after a frivolous beginning and many escapades, settled on Long Island. He was converted by a remark-

[8] Joseph Fry was not a business success. At first his brothers-in-law, Samuel and Joseph John Gurney, saved him by their heroic efforts, but in 1828, he became bankrupt.

[9] Savery's *Journal, Friends Library*, Vol. I, p. 453.

able combination of influences, including the written word, the spoken word, and silence. The written word was Penn's *No Cross No Crown*, which Grellet read with the help of a dictionary, looking up nearly every word. The spoken word was that of an English Quaker lady, Deborah Darby, who had a gift for discerning future possibilities and who also influenced Elizabeth Gurney. Concerning the silent meeting, at Newton, on Long Island, Grellet reported, "great was the awfulness and the reverence that came upon me." In 1797, he began a truly wonderful work as a Quaker evangelist, in which capacity he visited London in the winter of 1812–1813 and paid a visit to Newgate prison. Because what he saw of exposure and filth was a shattering experience for the sensitive man, he went straight to Mildred's Court and told Elizabeth Fry. The seed had ripened.

Elizabeth and Joseph John were the two brightest stars in the Gurney firmament. Joseph John Gurney (1788–1847) combined many elements in one composite career.[10] He was scholar, banker, author, preacher, philanthropist, and cultivated gentlemen. He remained a banker to the end of his days, though constantly tempted to abandon the work in order to give full time to other pursuits, but always he decided that the combination constituted his most productive way of life. For one thing, the banking business provided income to make possible the vast travel in the ministry as well as his increasingly generous philanthropy. The bank which he headed in Norwich became, later, the number one branch of the great banking chain known as Barclays, and Joseph John's descendants are officers of the local branch to this day. One of them, Richard Gurney, has recently been Lord Mayor of the city of Norwich.

As a youth, Gurney did so well at school that his father was advised to give him an advanced education, which the elder

---

[10] The need for a full-length contemporary biography of Joseph John Gurney is now met. The book is: David E. Swift, *Joseph John Gurney, Banker, Reformer and Quaker* (Middletown, Conn.: Wesleyan University Press, 1962).

Gurney was delighted to do. The boy could not, however, qualify for Oxford or Cambridge, since he was not an Anglican. True to the Quaker idea that the reality is worth more than the words on paper, Joseph John went to Oxford to study under a tutor, not greatly concerned over the fact that he could never be granted a degree. He recalled later the experience of reading fourteen hours a day. The tutor, John Rogers, wrote to the boy's father to say, "You will not be surprised, I am well convinced, when I assure you that your son Joseph is one of the most amiable and most industrious young men that were ever intrusted to my care." Some notion of young Gurney's progress is indicated by the fact that, at sixteen, he was reading both the Italian of Dante and the Hebrew of the Old Testament.

At seventeen Gurney left his formal studies and returned to Norwich to start his career in the bank, a career which he continued for more than forty years. It must not be supposed, however, that the beginning of banking was for him the end of scholarship. His study room at Earlham Hall became the chief physical center of his life. There he continued the life of a scholar with the consequence that he became, along with Barclay and Penn, one of the few systematic theologians in the entire history of Quakerism.

It is still delightful to picture the scholarly banker, as he sat in his study and watched a fourteen-year-old boy, George Borrow, fishing in the River Yare, where it flows through Earlham property. Years later, Borrow, in his book *Lavengro*, told delightfully of the friendly encounter.

"Canst thou answer to thy conscience for pulling all those fish out of the water, and leaving them to gasp in the sun?" said a voice, clear and sonorous as a bell.

I started and looked round. Close behind me stood the tall figure of a man, dressed in raiment of quaint and singular fashion, but of goodly materials. He was in the prime and vigour of manhood; his features handsome and noble, but full of calmness and benevolence; at least I thought so, though they were somewhat shaded by a hat of finest beaver, with broad drooping eaves.[11]

Gurney was married three times, first to Jane Birkbeck, at the age of twenty-nine, second, to Mary Fowler, nearly ten years later, and third, to the American Quaker, Eliza Paul Kirkbride, at fifty-three. He was the father of one son and one daughter. Earlham Hall was always his home, but it soon became far more than a home in the ordinary sense of the word. It was, in fact, an exciting center of social concern, where ideas were shared and where movements were originated. With Joseph John Gurney as the master of the house, it was reasonable that the abolition of slavery should have become a common topic of discussion. This was facilitated by the frequent visits of his brother-in-law, Sir Thomas Fowell Buxton, who married Hannah in 1807. Buxton was Wilberforce's successor in Parliament, as leader in the drive to abolish slavery. Gurney, who had known Buxton since boyhood, urged him to enter politics and there to take up "one great object."

The vivid discussions at Earlham Hall were carried straight to Parliament by Sir Thomas Fowell Buxton, where he was the leading abolitionist prior to the vote, in 1833, which ended slavery in the British colonies. This victory came at the conclusion of ten years of aggressive efforts to influence public opinion after Wilberforce had published, in 1823, his "Appeal on behalf of the Slaves" and the Anti-Slavery Society had been formed. Joseph John Gurney was the chief organizer for the anti-slavery cause in the Norwich area.

Earlham Hall was the scene of the annual meetings of the Bible Society from 1811 to 1836. Though the hospitality necessarily ended when Gurney made his long American visit, it had been a major feature of his life for a quarter century. Many visitors stayed for two or three days, enjoying an experience not unlike that of the

[11] Borrow's description accords well with the portrait of Gurney painted by Richmond. The portrait hangs in Bawdeswell Hall, Norfolk, the home of Quintin Gurney. Borrow's description of the incident is in *Lavengro* (London, 1923), Vol. I, p. 158. It occurred in 1817.

"retreats" now common in America, particularly in the laymen's movements. The capacious house could accommodate at least thirty overnight guests. This is not wholly surprising when we realize that, immediately after World War II, the house was used as a school for three hundred small children. Those who came as guests at these conferences were of all persuasions. A Baptist visitor wrote glowingly on September 13, 1811, of the first Earlham gathering, when Elizabeth Fry was present, giving assistance to her favorite brother.

Our host and hostess were Quakers, but, with the most cordial concurrence of the family, a clergyman read a portion of the Scriptures morning and evening. . . . After dinner on the day of the meeting, the pause encouraged by the Society of Friends was succeeded by a devout address from a female minister, Elizabeth Fry, whose manner was so impressive and whose words were so appropriate that none present can ever forget them. The first emotion was surprise; the second, awe; the third, pious fervour.[12]

Gurney's decision to become a Quaker in fact, and not merely by inheritance, was made only after agonizing meditation. The decision involved the use of plain dress and plain speech and withdrawal from most social life, though the gracious entertainment of Christian bodies at Earlham came to be something of a substitute for the social occasions which had been given up with such struggle. As Gurney's critics were quick to point out, however, the plainness which Gurney adopted did not give the appearance of really severe hardship. In the Richmond portrait, for example, we hardly notice the absence of a collar to the coat, in view of the fact that it is evidently made of the best cloth and is well cut. On his American visit some critics were envious of Gurney's beautifully matched team of horses, David and Jonathan. It is said sometimes that Gurney inaugurated a continuing tradition of plain Quakers who now demonstrate their plainness by making sure that their fine cars are painted black.

[12] J. B. Braithwaite, *Memoirs of Joseph John Gurney* (Philadelphia, 1854), Vol. I, pp. 79 f.

In 1818 Gurney was recognized as a minister and a sound one. Thereafter he felt free to travel as a minister and, consequently, to do a great deal of preaching. Though he loved this service, it was always difficult for him. "I sometimes think," he said, "that the ministry of the Gospel is the only thing I know which practice *never makes easy*."[13] This revealing comment came after he had been in the public ministry for twelve years. To the ordinary difficulties of public speaking were added his own peculiar ones, which arose out of the envy of those who thought he was too handsome, too eloquent, too rich, and too successful. He suffered from the resentment which mediocrity so often exhibits in the presence of excellence. By contrast, his admirers were ecstatic. One listener, in 1820, recorded having been powerfully struck by "his fine person, his beautiful dark, glossy hair, his intelligent, . . . and truly amiable countenance." When Gurney spoke at an "appointed meeting" at Springfield, Ohio, a young woman wrote to her mother, "It has never been my lot to be present at so highly favoured a season. . . . There seems to be a constantly overflowing spirit of love to all around him."[14]

To the natural envy of competitors for leadership there was added the constant suspicion that Gurney was unorthodox. His supposed unorthodoxy was not, as we might think, that of not being sufficiently evangelical, but rather that of being too much so. He studied the Scriptures daily, reading them in the original tongues; he deeply believed in the divinity of Christ; he stressed, as did his ancestor, Barclay, the indwelling of the Living Christ in the heart of each individual. Friends who were eager to keep Quakerism separate from the contamination of the world were deeply worried by the fact that Gurney mingled freely with non-Quakers. He was a close friend of the Bishop of Norwich and of many other Anglicans, particularly those who, like Charles

[13] *Ibid.*, Vol. I, p. 466.
[14] The letter, from which this is taken, belongs to Mrs. Arthur Eddington, of Norwich, England.

Simeon, of Cambridge, were openly evangelical. Even though he defended, in his published writings, the main tenets of Quakers, the conservative party did not like the way in which he did so. For one thing, he quoted the Bible too much, they thought, and was too successful in introducing the study of the Bible at Ackworth School. In America, he encountered the bitter opposition of a Rhode Island Quaker named John Wilbur. The consequence was an unhappy division, in which the contending parties were popularly designated Wilburites and Gurneyites.

It was the purpose of Joseph John Gurney to be, first of all, a loyal follower of Christ. Though he valued the Quaker witness, he was certainly a Christian first. He was well aware of the fact that his path would have been an easier one if he had elected to be more sectarian, but he was sure that this would have meant disloyalty, not only to Christendom in general, but also to Quakerdom in particular. He elected the middle way because he thought that the truth lay there, realizing full well that he would consequently be hit on both sides. "I adopt," he wrote in his manuscript Journal, "and have professed with the utmost openness the middle line, on which account my name is cast out as evil on both sides to a remarkable degree. I wonder I do not mind it more."

Gurney's three years in the United States and the West Indies (1837–1840), constituted, for the most part, a triumphal tour. Immense crowds appeared nearly everywhere he went. He reported that, at Richmond, Indiana, "It was supposed that about 3,000 were accommodated within the walls; and nearly as many, unable to obtain a place in the house, were promenading by the hour together on the premises." One result of his striking success in frontier Indiana was the subsequent naming of Earlham College for his beautiful estate. It opened as a boarding school in 1847, the year of his death, with some gifts from English Quakers, including the Gurney family. The name Earlham was adopted in 1859, when the school became a college, and the institution has always maintained the East Anglian connection. One evidence is the obvious fact that the campus is laid out after the manner of an English park.

The visit to North Carolina was so influential that Gurney is still used as a Christian name in the Guilford area. In Washington, Gurney felt led to arrange a Sunday morning meeting for congressmen, cabinet members, and the President. The meeting was held in the hall of the House of Representatives, with a glittering company present, including President Martin Van Buren. Among those who greeted the speaker afterward were Henry Clay and John Quincy Adams. While in Washington, he sought and obtained an interview with the President, much as his surviving widow, Eliza, was to do later during the presidency of Abraham Lincoln. The major topics of the interview were the slavery issue and the injustices suffered by Indians. This was twenty-three years before the outbreak of the Civil War. Part of the Presidential interview was devoted to Gurney's report to Van Buren of his brother-in-law Buxton's plan for a union of governments in Europe, reminiscent of the earlier plan proposed by William Penn.

One of the results of Gurney's American tour was his friendship with Eliza Paul Kirkbride. She became his third wife and the gracious mistress of Earlham Hall in October, 1841. The last five years of Gurney's life were spent happily, with Eliza as his competent wife and with Earlham Hall as a base for extended labors in the ministry in addition to continued work at the bank. It was a mark of the man's integrity that, while he was in the Western Hemisphere, he saw to it that he received no salary from the bank, the amount saved going to others whose responsibilities were correspondingly increased.

The death of Joseph John ended one great period for the Gurneys of Earlham and was nobly marked in the city of Norwich. During the week between his death and his funeral, the general loss was indicated by half-closed shops and darkened windows in private homes throughout the ancient city. On the

THE GURNEYS OF EARLHAM

Sunday after his death funeral sermons were preached in a number of churches. At the famous Cathedral the bishop, Edward Stanley, declared that Gurney's "peaceful life was one unwearied comment on evangelical charity in its fullest and most expanded sense."

With the master of the great house gone, Eliza Gurney decided to return to America to live out the remainder of her days. She was, herself, a recorded minister, and had great influence among her native Philadelphia Friends. Her fabulous reputation is humorously told by Logan Pearsall Smith, in his memoirs of his own Philadelphia boyhood. The reference to Mrs. Gurney is as follows:

Had they not indeed among them a living representative of that splendor in the Eliza Kirkbride who had reigned at Earlham, and with whom my grandfather had dined in England, and who, after the decease of her husband—that eminent evangelist, Joseph John Gurney, —had returned to her native city, where, preaching with great acceptance, she now reigned as a kind of Quaker queen.[15]

Eliza was still one of the Gurneys of Earlham, though an adopted one, to the end of her fruitful days. Her fine house, at Atlantic City, from which one of her letters to President Lincoln was addressed, was called "Earlham Lodge." Fifteen years after her husband's death, in the autumn of 1862, she sought and obtained an interview at the White House. Going on Sunday and taking a few other Friends with her, Mrs. Gurney turned the interview into a small meeting for worship. Both prayer and a spoken message were provided by Eliza after which came a spoken message from President Lincoln. His words, recorded by one of his secretaries who was present, were among the most important of his entire career. They provide us with the best single statement which we have of the content of the President's religious faith.

Another valuable insight into the development of President Lincoln's mind, in the agonizing days of decision, appears in his letter to Mrs. Gurney, dated September 4, 1864, and written with

[15] Logan Pearsall Smith, *Unforgotten Years* (Boston: Little, Brown and Company, 1939), pp. 24–25.

his own hand. The letter sounds almost like a first draft of the famous Second Inaugural, partly because he is so clearly meditating on the mystery of the divine will and on man's capacity to be an instrument of it, in spite of the human tendency to err. The basic faith, as Lincoln stated it to the widow of Joseph John Gurney, is to the effect that, "Surely He intends some great good to follow this mighty convulsion, which no mortal could make and no mortal could stay."[16]

The international character of the Quaker itinerant ministry is nowhere better exhibited than in the careers of the daughter and son of John Gurney of Earlham. The pattern of life which centers at Earlham Hall, and which is so deeply involved in the total Quaker scene, is one which is woven back and forth across the Atlantic. It starts with the visit of William Savery, going from America to England, and it continues to this day. Apart from the visit of Savery, the new fire in the hearts of Elizabeth and her brother might never have been kindled. Apart from Joseph John's American visit, American Quakerism would today be utterly different and, in many parts, might not even exist. Eliza Gurney's origin in America and later return to America are brilliant parts in the trans-Atlantic pattern of Quakerism. The pattern reached a climax in the White House, in 1862, in what Abraham Lincoln, himself a product of Quaker forebears, said was an occasion that he had not forgotten and "probably shall never forget."

[16] The Lincoln-Gurney correspondence is available in the Library of Congress. I have published the relevant parts of it in *The Christian Herald*, July, 1965, pp. 24–27.

10 / The Struggle for Peace

I am only too conscious that only a tiny fraction of
Christians in the world accept the position which I hold
and I feel humble about holding it in the face of the fact
that the vast majority of Christians walk a different path
from mine.

RUFUS M. JONES

The Quaker witness for peace is recognized by millions who know
little else about the Quaker Movement. It is widely understood
that Quakers have long seen war as evil, rather than essentially
glorious, and that many Quakers have, in the crises of actual wars,
been conscientious objectors to either participation in war or
preparation for war. But the general understanding of the complexities of the problem is obviously slight. Even among those who
are themselves Quakers there is often demonstrated a severe lack
of comprehension of the complexity of the moral issues involved,
some speaking of the "Peace Testimony" as though it were simple,
clear, and universally accepted, after the fashion of a creed. Such
widespread misunderstanding necessitates careful examination.

It is important, in the first place, to see the wide difference there
is between the peace problem and other social problems. Some
chapters in social progress have an ending, even though other
problems follow the ones which are solved. Thus, though the
world is still torn by racial strife, legal human slavery, in most parts
of the world, was ended in the nineteenth century. The fight for
the elimination of cruel treatment of the insane, begun by William Tuke and other Quakers, when they established The Retreat
at York in 1796, has largely ended in victory, even though mental

187

illness is still baffling. But there has been no comparable victory in the struggle for peace. Because of the crucial atomic discoveries of our generation, we are, increasingly, in a situation in which war on a planetary scale might destroy almost all else that men have learned to value and which has been built up with such slow and agonizing efforts. Since the events of 1945, it has been obvious to all thinking people that we are in a new age of danger, different, not merely in degree but in kind, from all that went before. The invention of gunpowder was revolutionary because it enabled the few to triumph over the many; the invention of atomic power may enable a few to triumph over *all*.

Some steps have been made, some excellent diplomacy has been practiced, and the beginning of a World Forum has been established, yet we are very far from the goal. Peace has been waged, but peace has not been won! The confident predictions of a warless world, which were voiced early in our century, even by a man as astute as Andrew Carnegie, now seem ridiculously Utopian. In the twentieth century we have experienced two global wars, perhaps the worst in all history, and today, after all of the efforts for peace, the United States of America spends more than half of its annual budget on what is called "Defense." Indeed, so deeply involved is our entire economy in Defense contracts that many careful scholars conclude that the economy could not stand the strain of the breaking out of real peace.

The outlook for peace is made dimmer, rather than brighter, in our day, because of a radically new factor with which our ancestors in other centuries did not have to contend. This new factor is that of a militant ideology which welcomes wars, at least wars of a particular kind, because wars produce a situation in which it is believed that ideological victory can be more readily achieved. In the full emergence of militant communism we have added to the causes of war something truly novel. We must now reckon, not merely with the economic and the political causes of war, but also with what we may, in honesty, call the "religious" causes. We miss the truth entirely if we fail to understand that there is, in the world, a new and virulent religion, for which men are wholly willing to die. The fact that it does not include belief in Almighty God is no reason for not recognizing it as a religion.

The present ideological conflict between Russia and mainland China is fundamentally a religious war, comparable, in many ways, to the struggles between components of the Biblical faith, though centering, naturally, on different issues. The war in South Vietnam is something which nearly every American deplores and wishes could have been avoided. By contrast many communists have reason to be glad. They are particularly glad whenever the war brings discomfiture and loss of prestige to the free way of life and government.

The truth is that, so far as the struggle for peace is concerned, we live in a hard time. It is obvious that peace does not come by wanting it. In many ways the problems of peace production are increased rather than diminished by the general progress of civilization. We want peace, but this is not *all* that we want; we also want freedom and maximum independence consistent with order. Many of our most difficult human problems arise, not because of a failure to recognize moral principles, but because there are so many which require recognition. In numerous cases the principles are clearly in conflict, a classic case of this being presented in the American Civil War. It was precisely to such a conflict of equally valid principles that President Lincoln was referring in his final letter to Mrs. Gurney, whose correspondence with Lincoln has been mentioned in the previous chapter. "On principle and faith," wrote Lincoln of Quakers, "opposed to both war *and* oppression, they can only practically oppose oppression by war. In this hard dilemma some have chosen one horn and some the other."

A modern illustration of the conflict of valid principles is provided by the agonizing decision of the eventual martyr, Dietrich Bonhoeffer, in Germany during the dark days of World War II. Opposed to murder and also opposed to the cruel injustice of the Nazi regime, which involved murder in wholesale dimensions, the moral struggle of the profound Christian thinker finally led to his decision to share in the plot to murder Adolf Hitler. The standard Quaker position, for better or for worse, has been to take the other horn of the cruel dilemma.

The fact that the Quaker rejection of war soon became recognized as an essential feature of the Movement is well attested by references in contemporary non-Quaker literature. Many of the references were naturally critical, one such being that found in Boswell's *Life of Samuel Johnson*. Partly because of a recent duel, in which a man had killed his antagonist, Boswell introduced, on April 28, 1783, the subject of self-defense for discussion. What is interesting is to see the way in which the reference to Quakers was quickly made, with the supposition that the Quaker opposition was purely and simply Biblical, in its ultimate support.

Johnson. "I do not see, Sir, that fighting is absolutely forbidden in the Scripture; I see revenge forbidden, but not self-defense."

Boswell. "The Quakers say it is. 'Unto him that smiteth thee on one cheek, offer him also the other.' "

Johnson. "But stay, Sir; the text is meant only to have the effect of moderating passion; it is plain that we are not to take it in a literal sense. We see this from the context, where there are other recommendations, which I warrant you, the Quaker will not take literally: as, for instance, 'from him that would borrow of thee turn not thou away.' Let a man whose credit is bad come to a Quaker and say, 'Well, Sir, lend me a hundred pounds;' he'll find him as unwilling as any other man."[1]

The original Quaker "testimony" against war was really surprising. Only in a mind as essentially uncomplicated and unspoiled as that of George Fox would it have been possible at all. The fundamental insight, in which Quakers at first were almost alone, was to the effect that war is intrinsically wrong and evil. This insight came at a time when the great majority of mankind,

[1] James Boswell, *Life of Samuel Johnson* (New York, 1887), Vol. IV, p. 298.

including the majority of professing Christians, thought of war as noble or at least inevitable. Hardships incident to war were naturally recognized, but the pains were accepted with the same resignation as that required in connection with the pains of child-birth or any other of the evils incident to the general human situation. The tremendous Quaker insight was that war is wrong, that it is not a necessary evil, and that no effort required in working for its abolition is to be accounted too great.

It must not be supposed that Fox went much further than this or that he even understood the thorny moral problems in connection with war which bothered the more sophisticated minds of Penington and Penn, or, later, of Eliza Gurney and Abraham Lincoln. Fox did not deal with disarmament, with the protection of the innocent from wanton aggression or with the problems of the military draft. Soldiering seemed to Fox primarily an occupation and it was one which he felt divinely led not to adopt. In essence he considered that it was a simple matter of obedience to Christ. "I told them," he said in 1650, "they were not to dispute of God and Christ, but to obey Him." These words were said at Derby where Fox was soon placed in the House of Correction, and where he had a chance to be free of imprisonment on condition that he join Cromwell's army. The necessity of a decision seems to have established a conviction about war which Fox had not consciously held previously. The passage in the *Journal* is revealing of Fox's mentality, with its mixture of pride, simplicity, and moral insight.

Now the time of my commitment to the House of Correction being nearly out, and there being many new soldiers raised, the commissioners would have made me captain over them; and the soldiers cried they would have none but me. So the keeper of the House of Correction was commanded to bring me before the commissioners and soldiers in the market-place; and there they offered me that preferment (as they called it), asking me if I would not take up arms for the Commonwealth against Charles Stuart? I told them I knew from whence all wars arose, even from the lust, according to James's doctrine; and that I lived in the virtue of that life and power that took away the occasion of all wars.[2]

This, by any standard, is a truly remarkable passage. That Fox could have been made a captain is easy to believe, for he was certainly a natural leader of men. What is surprising is that this unschooled man of twenty-six, with no theological background except that of the New Testament to which he made reference, should reject an attractive military solution to his problems, on moral and spiritual, rather than prudential, grounds. In all honesty we must point out that Fox did not wholly tell the truth. He was claiming a kind of perfection and his claim was patently false. He did not, as a matter of fact, live "in the virtue of that life and power" which takes away the occasions of all wars. To James Nayler he was harsh and unloving for a long time, and he rejoiced far too much in the sufferings of his persecutors. A vivid example of this is provided by Fox's encounter with a fellow prisoner in Scarborough Castle, named William Wilkinson, who challenged Fox to a fight, knowing well that, on principle, Fox would not protect his own body. Soon, Fox says, the man took the oath, gave bond, and was released, but, Fox adds, with evident glee, "the Lord soon cut him off in his wickedness."[3]

Though Fox was not always a loving man, he was a great man who must be forever honored in that he, more than most men, created the fountainhead of the stream of antiwar conviction in the modern world. This is part of what Thomas Carlyle meant by saying, with evident exaggeration, that the start of Fox on his itinerant ministry was the greatest incident in modern history. It took a high degree of courage, as well as of moral insight, to challenge a system which almost everyone else accepted without serious argument. One consequence was that the refusal to participate in war or preparation for war became one of the most obvious marks of a Quaker.

[2] *Journal*, 1650.
[3] *Journal*, 1666.

With the Restoration of the Stuart monarchy in Britain the still fluid Quaker Movement had a rare opportunity to make its political position clear. There was naturally a strong desire to avoid further imprisonment caused by religious activity, and there was considerable hope that the new king meant what he had said, on April 4, 1660, in the Declaration of Breda. Though the worst of Quaker imprisonment came after Charles II had ascended the throne, his words at Breda specifically promised otherwise.

We do declare a liberty to tender consciences, and that no man shall be disquieted or called in question for differences of opinion in matter of religion, which do not disturb the peace of the kingdom, and that we shall be ready to consent to such an Act of Parliament as, upon mature deliberation, shall be offered to us, for the full granting that indulgence.

The careful reader of the new King's words is quick to note that the disturbance of the peace of the kingdom is the key consideration. When Charles was proclaimed King and entered the capital in May, 1660, there was widespread rejoicing, but the royal party was well aware of underground opposition. This is why so much stress was placed upon the Oath of Allegiance. The majority of Quakers who were imprisoned during the next twenty-five years were punished more for the rejection of the oath than for any other single reason. It was naturally difficult for all the magistrates to make a fine distinction between those who rejected the oath because they hated King Charles and those who rejected it because *any* oath of any kind seemed to be an act of disobedience to the specific command of Christ (Matt. 5:34–37) and a rejection of the single standard of truthtelling, to which sincere Christians should adhere.

A leading Quaker, Richard Hubberthorne, had what appeared to be a highly fruitful conference with the King soon after he ascended the throne. In the course of the conversation the King said, "Well, of this you may be assured, that you shall none of you suffer for your opinions or religion, so long as you live peaceably,

and you have the word of a king for it." Charles may even have
been sincere in making this clear promise, but, in any case, the
promise was not kept.

The Quaker decision was to make a public statement to set the
King's mind at rest, so far as the danger of Quaker subversion or
incipient military revolt was concerned. Quakers were suspect
because they were undoubtedly an extreme group and because
they had certain external similarities to groups of people who were
potentially subversive. The most dangerous of these, the Fifth
Monarchy Men, being devoted to the overthrow of the government in order to bring in their own version of a Christian order,
actually engaged in an uprising in the opening days of 1661. This
aroused the authorities so greatly, in their dread of the action of
the extreme Puritan sects, that there resulted the wholesale imprisonment of Quakers, who had no part whatever in any armed
revolt. Influential Friends had done all that they could, but their
efforts were not availing to give protection. Fox reports that
"Margaret Fell went to the King,[4] and told him what sad work
there was in the City and nation, and shewed him we were an
innocent, peaceable people, and that we must keep our meetings
as heretofore, whatever we suffered, but that it concerned him to
see that peace was kept."[5]

The public statement, on the part of those who rejected all
oaths, was essentially a declaration of loyalty to the regime and the
assertion of completely peaceable intentions, so far as the Quaker
community was concerned. Fox says that copies of the declaration
were sent to the King and Council. They were also sold in the
streets and at the Exchange.

That Quakers needed to do something drastic in order to make
their position clear is obvious to us when we read their sometimes
violent language. Because they did not hesitate to use military
metaphors, speaking often of the "Lamb's War," they were

[4] Later, in the *Journal*, Fox says "Margaret Fell went often to the King."
[5] *Journal*, 1660.

naturally under suspicion. Fox found it necessary to say that "our weapons are spiritual and not carnal."[6] The now-famous Quaker Declaration against plots and fightings was written by Fox and Richard Hubberthorne and presented to the King on January 21, while the memories of the Fifth Monarchy uprising were still sharp.

The Declaration is a long one and has often been reprinted, particularly in the official Quaker books of discipline. The heart of the statement, intended to allay any remaining fears of an armed Quaker uprising, is the following sentence:

All bloody principles and practices as we to our own particular do utterly deny, with all outward wars and strife and fightings with outward weapons for any end or under any pretense whatsoever; and this is our testimony to the whole world.

What started as a solution of a particular practical problem became, in the process, the statement of a principle of far-reaching effect. The important document was reissued, with the approval of the Morning Meeting, in 1684, along with the assertion that Friends as a body could not wage war with outward weapons. This has been restated, many times, by Quakers in many different parts of the world and by all branches of the Religious Society of Friends.

In the succeeding years the Quaker attitude toward war has been, in one way, well understood and, in another, poorly understood. Naturally, outsiders have looked upon the rejection of war as something which involves the fixed character of a creed, but this is a mistaken judgment. Actually the fact that Quakers have no fixed creed is a very important feature of the Movement and has applied to pacifism more vividly than to almost anything else. In some instances, during three hundred years, Quakers have been disowned for joining armed forces, just as they have been disowned, in the same period, for marrying non-Quakers. Such practices are completely rejected by the vast majority of Quakers

[6] See Braithwaite, *The Beginnings of Quakerism*, p. 462.

today, because Quakers are as much opposed to moral dogma as they are to war. During World War II, partly because of the special character of the Nazi terror, the majority of Quakers who were subject to the draft entered the armed forces, many of them doing so after an agonizing period of decision and with the conviction that they were following the leading of the Living Christ. Others, sometimes from the same families, became conscientious objectors, after similar agonizing periods of decision. Today, Quakers follow both sets of young men with equal affection and respect, because Quakers are devoted to freedom as well as to peace and nearly all realize that the road to peace is far from simple.

In several of the wars which have occurred during the last two centuries the decision of idealistic Christians has been a very difficult one, because, in the Revolution, in the Civil War, and in the two World Wars the conflict has seemed to be between devotion to peace and the devotion to freedom. This is what Abraham Lincoln understood so well and what he expressed, in imperishable form, in his correspondence with the widow of Joseph John Gurney. At the time of the American Revolution a number who felt led to join the Revolutionary Army formed their own Society and were called Free Quakers. The meetinghouse they erected is being kept as a permanent monument in the open mall north of Independence Hall in Philadelphia.

Quakers have differed markedly, through the years, from the others known sometimes as Peace Churches, i.e., Amish, Mennonites, etc., in that Quakers have been, on the whole, far more involved in the events of the world than have these others. Such involvement has made the decision more difficult, because the more involved one is, the more complex the issues are seen to be. Though a minority of Quakers now identify pacifism and Basic Christianity it would be grossly inaccurate to attribute such a simple view to most contemporary Quakers.

On the whole, in spite of the refusal of Fox to accept a

commission in Cromwell's army, and in spite of the published statement of January, 1661, pacifism, as we understand it, did not play as large a part in the life and thought of early Quakers as it has in the thought of some subsequent generations. It is a little surprising to the beginner, for example, to realize that, in his famous *Apology*, Barclay actually assigns more space to the Quaker opposition to oaths, than he assigns to the Quaker opposition to war. William Penn is very brief in his references to what we might call pacifism, in his *Rise and Progress of the People Called Quakers*. He says Quakers have been known for "not fighting, but suffering." He connects the rejection of fighting with the rejection of oaths, saying, "Thus, as truth-speaking succeeded swearing, so faith and patience succeeded fighting, in the doctrine and practice of this people."[7]

In no known instance did the earliest exponents of the Quaker faith deal with a question such as that which arose, before the start of World War II, in the persecution of the Jews and the existence of concentration camps involving torture. The issue was uniformly stated in terms of what the individual should do when he becomes the personal object of attack or aggression, rather than in terms of what the Christian's duty may be when the victim is a third party. It is obvious that the moral situation is widely different in the two situations. The really difficult question before Quakers through the generations has not been, primarily, what a person ought to do if someone smites him on the cheek, but rather what he ought to do if someone is held in bondage who might be released or whose life might be saved, through the action of the person who is not personally threatened, but who knows that he is his brother's keeper. It is unfortunate that the Quakers of the earlier period of tremendous spiritual and moral vigor did not address themselves to this question, but the truth is that, for the most part, they did not.

The closest which early Quakers came to facing an issue like

[7] P. 26.

that just mentioned was in reference to the question whether
Quakers should oppose the very existence of a national army. This
question was, apparently, not faced by George Fox nor was it a
question which his mind was capable of facing. His own decision
was essentially simple, and was really for him alone. He felt led not
to fight with physical weapons, and, for him, that was the end
of the matter. But it could not be the end of the matter for
Barclay, Penington, and Penn, the three outstanding public
thinkers of seventeenth-century Quakerism. These men were far
closer to government than Fox ever was, Penn sometimes being at
Whitehall every day. In Penn's closeness to the King he was
naturally thrown with army officers, many of whom he was bound
to admire. The experience of such a man was so broad that he
could not possibly, with any sincerity, claim that all who were in the
army were thereby failing to be followers of Christ.

If the problem of the Quaker pacifist regarding the injured third
party, for whom he cannot honorably renounce all responsibility, is
a difficult one, the problem of the relationship to his own fellow
countrymen or even brothers, who are members of the armed
forces, is an equally difficult one. Starting, as he is tempted to do,
with the proposition, "All true Christians reject military service,"
he is bound, if he is intellectually consistent, to accept also the
contrapositive, "No one in the armed forces is a true Christian."
Almost anyone can see, at once, that such a position is intolerably
self-righteous. It makes a judgment that is really monstrous in its
harshness and one which is not consistent with the other evidence
available. Certainly it cannot be made consistent with the spirit of
Christ who gave his greatest reported approbation to a military
man, the centurion whose aide was ill (Matt. 8:5–13, Luke
7:2–10). When forced to look directly at the proposition mentioned above, especially in the light of its immediate logical
inferences, almost any contemporary Quaker will reject it. He will
be quick to say that, even though he may feel led to reject military
service himself, he is conscious of the existence of many soldiers, of

the eminence of George Washington or of lesser eminence, who are far better Christians than himself.

Both Barclay and Penn faced this question directly in their published writings. Barclay was such a good logician that he sensed at once the immediate inferences of a propostion and saw that what he, as a Quaker, said, might seem to be harshly derogatory to others who took a different position. He was too kind and also too wise to engage in wholesale condemnation of others. Accordingly, he held, on the one hand, that, while the ultimate Christian ideal is that of absolute nonresistance, so far as an attack on oneself is concerned, the actual situation which faces any government is a highly complex one. Most of the inhabitants of any state are by no means ready for a program of nonresistance which would, indeed, be meaningless to them. We must, then, as realists, recognize the state they are in. The best decision, in practice, is not the abstract best, but is always *the best under the circumstances.* "And, therefore, while they are in that condition," wrote Barclay in a memorable sentence, "we shall not say, that war, undertaken upon a just occasion, is altogether unlawful to them." If this sentence, and the reasoning which leads up to it in the total philosophy of Barclay, had been better understood, much of the criticism leveled at Quakers in various generations could have been avoided.

Isaac Penington, the leading mystic of early Quakers and the clearest reporter of firsthand religious experience, possessed the kind of intellectual sophistication to make him troubled by the same problem which troubled Barclay. Penington arrived at the same solution of the problem which Barclay reached, but with an important difference in that he was more explicit and more detailed. After holding that the ultimate Christian ideal is one in which each man, as he is touched by the Spirit of Christ, turns the other cheek when smitten, Penington went on to face the obvious fact that there are great numbers, in a modern nation, who are not ready for this, and, indeed, have not even heard of it. What, then, are they to do? Penington's statement, in which he makes a delicate distinction, is one which requires close attention if it is to be understood. He sees a time when an entire nation will depend on God's preservation and nothing else, though this is by no means a present possibility. His dream is of a time when "the gospel will teach a nation (if they hearken to it) as well as a particular person, to trust the Lord and to wait on him for preservation." But it is in regard to the present existential situation that Penington makes his clear statement.

I speak not this against any magistrate's or people's defending themselves against foreign invasions, or making use of the sword to suppress the violent and evil doers within their borders (for this the present estate of things may and doth require, and a great blessing will attend the sword where it is borne uprightly to that end, and its use will be honourable; and while there is need of a sword, the Lord will not suffer that government, or those governors, to want fitting instruments under them for the managing thereof, to wait on him in his fear to have the edge of it rightly directed); but yet there is a better state which the Lord hath already brought some into, and which nations are to expect to travel towards.

Penington seems to have wrestled with the problem more thoroughly than has any other Quaker who has lived and written. It is important to know that Professor Reinhold Niebuhr, whose vigorous attack on most forms of pacifism has been extremely effective, particularly in Protestant theological seminaries, has nothing but admiration for the kind of pacifism which the words of Isaac Penington express. Niebuhr, having been a pacifist, in his young manhood, later became a powerful critic of pacifism, especially of the kind which seemed to deny the rightness of the existence of any military power. Such pacifism seemed to him to be intellectually muddled because it did not make a distinction between what may be required of a special religious society within a state and what is morally required of a nation which is certainly "in the mixture." Since, in the ten years before the beginning of World War II, Reinhold Niebuhr was rapidly becoming the leading theological thinker of America, his criticism was one which all avowed pacifists, of whatever variety, were forced to take seriously.[8] Niebuhr's really damaging conclusion was that "most modern forms of Christian pacifism are heretical."[9]

In the influential seminaries, such as Union in New York, and Yale, the effect of Niebuhr's analysis was instantaneous. Accordingly, by the time America entered the war, in 1941, the number of Christian leaders who called themselves pacifists was sharply reduced, and the number has never again been as large as it was in the third decade of the twentieth century.[10]

A striking symptom of change in the intellectual climate, so far as peace is concerned, was that of the establishment of a new journal of Christian opinion, *Christianity and Crisis*, in 1941. Among the founders were men deeply committed to peace and also deeply committed to freedom and justice. These men, when they saw the clouds gathering, believed that peace bought at the price of totalitarian domination, which seemed so close to reality, in the Battle of Britain, was not a Christian ideal. Representative of those men was John Bennett, now President of Union Theological Seminary, whose devotion to the production of peace has been constant and whose connection with Quakers, particularly in early days, has been close. Among these men the kind of pacifism expressed by Isaac Penington has been almost universally admired.

On the whole, the criticism which Quakers have had to endure has been wholesome. A Quaker is a better Christian if he is forced to examine his premises. The result is that, though we have some strong Quaker pacifism today, very little of it is of the dogmatic variety. Not many today would say, "Jesus would be a pacifist if He were alive today, so I, as His follower, must be." This is seldom

[8] I heard him, in March, 1929, at Philadelphia Yearly Meeting of Friends, as he was beginning his attack. He soon put this into a book.

[9] *Christianity and Power Politics* (New York: Charles Scribner's Sons, 1940), p. 6.

[10] Another voice which made Quakers look humbly and critically at their position was that of William Temple, Archbishop of Canterbury. This deeply Christian man supported the war as the lesser of possible evils and suggested that a sincere pacifist should indicate his willingness to contract out of the advantages as well as out of the obligations of citizenship.

heard today because we clearly do not know what position Jesus would take in our complex modern world. We do not know whether Bonhoeffer, in his decision to try to kill Hitler, and thus avoid bloodshed and suffering on the part of millions, was following Christ or not. All that we know is that he *thought* he was.

Though a small minority of contemporary Quakers claim that they favor, for their own nation, unilateral disarmament *now*, they are by no means representative. Actually, most Quakers, including those who register in the draft as conscientious objectors and perform what is called "alternative" service, will say, if pressed, that they would not eliminate the armed forces of their nation, *at this moment*, even if they could. This is not because of any lack of devotion to peace. Indeed they can see, without much difficulty, that the immediate total elimination of our armed forces would, in all probability, *create* war, the very thing which they are seeking to avoid. It is obvious, for example, that the existence of the United States Fleet, in the Taiwan Straits, *prevents* an invasion of either the Communists or the Nationalists. It would be an extremely confused lover of peace who wished for the elimination of this means of prevention of something that would involve untold murder and violence.

Inasmuch as the classic Quaker position regarding the armed forces is based on what is really a sophisticated analysis of the human situation, there are always some who misunderstand it or who make criticisms on superficial grounds. Supposing that they are applying the principle of consistency, they say that a Quaker who adopts the position of a conscientious objector *ought* to denounce the very existence of the army or the navy. To the young man, who refuses to don the uniform, they say, "You ought, in consistency, to condemn all who do don the uniform. Don't you accept a single standard? How could one position be right for you and the opposite position be right for your brother?"

Because the above criticism is often heard and perhaps has even occurred to the mind of the friendly reader, it requires careful and sustained attention. We have made a big start on a reasonable answer when we realize that moral duty is never abstract. What we ought to do is inevitably concrete and really means what we ought to do in particular situations, each situation requiring analysis. One of the most helpful of all philosophical approaches to such questions was that provided by Professor F. H. Bradley, of Oxford University, in an essay which has already become a modern classic, "My Station and its Duties."[11] No man, argues Bradley, can know what he ought to do until he first knows who he is and what his peculiar situation entails. In many predicaments the duty of the bachelor is not identical with that of the married man.

To the Christian there is one and only one absolute, the kind of love in which we truly care for individuals. This, of course, includes caring for the victim of the aggressor as for the aggressor. Our responsibility is to the murderer and also to those whom he is about to murder. Though love provides the major premise of our Christian syllogism, it never provides the minor premise. The minor premise is arrived at only by reason and common sense and experience. Love may certainly mean different things in different situations. That is why no man can rightly dogmatize, or universalize his own judgment, on moral issues. There is, in every situation, a real right, but people who live in the finite predicament can never know, absolutely, what that real right is. All that we can do is to *try*, and to be tender in our judgment of others whose decisions are not identical with our own.

The most active intellectual frontier in Quaker thought today is in the area of the witness for peace. This is because a number of the best minds are keenly aware of the fact that peace is a subject so complex that it is one on which it is wrong to be doctrinaire. Some in the recent past have been doctrinaire, with a fundamentalist cast of mind about what they call the peace position of Friends, as though this were a fixed and well-known entity. But to make any secondary position a fixed one is to confuse the true

[11] *Ethical Studies: Selected Essays* (New York: Liberal Arts Press, 1951).

picture. There is only one fixed point in the spiritual firmament, so far as a Christian is concerned. The wisest words of our generation on this topic are those of Professor Herbert Butterfield when he ended a great book by saying, "Hold to Christ and for the rest be totally uncommitted."[12]

If this philosophy is truly understood and accepted, we are ready to see the wisdom of Penington's position. The truth is complex! It is right, at this juncture of history and in the light of the plural society which our government represents, that armed forces should exist. This is right because any conceivable alternative would be worse in terms of human consequences and suffering, which are the only terms on which it is reasonable to argue. The person who says of an action, "It is right, even though it will harm the human race," is simply confused and in any case he is not a follower of Christ, whose concern was for the little ones. If Herbert Hoover, the only Quaker to become President of the United States, had, upon the assumption of the highest office, immediately disbanded all of the armed forces, he would not have been a compassionate man and he would not even have been a good Quaker.

There is more fresh thinking on the subject of Quaker pacifism today than there has been for many decades. The result is a truly agonizing reappraisal, such as that of Gerald Bailey who has often represented the Friends World Committee for Consultation at the United Nations. Gerald Bailey's most careful thought, reflecting the missile crisis in Cuba, is seen in his Lilly Lectures, *The Politics of Peace.*

In similar vein, E. B. Castle has written a searching chapter called "Christ and Caesar." In asking contemporary Quakers to be intellectually honest, in the light of political complexities, he writes:

But too few Friends have honestly admitted that there is a gap between their long term policy of non-violence and the exigencies of

[12] *Christianity and History* (New York: Charles Scribner's Sons, 1950), p. 146.

modern civil and international affairs. To admit this would clear the air and provide Friends with a more realistic view of what their function in peace-making ought to be. No interpretation of Christianity permits Christians to remain snug in any ivory tower.

The major contribution of a writer like Castle is the recognition, similar to that of Penington long ago, that a dilemma exists. He writes:

The Quaker dilemma, as far as I can see, can be resolved in two ways. In the first place the Quaker witness against all war must be maintained, because it is founded on Christian truth and because this truth must be declared. The educative value of this persistent witness has been shown in its increasingly wide acceptance among members of other branches of the Christian Church. In all great causes there must be pioneers whose function it is to point the way. Otherwise the world remains forever in the realm of the second-best, governed by expedients that can never hold back the flood of evil. On the other hand it is of the utmost importance that Friends should recognize the nature of the responsibilities of men who hold positions Friends themselves would not feel free to occupy.[13]

Another contemporary English writer, Harold Loukes, shows how the moral question of involvement in war comes today in a new and particularly difficult form.

Would you be ready to fight in a United Nations force, dedicated to the maintaining of law when "glorious liberty" is impossible and inglorious anarchy imminent? This issue the Society of Friends has not yet faced; and it may well be that the next Friendly rumpus will be about a pamphlet "Towards a neo-Quaker view of war." In the meantime, most Quakers remain with a clear sense of individual vocation, but no general, applicable statement on the political realities of a world not yet in the "life and power" that takes away "the occasion of all wars."[14]

Perhaps the biggest step forward in the present Quaker rethinking about peace and war is the recognition that, with no inconsistency whatever, it is possible to honor the work of the conscien-

[13] *Approach to Quakerism* (London: Bannisdale Press, 1961), p. 158.
[14] *The Quaker Contribution*, p. 116.

tious participator and, at the same time, insist upon the vast importance of the witness provided by the conscientious objector. Indeed, even though the majority of young Quakers have, at least in the recent past, accepted the draft, there is no known body of Quakers which has not defended, with vigor, the position of the conscientious objector. All have recognized the important distinction between conscientious objection, on the one hand, and draft evasion, on the other. No thoughtful Quaker has ever defended the draft evader. Like Socrates in prison, as reported in the *Crito*, the Quaker has always recognized an enormous debt to the state and to its laws. It is recognition of such a debt that prohibits an honest man from running away. He may differ from his government, but he will differ openly and he will take the consequences, even if, as in the case of Socrates, these are imprisonment and death. The conscientious objector, when sincere, is not a coward, but often a superlatively brave man, for he is brave enough to face the inevitable unpopularity of his position.

The Quaker pacifist, even when he is humble enough not to claim that he presents a viable position for the state *now*, has the right to recognize that he, also, is a contributor. By his extreme position he is helping the state to avoid settling back into a mood in which war and the preparation for war are taken for granted. He is the gadfly of his civilization, somewhat as Socrates was the gadfly of the Athenian civilization. It is right that some, without being censorious of others, and being genuinely loving, should, in the course of their present lives, provide a modicum of the pattern "which nations are to expect and travel towards." The position of the conscientious objector is morally justified if he makes peace more likely, not today, but in the long run.

That there is a firm determination among Quakers to engage in new thinking on the problem of peace is increasingly evident. The general conviction is that the repetition of old formulas is not sufficient. One of those most active in this development is Dr. Errol T. Elliott, former editor of *The American Friend* and former chairman of the Friends World Committee. What Dr. Elliott and many other influential Friends are insisting is that the "Quaker Peace Testimony" must never be equated with either negativity or neutrality. When we realize, he says, how much of human welfare is at stake in the tragedy of war, both hot and cold, our responsibility is tremendous. This responsibility is to engage in imaginative acts of *peace-making* and never to be satisfied with a mere antiwar stand.

Quakers may not be able to "answer" complex human problems, but their entire heritage prepares them to "respond" to such problems. Examples of such response in Quaker history are already numerous, ranging from the establishment of work camps in areas of tension to the support of interracial housing projects and the schools for young diplomats. There are probably many new developments which Quakers should sponsor, but which are waiting for the emergence of a dedicated imagination. What is needed is not a static position, but new wine in new wineskins. The testimony which the time requires is a "Testimony of responsibility."

The Quaker dedication to peace, when rightly understood, is something which is cherished not for the sake of a doctrine and not even for the sake of Quakers. It is cherished for the sake of the *world*. The only purpose is to aid, as imaginatively and as bravely as possible, in taking away "the occasion of all wars."

11 / Quaker Writers

The chief glory of every people arises from its authors.
SAMUEL JOHNSON

Quakers are a highly articulate people. So great has been the addiction to the written word that there are several large libraries devoted exclusively to Quaker books.[1] Indeed, the total production is amazing in view of the relative smallness of the Quaker population either today or in former generations. That a people so famous for silence should have been so verbose is, to say the least, slightly paradoxical. There have even been voluminous writings on silence itself! Perhaps the book or the pamphlet has been an escape from silence. In any case, whatever the true explanation may be, the sheer volume of Quaker literature is impressive, and is an important means of understanding the Quaker way of life.

Quaker books, partly because they are so numerous, have exerted a strong influence, not only on Quaker readers, but on the mind of the general public. In this way Quakerism has escaped the fate of an unknown inarticulate sect, and has become a topic of conversation among general readers. An example of influence on letters is that provided by the autobiographical account of Robert Louis Stevenson, when he was lonely and ill in San Francisco, in December, 1879. In a secondhand bookstore, Stevenson found a copy of Penn's *Some Fruits of Solitude* which turned out to be exactly what he needed at the time. Of Penn's book of spiritual

---

[1] The chief Quaker libraries are four. They are the Friends Reference Library, Friends House, London, and the Quaker collections of Haverford College, Swarthmore College, and Earlham College. There are others which are smaller.

wisdom he wrote to Horatio F. Brown, to whom he gave the volume:

If ever in all my "human conduct" I have done a better thing to any fellow creature than handing on to you this sweet, dignified, and wholesome book, I know I shall hear of it on the last day. To write a book like this were impossible; at least one can hand it on, with a wrench, one to another. My wife cries out and my own heart misgives me, but still—here it is.

I hope, if you get thus far, you will know what an invaluable present I have made you. Even the copy was dear to me, printed in the colony that Penn established, and carried in my pocket all about the San Francisco streets, read in streetcars and ferryboats, when I was sick unto death, and found in all times and places a peaceful and sweet companion. But I hope, when you shall have reached this note, my gift will not have been in vain; for while, just now, we are so busy and intelligent, there is not the man living—no, nor recently dead—that could put, with so lovely a spirit, so much honest, kind wisdom into words.[2]

As might be supposed, the earliest Quaker books were, for the most part, sharply controversial and, consequently, of little permanent value. They dealt with issues and personalities in which we have little or no interest and many of them are far from admirable. The earliest Quaker writers were extravagant in their claims and attacked their intellectual enemies with unsparing aggressiveness. An outstanding early title is that of the book which George Fox prepared in 1657 and published in 1659, *The Great Mistery of the Great Whore*. All of it now seems severely dated and merely disputatious, but it was important at the time as an indication of the way in which Quakers were attempting to meet every public criticism. The book to which Fox gave the curious and offensive title is fundamentally his answer to one hundred anti-Quaker publications. It is not a systematic statement of Quaker principles, but rather a series of rejoinders in which there is demonstrated a rude brilliance of debating style.

[2] *Some Fruits of Solitude* (Philadelphia: David McKay Company, 1900), pp. 5–7. The Stevenson letter is quoted in a valuable Introduction by Edmund Gosse.

If Fox had to be remembered for his crude controversial writings he would not be remembered at all. But he will be remembered, for generations, for something of a very different character, the story of his own life. In writing his *Journal* Fox, though he could not know it at the time, was originating a new subspecies of literature. By this we do not mean to say that Fox was the first man to write about himself, for in that he had many predecessors. We find evidences, for example, of what appears to be a travel diary imbedded in the Book of Acts, and all literate people know of Augustine's *Confessions*. But the former is certainly a mere fragment and the latter is, as it advances, more and more a theological treatise. What Fox did was to combine the travel diary with the detailed account of how God had reached him and used him. Before Fox, there were only approaches to this literary pattern; since Fox, the pattern has been faithfully followed in hundreds of instances. He set a new style of autobiographical devotional writing which has become the style, not merely for Quakers, but for many who are wholly outside the Religious Society of Friends. The famous *Journal of John Woolman* is an illustration of the adoption of the pattern within the Quaker fold, while the *Journal of John Wesley* is an illustration of its external adoption.

Much of the secret of the power of the literary form which, at least so far as the author was concerned, was original with Fox, lies in his clear purpose. He was writing a new unit in the *literature of witness*. His intention was not to tell an interesting story, to preach a sermon, or to glorify Fox, but rather to tell how the Lord had dealt with him. After all, this is the chief thing that any truly devout man has to say. The ultimate testimony is not argument or speculation or dialectic, but the simple record of what has occurred. The characteristic Quaker language is the language of empirical evidence which, though it may be criticized, cannot be transcended. The mood in which Fox and his many imitators wrote was that which has been given vivid modern expression by the contemporary French existentialist philosopher, Gabriel Marcel. "I am obliged," writes Marcel, "to bear witness because I hold, as it were, a particle of light, and to keep it to myself would be equivalent to extinguishing it."[3] This powerful motive is expressed in the opening words of the remarkable document which, in 1675, or possibly in 1674, Fox dictated to his stepson-in-law, Thomas Lower:

> That all men may know the dealings of the Lord with me, and the various exercises, trials, and troubles through which he led me, in order to prepare and fit me for the work unto which he had appointed me, and may thereby be drawn to admire and glorify His infinite wisdom and goodness. . . .

So influential was the example of Fox that great numbers of Quakers, particularly in the eighteenth century, wrote journals in the same style. This is the chief reason why the Quaker libraries are so large. Though some journals were never printed, a great many of them were, and were cherished by entire generations. Always these works have the same theme, the theme of experience. Thus the *Journal of the Life of Thomas Story* begins:

> The following work is intended to record the tender mercies and judgments of the Lord; to relate my own experience of his dealings with me through the course of my life; and to write a faithful journal of my travels and labours in the service of the gospel.

The beginning of the *Journal of Thomas Chalkley* is similar:

> Having great cause to acknowledge the regard and protection of divine Providence in the several stages of my life, i think it may be of service to others, to leave behind me the following account of my life and travels.

Because most influential Quakers, at least during the first two centuries, engaged in the traveling ministry, the characteristic spiritual autobiography records a prodigious amount of travel. It must be understood that the itinerant ministry was a necessity

[3] *The Philosophy of Existence* (London: Harvill Press, 1948), p. 67.

when there were no settled pastors, if the fires of the spirit were to be rekindled and fueled. It is by perusing the pages of the old journals that we understand how arduous the travel was until the advent of the railroad. Even after the invention of the railroad, Joseph John Gurney, in traveling from Harrisburg to Ohio, went by boat up the Susquehanna and Juniata Rivers and then crossed the main grade of the Allegheny Mountains, not far from Altoona, by a series of levels and inclines, the cars being drawn by horses on the level stretches, and up the steep inclines by ropes and pulleys, powered by stationary steam engines.[4]

Gurney's travel in 1837 was luxurious in comparison with that of Quaker preachers of earlier generations who often went where there were no roads at all. The usual travel, especially in the remote settlements, where religious visits were so needed and so appreciated, was by foot or, at best, on horseback. It is difficult for us to realize how long some of these journeys were. Thus, in the *Journal of Joshua Evans* we read, "On the 1st day of the 12th mo 1797, I returned to my own home; having been absent nearly fourteen months and travelled upwards of five thousand miles."[5] Evans, at the time of the completion of this arduous travel, was sixty-six years of age. Travel, early in the nineteenth century, was still very uncomfortable and consequently tiring, but the Quaker travelers seldom complained. In 1811, John Hunt wrote, "In this journey, I was from home two weeks, and was able to bear the ride over rough stony, mountainous roads, with my dear Companions, each of us upwards of seventy years of age."

As the old volumes reveal, one of the chief means of nurture in the eighteenth century was the practice of going to a community and visiting nearly every family, particularly those in the Quaker community. A good account of such a visit is provided in John Hunt's *Journal* for the year 1784.

[4] *A Journey in North America, Described in Familiar Letters to Amelia Opie* (Norwich, 1841), p. 18.
[5] Friends Miscellany, Vol. X, p. 197.

In the 8th month, I joined my friends Isaac Zane of Philadelphia, John Collins, Elizabeth Collins and Sarah Evans, in a visit to the families of our meeting at Moorestown. We visited about seventy-five families, and parted with feeling nearness and uniting regard; having been much united in close labour through this arduous visit. Although at times we had dipping stripping and baptizing seasons we were helped with a little of the *best* help in the needful time; insomuch that the careless and lukewarm were faithfully warned, and the honest-hearted encouraged and invited.[6]

The general reader, as he scans these old books, must determine, in advance, that he will not be thrown off by what seems to us to be stilted language, and some translation is needed, but, if these steps are taken, the rewards are great. We get the sense of magnificent self-giving on the part of men and women of modest endowments. We also get from reading the journals numerous facts which otherwise might not be known or verified. Several of these have to do with the violent struggle over slavery. For example, in Hunt's account of what occurred in 1798, we learn the sad fact that one hundred thirty-four Negroes, who had been set free by the Carolina Quakers, at great financial loss to themselves, were caught by slave traders and sold back into slavery. Most of these were in the Albermarle Sound area, in what are now Pasquotank and Perquimans Counties. The outrage of stealing and reselling former slaves hastened the migration to Indiana, several Quaker families taking their former slaves with them to insure their freedom in the new state where slavery was forever outlawed.[7]

In contrast to such a sad note, John Hunt sometimes gives us a light touch, especially in reference to Joshua Evans' beard. It must be remembered that most Quakers, like other men of the eighteenth century, shaved. Consequently, a Quaker with a beard was

[6] *Ibid.*, p. 237.
[7] This was true of John Smith, a pioneer settler of Richmond, Indiana, who emigrated from Elizabeth City, North Carolina, to help found a Quaker community in 1806.

looked upon as an oddity, perhaps as one who was trying to attract attention to himself. This is the point of the following *Journal* entry, dated 1786.

Met a committee appointed by our last select meeting held at Salem, on account of Joshua Evans' wearing his beard, and other singularities. The conference was long, but good order and good temper were maintained, tho very different sentiments prevailed. It was a good edifying season, and I believe the opportunity will be useful; though he was left with his beard on, much as we found him, none having the power, or a razor to cut it off.[8]

It is chiefly by means of the old journals that we learn of the development of Quaker ideas, such as one which is mentioned in the *Journal of John Churchman*, a Quaker of Northern Maryland, writing in 1740.

In this journey, travelling in Talbot County, an elderly man asked us if we saw some posts to which he pointed, and added, the first meeting George Fox had on this side of the Chesapeake bay, was held in a tobacco house there, which was then new, and those posts were part of it. John Browning rode to them, and sat on his horse very quiet; and returning to us again with more speed than he went, I asked him what he saw amongst those old posts; and he answered, "I would not have missed what I saw for five pounds, for I saw the root and ground of idolatry. Before I went, I thought perhaps I might have felt some secret virtue in the place where George Fox had stood and preached, whom I believe to have been a good man; but whilst I stood there, I was secretly informed, that if George was a good man, he was in heaven, and not there, and virtue is not to be communicated by dead things, whether posts, earth, or curious pictures, but by the power of God, who is the fountain of living virtue." A lesson, which if rightly learned, would wean from the worship of images and adoration of relicks.[9]

It is an easy step from the spiritual autobiography to the consciously devotional book, which is written deliberately to stir up the spiritual life of the reader. Though Penn's *No Cross No*

[8] *Ibid.*, p. 241.
[9] *Friends Library*, Vol. 6, p. 193.

Crown is hard to classify, it belongs more to the category of devotional literature than to any other. The same is true of Penn's *Some Fruits of Solitude* and its sequel, *More Fruits of Solitude*. This was not a new type of literature in the world, for the type is illustrated in *The Imitation of Christ* and so much more, but, with Penn, it was new for Quakers. Many of the best ideas of Penn have ceased to be the peculiar possession of the people called Quakers and now belong to literate men and women everywhere. Two of these are especially worthy of present attention. The first has almost become the golden text of the ecumenical movement.

The humble, meek, merciful, just, pious and devout souls are everywhere of one religion; and, when death has taken off the mask, they will know one another, though the divers liveries they wear here makes them strangers.[10]

The eloquence of William Penn was never greater than when he dealt with the reality of eternal life. Hence a famous passage from *More Fruits of Solitude.*

They that live beyond the world cannot be separated by it. Death cannot kill what never dies, nor can spirits ever be divided that love and live in the same Divine Principle, the root and record of their friendship. If absence be not death, neither is theirs: death is but crossing the world, as friends do the seas; they live in one another still. For they must needs be present that love and live in that which is omnipresent. In this Divine Glass they see face to face; and their converse is free as well as pure.
This is the comfort of friends, that though they may be said to die, yet their friendship and society are in the best sense ever present, because immortal.

One of the ways in which the present literary output of Quakers has more similarity to that of the seventeenth century than to that of the long intervening period is in the strong emphasis upon devotional writing, especially that aimed more at the general thoughtful reader than at the conscious Quaker member. Apart

[10] There are many editions of *Fruits of Solitude*. The best is that edited by Edmund Gosse in 1900. See pp. 99, 100.

from the work of John Woolman it is hard to point to any first-class devotional writing in the quietest period. Whatever spiritual vitality found expression at this time by means of the written word, normally took the form of the journal. Now, however, for the greater part of a century, Quakers have produced devotional writing of high quality and wide acceptance, so far as the reading public is concerned.

There are many reasons for this new burst of devotional writing, but one of the most important among them is the renewed emphasis upon the authority of religious experience. If any one man is more responsible than others for the new life in Quakerism in the twentieth century it is John Wilhelm Rowntree, a member of the famous chocolate-producing family of York, England, who died in the United States in 1905. Now the body of his friend, Rufus M. Jones, lies next to his in the Quaker burial ground at Haverford, Pennsylvania. Rowntree was convinced that the basic Quaker message of the Inward Light, interpreted as the Living Christ, was vital and relevant to the lives of modern men. "There is room yet," he wrote, "for the teaching of the Inward Light, for the witness of a Living God, for a reinterpretation of the Christ in lives that shall convict the careless, language that shall convince the doubting."[11]

Rowntree was aware of the difficulties of a mere doctrine of the Inward Light, separated from the incarnation. It could, he thought, become so general and vague that it would lose its essential strength. But emphasis on the availability of the Living Christ was a different matter and herein lay Rowntree's power in devotional writing.

The difficulties of the doctrine of Inward Guidance are, as James Nayler's experience reminds us, serious and practical. I would suggest that the solution lies in a deeper interpretation of the person and message of Jesus Christ. Apart from the thought of God as we see Him set forth in Jesus, and the common consciousness of truth as revealed in lofty souls who have been touched by His spiritual fire, it is not

[11] *Essays and Addresses*, 1905, p. 75.

evident how the faults of individual interpretation are to be corrected.
. . . [But] with Jesus as the Gospel, witnessed in the conscience of a
civilization infected by His Spirit, I see the balance-wheel to the
doctrine of the Inward Light.[12]

The crucial date for the vision of a new vitality among Quakers,
especially in Britain, was November, 1895. John Wilhelm Rowntree, then only twenty-seven years of age, like Barclay when the
Apology first appeared, moved a Conference at Manchester with a
truly stirring appeal. At the end of his memorable address, the
young man uttered a prayer which is today the best loved of all
Quaker prayers and one which is appreciated by many as a part of
the classic devotional literature of the world.

Then, O Christ, convince us by Thy Spirit, thrill us with Thy
Divine passion, drown our selfishness in Thy invading love, lay on us
the burden of all the world's suffering, drive us forth with the apostolic
fervour of the early Church! So only can our message be delivered:—
"Speak to the Children of Israel that they go forward."[13]

The same devotional mood was central in the life of Rowntree's
friend, William Charles Braithwaite, whose volumes of history
include devotional passages. In one of these, Braithwaite wrote of
the reality of direct religious experience, as he had known it,
mentioning the sense of Presence in scenes of natural beauty. "We
dwell again, very near to God," he wrote, "on some wide-viewed
hill, the clamour of the world hushed, the peace of the blue sky
around us and the grateful green of dewy mountain lawns." But all
this, he reported, was inadequate without something still more
firm. "The experience, however, is precarious and fugitive," he
continued, "until we come into some sense of vital union with
Christ. With us the aim and the achievement lie woefully apart;
with Him they come together naturally, inevitably."[14]

John Wilhelm Rowntree and William Charles Braithwaite were

[12] *Ibid.*, pp. 244, 245.
[13] *Proceedings of Manchester Conference*, p. 83.
[14] *The Second Period of Quakerism*, pp. 307, 398.

closely associated with Professor Rufus M. Jones, of Haverford College, with whom they planned the series of Quaker histories now known as the Rowntree Series. Rufus Jones became the most prolific of Quaker writers, completing fifty-six books and working right up to the day of his death in 1948. The best known and probably the most enduring of these books are devotional in nature and all deal, in one way or another, with the reality of direct religious experience. *Pathways to the Reality of God* is a characteristic title. Rufus Jones produced something of a cross between the ancient Quaker journal and the modern devotional essay in a series of books about his own life. These are *A Boy's Religion from Memory, Finding the Trail of Life,* and *The Trail in the Middle Years.*

In something of the spirit of the early Quaker journal writers, Rufus Jones recounted his own experience of how God had touched his own life. For example, he tells how, on a voyage to England in 1903, his only child, a boy of eleven named Lowell, died in America.

The night before landing in Liverpool I awoke in my berth with a strange sense of trouble and sadness. As I lay wondering what it meant, I felt myself invaded by a Presence and held by Everlasting Arms. It was the most extraordinary experience I had ever had. But I had no intimation that anything was happening to Lowell. When we landed in Liverpool a cable informed me that he was desperately ill, and a second cable, in answer to one from me, brought the dreadful news that he was gone.[15]

As long as Rufus Jones lived, the portrait of this boy hung over the fireplace mantel in his study at Haverford.

Much influenced by William James and impressed with the great impact made by James's Gifford Lectures, *The Varieties of Religious Experience,* Rufus Jones determined to make his "life clue" the study of that firsthand experience to which so many had testified. Nowhere did he find better evidence than in the life of

[15] *The Luminous Trail* (New York: The Macmillan Company, 1947), p. 163.

his friend and associate, John Wilhelm Rowntree. Soon after Rowntree's untimely death in 1905, Professor Jones told of the young man's transforming experience of the love of God, as he faced calamity.

Just as he was entering young manhood and was beginning to feel the dawning sense of a great mission before him, he discovered that he was slowly losing his sight. He was told that before middle life he would become totally blind. Dazed and overwhelmed, he staggered from the doctor's office to the street and stood there in silence. Suddenly he felt the love of God wrap him about as though a visible presence enfolded him, and a joy filled him, such as he had never known before. From that time . . . he was a gloriously joyous and happy man.[16]

The first Quaker of the past century to attempt to write devotional literature for the general reader was a gifted woman of Philadelphia, Hannah Whitall Smith. She broke out of the narrow Quaker mold, somewhat after the manner of Joseph John Gurney, and preached acceptably on both sides of the Atlantic. Though she was a leader in the causes of temperance and woman suffrage, she is remembered chiefly for her genius as a spiritual guide. Affected by the holiness movement, she appealed for the expectation of perfection in something of the manner of George Fox. Her book *The Christian's Secret of a Happy Life* not only had a phenomenal sale as soon as it was first printed in 1870, but has continued as a favorite of thousands of readers to this day. Fully two million copies have been sold. In short, Mrs. Smith's is one of the most successful devotional books of all time.

The response to Mrs. Smith's writing seems a bit surprising when we realize that she said nothing that was profound and nothing that was really new. She simply conveyed her absolute trust in the Living Christ, which was the great thing that her Quaker nurture had given her. We understand the heart of her

[16] This appeared originally in *The American Friend*, March 16, 1905. It was reprinted in John Wilhelm Rowntree, *Essays and Addresses*, 1905, p. 434.

message when she asks us to say with her the following commitment:

Lord Jesus, I believe that thou art able and willing to deliver me from all the care and unrest and bondage of my Christian life. I believe thou didst die to set me free, not only in the future, but now and here. I believe thou art stronger than sin, and that thou canst keep me, in my extreme of weakness, from following into its snares or yielding obedience to its commands. And, Lord, I am going to trust thee to keep me. I have tried keeping myself and have failed, and failed most grievously. I am absolutely helpless. So now I will trust thee. I give myself to thee. I keep back no reserves. Body, soul, and spirit, I present myself to thee as a piece of clay, to be fashioned into anything thy love and thy wisdom shall choose. And now I *am* thine . . . I trust thee utterly, and I trust thee *now*.[17]

The "secret" which Hannah Whitall Smith disclosed was the simple one of absolute trust. Of such trust, she advised her many readers to make it "a daily, definite act of your will, and many times a day recur to it, as being your continual attitude before the Lord. Confess it to yourself. Confess it to your God. Confess it to your friends." She urged readers to say over and over "Lord, I am thine; I do yield myself up entirely to thee, and I believe that thou dost take me. I leave myself with thee. Work in me all the good pleasure of thy will, and I will only lie still in thy hands and trust thee."[18]

There is a sense in which Hannah Whitall Smith was truly a Quaker, but part of her Quakerism was her willingness to rebel against the limitations of the Quakerism which she knew. Her brilliant son, the essayist, Logan Pearsall Smith, edited her letters under the appropriate title A *Religious Rebel*. She had many sorrows, especially in her own family. The best evidence of the unity of Mrs. Smith's life and message was the way in which she grew old gracefully. In 1903, at the age of seventy-one, she wrote,

17 *The Christian's Secret of a Happy Life* (Westwood, N. J.: Fleming H. Revell Company, 1952), p. 54.
18 *Ibid.*, p. 67.

"I am convinced it is a great art to know how to grow old gracefully, and I am determined to practice it. . . . I always thought I should love to grow old, and I find it is even more delightful than I thought."[19]

Thomas R. Kelly (1893–1941) must be acclaimed the outstanding Quaker devotional writer of the twentieth century. Growing up in Ohio and attending Wilmington College, he early decided to be a philosopher and came under the influence of Rufus Jones in his graduate study at Haverford. Most of his adult life was spent teaching philosophy at two Quaker colleges, Earlham and Haverford. After his death in 1941, his friends collected some of his devotional essays and addresses and published them, with an Introduction by Douglas Steere, as *A Testament of Devotion*. The book has become a modern classic, perhaps the only true devotional classic of this generation. The volume which Thomas Kelly never saw, and never expected to have published, has been reprinted more than twenty times and has all of the marks of permanence. The secret of this response is that Kelly had found life "glorious and new," and consequently his heart sang. He had learned that "God *can* be found." He tried, he said, to keep his "inner hilarity and exuberance" within bounds, lest, as was true of the men of Pentecost, he be suspected of being filled with new wine. Perhaps the deepest of all his spiritual insights was that concerning the reality of the "gathered meeting."

In the gathered meeting the sense is present that a new Life and Power has entered our midst. . . . We are in communication with one another because we are being communicated to, and through, by the Divine Presence. . . . for we have experienced a touch of that persuading Power that disquiets us until we find our home in Him. . . . When one rises to speak in such a meeting one has a sense of *being used*, of being played upon, of being spoken through. It is as amazing an experience as that of being *prayed through*, when we, the praying ones, are no longer the initiators of the supplication, but seem

[19] *A Religious Rebel, the Letters of H. W. Smith*, ed. Logan Pearsall Smith, 1949, p. 156.

to be transmitters, who second an impulse welling up from the depths of the soul.[20]

Of living Quakers, the leading devotional writer is Douglas V. Steere, now Emeritus Professor of Philosophy at Haverford College. Professor Steere has established a firm reputation as a scholarly interpreter of the devotional classics. Among his most important books are *On Beginning from Within, Prayer and Worship,* and *Doors into Life.* He has been especially effective in introducing to English-speaking people Søren Kierkegaard's *Purity of Heart is to Will One Thing* and in making better known the devotional contribution of the Roman Catholic layman, Baron Friedrich von Hügel.

Quakerism was marked, very early, by a strong determination to recount faithfully the history of the Movement. The monumental work of this character is chiefly that of William Charles Braithwaite, the Banbury banker, and Rufus M. Jones. After the death of John Wilhelm Rowntree these men set to work to produce the large volumes of the series now named for their friend and inspirer. Braithwaite brought out *The Beginnings of Quakerism* in 1912 and *The Second Period of Quakerism* in 1919. *The Quakers in the American Colonies,* the work of Rufus Jones, with the help of Isaac Sharpless and Amelia Gummere, was published in 1911. Rufus Jones brought out the two volumes of *The Later Periods of Quakerism* in 1921. All of these authors profited by using the material which Rowntree had collected, in the hope that he could write a history of the Society of Friends "which should adequately exhibit Quakerism as a great experiment in spiritual religion, and should be abreast of the requirements of modern research."[21]

This ambitious Rowntree Series of histories also includes two preparatory volumes by Rufus Jones, *Studies in Mystical Religion,* 1909, and *Spiritual Reformers in the 16th and 17th Centuries,*

[20] This paper was written for *The Friend,* while I was editor, in 1940. It is printed in Vol. 114 (1940–1941), pp. 201–5. The sense of excitement, when Thomas Kelly's essays began to come to the editorial desk, is still vivid.

[21] *The Beginnings of Quakerism,* 1st Ed., 1912, p. v.

1914. To keep the basic works in line with current historical research and thinking, *The Beginnings of Quakerism* and *The Second Period of Quakerism* have now appeared in revised editions, made possible by the meticulous and painstaking work of Henry J. Cadbury and published by the Cambridge University Press.

The first important Quaker history was written by a Dutchman, William Sewel, whose biography has been written by the late William I. Hull, of Swarthmore College, in *Willem Sewel of Amsterdam, 1653–1720: The First Quaker Historian of Quakerism* (1933). Charles Lamb, in a famous passage, directed many to Sewel's work:

> Reader, if you are not acquainted with it, I would recommend to you, above all church-narratives, to read Sewel's *History of the Quakers*. It is in folio, and is the abstract of the journals of Fox, and the primitive Friends. It is far more edifying and affecting than anything you will read of Wesley and his colleagues. Here is nothing to stagger you, nothing to make you mistrust, no suspicion of alloy, no drop or drug of the worldly or ambitious spirit.[22]

Quaker writers have long been intrigued with the possibility of a great Quaker novel, but the dream never materializes, though many try. For some reason, most Quaker fiction writers are women. Daisy Newman has, in *Diligence in Love*, recreated an appealing Rhode Island scene, and Elfrida Vipont, in *Blow the Man Down*, has provided a racy account of the life of an early Quaker, Thomas Lurting, but the Quaker novel on the grand scale remains to be written. On the other hand, collections of Quaker short stories are remarkably successful. One attractive set of stories is *Wedded in Prison*, by Maude Robinson. Much the greatest Quaker success in fiction is that of Jessamyn West in *The Friendly Persuasion*. This book presents stories of Quaker life in southern Indiana which have appealed to vast numbers, both through the printed book and also through the motion picture, the latter being generally considered one of the best in an entire generation.

[22] *Essays of Elia*, "A Quaker's Meeting."

Millions know a little about the people called Quakers, simply as a result of Gary Cooper's fine depiction of a sensitive Quaker father of the period of the American Civil War.

Jessamyn West's resounding literary success suggests that the Quaker story appears at its best in slight vignettes, like that concerning the organ being played in the attic while the leading Quakers are present on a ministerial visit. In short, there is something about Quakerism which lends itself remarkably well to humor. One current form of Quaker writing is that of the collection of humorous Quaker anecdotes. One of these, easily available at Friends Book Stores, is *Quaker Chuckles*, by Helen White Charles. The reader soon notes that the characteristic Quaker humor is never really damaging to the object of laughter. Indeed, the butt of the Quaker joke is usually the Quaker himself. One of the outstanding assets of Rufus Jones was his ability in the employment of humorous illustrations, of which his store seemed to be limitless.

Perhaps the most surprising fact about the multiplicity of Quaker writings is that no Quaker has composed any really great poetry. It may be that the moral conflicts of Quakers are not of sufficient intensity to produce novels on a level with those of Dostoevski, but the conditions of poetry might reasonably be expected to appear. After all, the lives of the primitive Friends were not wholly different from that of their magnificent contemporary, John Milton. Quakers, from the beginning, would seem to have in them what a Harvard scholar suggests is the very stuff of poetry, in their emphasis on what is "permanent and ordered rather than isolated and particular."[23]

The closest connection between Quakerism and great poetry is that provided by the career of Walt Whitman. Whitman was never a Quaker, but he grew up in that part of Long Island where Quaker influence was strong, and he was a lifelong admirer of

[23] Walter Jackson Bate, *Prefaces to Criticism* (Garden City, N.Y.: Doubleday Anchor Book, 1959), p. 5.

Elias Hicks. Whitman, as a boy of ten, heard Hicks in Brooklyn when the eloquent farmer-preacher was on his last tour in the ministry. The memory of the rude eloquence of Hicks never left him, and he showed his admiration by keeping a bust of Hicks in his home in Camden, New Jersey.

The Quaker influence in Whitman's poetry is seen not primarily in the fact that he used the plain Quaker language, as in the line

Of earth, rocks, Fifth-month flowers
experienced, stars, rain, snow, my image,

but in two much more important ways. First, there is the Quaker insistence on experience at firsthand.

You shall no longer take things at second or third hand, nor look through the eyes of the dead, nor feed on the spectres in books,
You shall not look through my eye either, nor take things from me.
You shall listen to all sides and filter them from yourself.[24]

The second Quaker influence observable in Whitman's poetry is seen in the way in which, without rhyme, it achieves a rhythm similar to that of the singsong preaching of the early nineteenth century, which he heard from the lips of Elias Hicks. It must be remembered that nearly all of the Quaker preaching of Whitman's day was delivered in what must be called a chant. Much of Whitman's poetry may be chanted in a similar fashion.

John Greenleaf Whittier (1807–1892) is often called the Quaker poet, but no critic today places him in the first rank. His "Snowbound" is pleasant, but it is severely local. Some of his poems have become hymns and are now used in many different denominations. There is a curious paradox in the fact that the hymns now sung, which bear Whittier's name, were not meant to be sung at all. Writing in 1852, he described his own scene of worship which included no music.

[24] Walt Whitman, *Leaves of Grass*, "Song of Myself," 2.

In calm and cool and silence once again
I find my old accustomed place among
My brethren, where, perchance, no human tongue
Shall utter words; where never hymn is sung,
Nor deep-toned organ blown, nor censer swung.

However pleased we may be, from time to time, with the Whittier hymns, like the one beginning

Dear Lord and Father of mankind,
Forgive our feverish ways,

we are finally forced to conclude that they are not equal, in poetic power, to those represented by Martin Luther's "A Mighty Fortress is our God," or Harry Emerson Fosdick's "God of Grace and God of Glory." Calmness is a virtue, but it is a minor virtue, and it was certainly not the outstanding virtue of early Quakers. If Whittier could have brought the passion of the antislavery crusade, which he felt deeply, into his religious poetry, greatness might have emerged. Only in this connection did he exhibit what William Hazlitt called "gusto." "Poetry," Hazlitt wrote, "is only the highest eloquence of passion, the most vivid form of expression that can be given to our conception of anything, whether pleasurable or painful, mean or dignified, delightful or distressing."[25]

Whittier knew what it was to be unpopular, and he was capable of the "eloquence of passion" when the sin of holding other men as merchandise was involved. Indeed, when he was an old man, he said to a fifteen-year-old boy, "My lad, if thou wouldst win success, join thyself to some unpopular but noble cause." How strange that his religious poetry never succeeded in reflecting this mood! Perhaps he did not understand fully that Christ came to bring, not peace but a sword. There will not be any really great Quaker poet until some writer learns how to depict a moral decision so as to provide a genuine *katharsis* for the reader. It is conceivable that this might be provided by a suitable response to the stirring times in which we now live.

[25] "On Poetry in General."

12 / The Life of Culture

> Joy is the strength of the people of God; it is their glory;
> it is their characteristic mark.
>
> RENDEL HARRIS

The widow of George Fox lived to be an old woman, and she was very wise. When she died, in 1702, she had been the leading feminine influence in the Quaker Movement for exactly fifty years. Though she never wavered after the day when she first heard George Fox at Ulverston, she kept a remarkable sense of balance and was wisely critical of some of the tendencies in the Movement to which she was devoted. She was especially troubled by the fact that Quakers, after the initial period of vitality, were becoming too deeply concerned with outward features such as the insistence that all should wear gray clothing of a special cut. The idea that every form of gay appearance should be avoided, which soon became a fixed and relentless rule, was already being expressed by those who were assuming positions of leadership. This seemed to the aged Margaret Fox to be something alien to the spirit of Christ who told His followers not to take thought about what to eat or drink or what they should put on, but, instead, to consider the lilies. Whatever else Christ meant about the lilies of the field, the old lady thought, it was at least clear that they were *bright*, rather than a dull gray. In sarcastic vein she said, "We must look to no colours, nor make anything that is changeable colours as the hills are, nor sell them, nor wear them: but we must be all in one dress and one colour." For this approach to the Christian life she had nothing but contempt, and in conclusion declared that "this a silly poor Gospel."

The terrible truth is that what Margaret Fox called "a silly poor gospel" prevailed. Some elements of greatness appeared in the succeeding period of rigid conformity, but they appeared in spite of the rigidity and the cultural poverty. That it is not necessary for a contemporary Quaker to defend this rigidity is shown by Harold Loukes, who is completely frank about the sectarian unloveliness. After describing the stereotype which began about the time of the death of the great leaders, Loukes writes, "It is an unexciting view of the Christian life, this: solid furniture, well-managed servants, a respectable bookshelf, a well-made will, and no gambling—it all seems a far cry from the tendering spirit and outgoing love that were the marks of the early Society."[1]

Though it seems very strange, the pithy judgment of Margaret Fox was not heeded. Indeed, her sane approach did not have full Quaker acceptance for two hundred years. The battle is over now, but it was a hard one while it was fought and it calls attention to aspects of Quakerism that, frankly speaking, are not admirable. The battle included the whole relationship between the Christian and the life of culture.

The paradox is that Quakers have excelled in some forms of culture while they have been almost totally ineffective in others. They have, for example, a very poor record in music and a very good record in natural science, though it is not wholly easy to understand why this should be the case. One might naturally suppose that the strong desire to sit under Christ as their Teacher would have led to music and dancing and colors as gay as those of the flowers, but that is not how Quakers moved. They tried to be faithful to what Christ was known to have said, but apparently they did not pay close attention to His words, "I am come that they might have life, and that they might have it more abundantly" (John 10:10). The very struggle for *survival*, under severe and long-continued persecution, seems to have been so great that it left little room for anything not deeply serious. Even the Quaker

[1] *The Quaker Contribution*, p. 65.

penchant for humor seems to have been, for the most part, a later development.

It is surprising that such a cultured Scottish gentleman as Robert Barclay lent his influence to the development of a pattern which was highly restrictive. In Proposition XV of the *Apology*, he dealt with the objection, already being voiced, that even the best people need relaxation in a variety of cultural pursuits. "But they object," he wrote, "that men's spirits could not subsist, if they were always intent upon serious and spiritual matters, and that therefore there is need of some divertisement to recreate the mind a little, whereby it being refreshed, is able with greater vigour to apply itself to these things." Barclay granted the validity of this remonstrance, but hastened to assert that a Christian must never engage in any species of recreation which causes him to "recede from the remembrance of God." Apparently he felt that music and dancing and artistic work in general would involve such forgetfulness. He went on to list the "innocent divertisements" that were allowable to a Christian, the list being mildly amusing to the modern reader. The relaxations he advocated were "for friends to visit one another; to hear or read history; to speak soberly of the present or past transactions; to follow after gardening; to use geometrical and mathematical experiments, and such other things of this nature."[2]

It is obvious that Barclay's position, even though it expresses a certain stern nobility, leads, if followed consistently, to the denial of most cultural expressions. A Quaker did not sing, owned no musical instrument, wore a plain collarless coat of a somber gray, gave up all bright colors, had no pictures in his house, and used what was called the plain language. By this it was meant that only the singular of the second personal pronoun was used in addressing an individual, that the days of the week and of the months of the year were referred to by numerals rather than by names such as Wednesday or January, which were derivations from what were

[2] *Apology* XV, ix.

called heathen divinities. Some, when they became interested in astronomy, even went so far as to refer to planets by number, rather than to use such blasphemous terms as Mars and Jupiter.

The plain, unadorned speech, which made either the production or appreciation of poetry difficult, had a deeper expression in the rejection of all exaggeration or the employment of any proposition beyond what was actually known to be the case. Thus a familiar story is that of a Quaker of the strictest type who, on riding past a farm, was addressed by a worldly companion who asked, "Do you see that flock of sheep that has just been sheared?" To this the careful Quaker replied, "I see sheep that have been sheared on this side."

The rejection of music was clearly a mistake because it involved a genuine impoverishment of the human spirit. There is something terrible about good people living as contemporaries of Mozart or Handel or Beethoven and never hearing one of the majestic musical productions of the minds of these truly great men. We understand the reason for the restriction, but we can only deplore the fact that the development proceeded as it did. Those who loved musical instruments were made to feel guilty, as is so well shown in the story of the secret organ in *The Friendly Persuasion*, and those who openly resisted the impoverishment were summarily expelled from the Quaker Community. The loss which came in this way is incalculable, but sad to contemplate.

Nowhere was the objection to cultural pursuits more rigid than in the frontier communities, to which Quakers flocked after the War of 1812. Many of the finest persons among the settlers wanted to be Quakers, but were either *expelled* or merely *repelled*, because they would not limit their speech to a stereotype, give up the music they loved, or say that they were sorry when they married outside the Quaker fold. To read the old minutes is a distressing experience. The reader soon concludes that the Quaker population might easily be ten times its present size, had not such restrictive practices been in vogue for generations. In no place were Quakers more strict in these matters than in the strong new Quaker community of Richmond, Indiana, as can be seen by reading the well-kept minutes of Whitewater Monthly Meeting. Though all music was denounced, "fiddling" was considered the worst, presumably because it was popularly associated with dancing and other gay enterprises. In the minutes of one monthly meeting, a complaint is made of one member "for buying, keeping and playing a fiddle," and, in a later month, we learn that the wicked man is disowned "for playing a fiddle for people to dance with."

That the exclusion of music from the life of Quakers for nearly two hundred years was a tragic mistake was clearly expressed by Rufus M. Jones, as he surveyed the history of these centuries.

The reasons which they gave for the exclusion are not convincing. It is true that music has a sensuous basis, but so, too, has almost everything else in a normal person's life. Senses and emotions are not to be despised. It is a fact, as was insisted, that music is often put to low uses, but so, too, is money often put to low uses, and many other things which the Quaker prized. It would have been more fitting to have discriminated between the high and low uses, and to have trained the character to balance and restraint.[3]

Today, of course, all this is changed. The majority of Quakers have musical instruments in their places of worship and nearly all have them in their homes. The Quaker schools and colleges train fine choirs and even sponsor operatic performances. But, even though this battle has been won and a movement in the direction of a fuller life has been encouraged, it is still the sad fact that there has never been a great musical composer among the People Called Quakers.

The change in regard to reading has also been a radical one. For several generations Quaker lives were sorely impoverished by the complete rejection of novels and romances. Even in the memory of living persons, the reading of Shakespeare's plays and love

[3] *The Later Periods of Quakerism*, p. 192.

poetry was forbidden in some Quaker schools. The greatest writer of the English language was left out of Quaker lives for what seemed to some a good reason, though it was, in fact, a very poor one. It is, of course, a fact that Shakespeare dealt with sinful human situations, but in complete consistency, the Quaker censors would have been forced to forbid the reading of many parts of the Holy Scriptures. Indeed, the Bible may be said to specialize in sin.

Cultural restrictions, such as those already mentioned, were bound, in time, to lead to a revolution, and so they did. If there had not been a revolution, Quakerism would have become nothing more than an ineffective sect in the modern world and would now be referred to, for the most part, as historically interesting, but contemporaneously irrelevant. The critical sign of a genuine change came in 1859, the same year in which Charles Darwin published the *Origin of the Species*. The outstanding Quaker event of this momentous year was the appearance of a prize essay by John Stephenson Rowntree, of York, called *Quakerism Past and Present; being an Inquiry in the Causes of its Decline in Great Britain and Ireland*.[4]

Rowntree was well equipped for his critical task and utterly frank in calling attention to weaknesses. He said that the peculiar form of Quaker worship had become, indeed, a "form," with the accent on silence pushed to an absurd extreme. He was bold enough to state that Quakers had suffered severely from the elimination of the fine arts and music and from their general rejection of the worldly culture about them. He saw that isolation from culture involves a static and therefore a decaying type of life. Worst of all, little things are emphasized, to the neglect of the really big ones.

[4] A prize of one hundred guineas, a large sum in the light of the relative lack of inflation at the time, was offered, by an anonymous donor, for the best essay on the subject of Quaker decline. The second prize, which was announced as fifty guineas, but later raised to one hundred because of the excellence of the work, was awarded Thomas Hancock, an Anglican clergyman whose essay, *The Peculiam*, is still worthy of attention because it is continuously relevant.

Only a year after the publication of J. S. Rowntree's crucial essay, a complementary development occurred in America, particularly in the Indiana Yearly Meeting of 1860. A number of young people, led by able men each of whom was about thirty years old at the time, staged a virtual revolt. They were permitted to hold an evening meeting for younger Friends, without the restraint of the sober elders. To the amazement of all, more than a thousand persons attended the meeting which continued past midnight. Because the old shackles seemed to be broken, large numbers spoke or prayed, many for the first time in their lives. These same young people could not long be held back from the use of music, even in gatherings for public worship. The occasion in 1860, concludes Rufus Jones, "marked the turning of the epoch."[5] Soon music was not only employed in practice, but actively defended in theory. The following question, once it was clearly asked, was not easy to answer. "Will a child [be led to] commit evil any more readily by improper music than by improper conversation, and would not the sensible plan be to endeavour to regulate both, not cut either entirely off?"[6]

For a variety of reasons the Quaker objection to art was not quite on a par with the rejection of music. One reason seems to be the fact that the painter normally works alone and may, therefore, not corrupt anyone else, whereas, the production of music is essentially public and communal. As we have already seen, that remarkable Quaker father, John Gurney, employed a competent artist to teach his children, nearly all of whom learned to paint with some degree of success. Over and over they painted their beloved home, Earlham Hall, which was clearly their favorite artistic subject. Some of Gurney's fellow Quakers doubted the wisdom of this worldliness, but he was never expelled from membership. Perhaps he would have been expelled, had he not been so rich.

[5] *The Later Periods of Quakerism*, Vol. II, p. 897.
[6] *American Friend* (old series), Vol. II, p. 130.

The most famous of Quaker painters have arisen on the American scene. Benjamin West (1738–1820) was born in Chester County, Pennsylvania, but spent much of his life in England. He became President of the Royal Academy and is buried, among other artists, in St. Paul's Cathedral. West was the artist who made the well-known painting of "Penn's Treaty with the Indians." This has appeared in many media, including China plates, and was an obvious exception to the general rule against pictures on the walls of Quaker homes.[7]

One of the most surprising features of Quaker culture has been the extraordinary growth in the reputation of Edward Hicks. Hicks was an unusually successful producer in the primitive style similar to that so much admired in our generation in the canvases of Grandma Moses. Hicks came from the delightfully simple rural atmosphere of Bucks County, Pennsylvania, where he was entirely self-taught and consequently uncorrupted. The rediscovery of the genius of Hicks has amounted to something of a fad in our day. The best collection of his works hangs in the permanent exhibit of primitives, called the Abby Aldrich Rockefeller Collection, at Williamsburg, Virginia.

Edward Hicks had two main themes which he was able to weave into nearly everything which he painted. One of these was the Delaware Water Gap, for which Hicks had an extraordinary affection, and which turned up in wholly inappropriate connections. The other theme was that of the Peaceable Kingdom. The painting of mild-looking wild and domestic animals, with a child supposedly leading them, was of course reminiscent of the prophetic passage (Isa. 11:6–9) and represented Hicks's rather simple-minded vision of ultimate peace. The versions of this scene which the gifted rural Quaker painted are numerous indeed and each version has a curious appeal to sophisticated men and women of

[7] Clarkson, in his *Portraiture of Quakerism* (Vol. I, pp. 292–94), says of English Quakers, at the beginning of the nineteenth century, that three pictures were tolerated. These were "Penn's Treaty with the Indians," the interior of a slave ship, and a plan of Ackworth School.

the twentieth century. Hicks's paintings are now generally regarded as the best of their kind. With all the cultural mistakes that the Quakers of his age were making, a certain cultural excellence was possible, and the peculiar excellence of Edward Hicks is unthinkable apart from the simple Quaker setting out of which it arose.

The paradox of Quaker culture is nowhere more sharp than in connection with architecture. George Fox must have looked many times at the magnificent medieval cathedrals of his country. How could he pass through York or Lincoln without seeing them? It was part of the limitation of his vision that he apparently had no appreciation at all of these glorious creations of the human spirit. He was content to call them steeple-houses, and probably did not even notice the carvings done so lovingly by anonymous workmen or the glorious colors of the famous windows. We know, at least, that he was near the three-spired cathedral of Lichfield. The visit to Lichfield is told in a well-known entry in the *Journal*, which has received careful comment from many writers, including William James.

Thus being set at liberty again, I went on, as before, in the work of the Lord; and as I was walking in a close with several Friends, I lifted up my head and espied three steeple-house spires, and they struck at my life. I asked them what place that was, and they said, Lichfield. Immediately the way of the Lord came to me that thither I must go.[8]

Then occurred one of the most embarrassing and mystifying scenes of the life of Fox. He felt led to take off his shoes and walk barefooted, though it was winter, through the streets, where he felt commanded to cry, "Woe to the bloody city of Lichfield." Later, Fox interpreted his action as referring to the bloodshed in the city during the Civil War when the cathedral was held at one time by the forces of the king and at another by the forces of the Parliament. Whatever the explanation, it is important, for our

[8] *Journal,* 1651.

present purposes, to note that the beauty of the building meant nothing to an otherwise great and sensitive man.

When meetinghouses were built by Quakers, they were plain unadorned structures, but it is part of the paradox that they were often designed with remarkable aesthetic taste. Today we see the ancient meetinghouses, like the stone building at London Grove, Pennsylvania, as beautiful structures. The beauty arises not from any decoration at all, but from the fine proportions and the evident honesty of the building. The result has some similarity to that achieved in the paintings which we term primitives.

However fine some of the Quaker architecture is, it is easy to admit now that the failure to see the glory of other and grander styles was a serious failure. There is no reason, whatever, for a Quaker to lack appreciation of a magnificent building or to fail to encourage architectural styles different from his own. The styles may be equally good, though radically different. The contemporary English Quaker, E. B. Castle, has spoken for many when he says that, looking at the medieval cathedrals, he always has a slightly guilty feeling. What he means is that he cannot really wish that the austere aesthetic position of Fox had come earlier and had become dominant, because, in that case, some examples of rare beauty would never have come into the world. We can now say this openly and with no sense of guilt or fear of inconsistency. Quakerism, however creative it is in some ways, is not creative in all ways. To know this is good for Quaker humility.

It is something of a surprise to discover that there have been a few, in the Quaker heritage, who have been brilliant students of architecture, including that of the Middle Ages. The outstanding example is that of Thomas Rickman (1776–1841), who wrote perceptively on architectural styles and who played a major part in the Gothic revival of the nineteenth century. Though not always a Quaker, he was one for a time and was influential in what we are beginning to call the Cambridge Movement.[9]

---

[9] See James F. White, *The Cambridge Movement* (Cambridge: Cambridge University Press, 1962), p. 9.

Though Quakers long made the mistake of repressing the enjoyment of the fine arts, there has never been any serious doubt of the necessity of education. In this regard the Quaker Movement has, from the first, been in marked contrast with that of sects in which education has been considered unnecessary or dangerous. It is true that Elias Hicks went to such extremes in the glorification of the Inner Light that he saw human learning as either unnecessary or positively harmful. "Now what vast toil and labour," he said, "there is to give children human science, when the money thus expended might be better thrown into the sea."[10] It is easy to see how an extreme theory of divine illumination could lead to such a conclusion, but it must be made plain that this extreme position is exceptional. The great majority of Quakers, beginning with George Fox himself, have placed stress on education, with the result that contemporary Quakerism is famous for the excellence of its schools and colleges.

As early as 1668, George Fox, working in the London area, arranged for the establishment of two schools. The most interesting part of this decision was the breadth of purpose which Fox expressed. The schools at Shacklewell, he said, should be "set up to instruct young lasses and maidens in whatsoever things was civil and useful in the creation."[11] If this purpose had been truly honored in succeeding generations, the omission of the arts from standard Quaker education would not have been possible.

On leaving England, in 1682, to begin his great political experiment, William Penn wrote a letter to his wife and children in which he expressed himself clearly on the subject of education. He desired to foster an education, he said, that should be both liberal and useful. He believed that "ingenuity mixed with industry is good for the body and the mind too." The only hint, in Penn's educational philosophy, of the negative attitude toward fashionable attainments which came, eventually, to mark so much Quaker

10 *The Quaker*, Vol. I, p. 252. This is a collection of sermons by Hicks, taken in shorthand.
11 *Journal*, 1668.

education, appears when Penn explains his full reason for teaching what is useful in practical daily life. "This leads to consider the works of God and nature, of things that are good, and diverts mind from being taken up with the vain arts and inventions of a luxurious world." If we understand that sentence we see why Quakers soon became so much more eminent in natural science than in other phases of human culture.

The record of Quakerism in both the theory and practice of education is a very striking one, with Quakers often in the fore-front of educational advance. There are many reasons for this, but the most important single reason seems to be the Quaker com-bination of respect and realism concerning each human being. Whenever we take seriously the idea that each person, including each child, is a creature made in the image of God, education is bound to become an exciting and even sacred undertaking. Be-cause no existing practice is ever good enough, there must be a continual process of re-examination. The motive will be love, but be-cause human nature is difficult as well as potentially noble, it must always be tough love. The characteristic Quaker schoolmaster has, therefore, not been tolerant of confusion or of undisciplined self-expression.

One of the most imaginative steps in educational theory and practice was that inaugurated by Joseph Lancaster (1778–1838). Though he grew up on the south bank of the Thames, without the culture which is supposed to be necessary for the development of a successful teacher, Lancaster, after a period of service in the British navy, became a Quaker and decided to make his ministry that of a teacher. In 1801, he opened a school in the Borough Road, London, and promised to educate all children who wished to come, regardless of their financial ability. Parents who could afford to do so paid a small fee, but the poor paid nothing. Having no money to pay assistants, this unusual man hit on the unusual plan of employing older pupils to teach the younger ones. The system worked beyond the founder's fondest expectations. Soon he had no fewer than a thousand pupils under his care. The greatest development, of course, came in the lives of the monitors who grew remarkably as a result of their responsibilities. Lancaster knew what others have discovered for themselves later, that the secret of success in education is *involvement*. Later, there was formed "The Royal Lancasterian Society for Promoting the Education of the Children of the Poor."

Because official Quaker education tended, at first, to be a "guarded education," there were many decades in which Quaker schools forbade the reading of Shakespeare's plays, as well as most novels, and also forbade every kind of music, but the modern reader must understand that such restrictions are not now in force anywhere. There are many existing Quaker schools, both boarding and day schools, and all of them accept the philosophy of wholeness, so far as educational philosophy is concerned. The chief contrast with other schools is found in a sincere effort to encourage a genuine simplicity of manner and conduct, with a rejection of all that is artificial.

The establishment of degree-granting institutions of higher learning is limited to Quakers of the United States, those of Great Britain making use of the established national and local universities. The oldest degree-granting Quaker college is Haverford, which was established, as an excellent boarding school in 1833. Haverford was founded as a direct result of the lamentable division of 1827, in which ignorance played a major role. In 1856, Haverford became a college and has granted degrees ever since. Three years later, in 1859, Earlham, at Richmond, Indiana, also became a college, having originally, like Haverford, been a secondary boarding school, established in 1847. The third institution to offer full collegiate work, of what is generally known as university grade, was Swarthmore, which opened in 1869 and was named for the home of George and Margaret Fox in Lancashire.

Seven other Quaker colleges now operate in the United States. These are Guilford, in North Carolina, Wilmington and Malone, in Ohio, William Penn, in Iowa, Friends University, in Kansas, Whittier, in California, and George Fox, in Oregon. In addition to the ten already mentioned, it is right to mention three important institutions, which, though not under Quaker government, were founded by three men who were born and trained in the Quaker fellowship. The first of these, Cornell University, was established in 1868 at Ithaca, New York, through the generosity of Ezra Cornell (1807–1874). Cornell's broad requirement was that the new institution should offer instruction in all branches of learning. Five years later, in 1873, Johns Hopkins, of Baltimore (1795–1873), gave the then immense sum of seventeen million dollars to found and support both a university and a medical hospital. Quakers were dominant on the new board, of which Francis T. King was president. In 1880, Dr. Joseph Taylor (1810–1880), of Burlington, New Jersey, bequeathed his large estate to the foundation of Bryn Mawr College, which opened in 1885. All of the trustees were, by provision of Dr. Taylor's will, to be Quakers.

All Quaker colleges are public rather than sectarian institutions, in the sense that they educate thousands who are not Quakers and all of them recognize a public responsibility. The financial and moral support of these institutions has seemed to modern Quakers to be one of the finest ways in which a contribution to the total culture can be made. There is a very serious effort to do more, in these institutions, than to copy the secularized colleges and their programs. In an age when higher education begins to take on many of the characteristics of a factory, with teaching often being almost entirely impersonal, it is clear that there is room for an operation in which each individual is seen as precious, made in the image of God, and consequently worthy of patient personal attention. One statement of this philosophy, which has received widespread assent, is the following:

Underlying all that Earlham tries to do and to be is the vision of wholeness. The lives of men and women must include both worship

and work, both discipline and freedom, both respect for the individual
and concern for the group, both the training of the mind and the
training of the body, both cultural breadth and vocational competence.

The Quaker penchant for the natural sciences has been frequently noted and considerable thought expended in the effort to
explain it. Whereas the love of the beautiful has often been
suspect, supposedly leading to an excessive interest in the artificial
and the luxurious, the love of truth has always been honored.
Quakers have been convinced that one of the chief ways of
showing reverence to God is that of studying His creation, and
particularly the animal creation. John Woolman expressed one
aspect of this motivation when he wrote, "I believe that where the
love of God is verily perfected, and the true spirit of government
watchfully attended to a tenderness toward all creatures made
subj   23-24   ced." The same philosophy which has
renc   66   orts, such as fox-hunting, has caused
Frie   82   creation with loving care and fidelity
to tr

Th   194   f science have worked in many fields,
the 1   227-28.   is that of the various branches of
biolo   e example of such scientific Quaker
schol   Cope (1840–1897), of Philadelphia,
one o   ence of paleontology and author of
many   logy. Cope discovered more than
one th   vertebrates, previously unknown.
The interest in zoology and botany has continued in the Cope
family and is exemplified in James Cope, one of the recognized
contemporary authorities on bats. The visitor to the Lake Mohonk
area, in Ulster County, New York, is reminded of this family
heritage when he enjoys the fine view from Cope's Lookout.

One of the best insights into the meaning of Quakerism is
provided by the consideration of a remarkable group of scholars
whose lives overlapped at Earlham College two generations ago.
These were Joseph Moore, David Worth Dennis, and Allen D.

Hole. All were first-class scientists, all were men who loved the outdoors, even more than the study, and all were recognized ministers of the Society of Friends. Joseph Moore made enough paleontological discoveries to start a museum which still bears his name; David Worth Dennis had a grasp of many sciences; and Allen D. Hole was a distinguished geologist. In such men we see Quakerism at its best, combining the love of God with the love of nature. Far from supposing that there is any real or serious conflict between science and religion, these men believed that every laboratory experiment was a process in which men asked God a question. They believed that true science is a matter of discovery rather than of invention, because the little that we learn is but a fragment of the truth and is merely a matter of thinking a few of God's thoughts after Him.

The most famous of all Quaker scientists was John Dalton (1766–1844), born near Cockermouth, in Cumberland, not far from the scene of the initial successes of George Fox. Very early Dalton showed an unusual interest in natural phenomena, keeping a weather journal of his own and, with surprising foresight, assigning a magnetic cause to the aurora borealis. His most creative human contact was with a blind man of Kendal, John Gough, who taught Dalton Greek and Latin and started him on his scientific investigations.[12] In 1793, Dalton moved to Manchester, where he became tutor in mathematics in Manchester College. At the age of thirty he turned his attention to the study of chemistry, which he revolutionized by his treatment of atomic theory. His distinctive contribution was the discovery of the relative and unvarying weights of the ultimate particles of matter. His conclusion was that the atomic weight of each elemental substance in the universe is unalterable. All Quakers can well be pleased to be represented by Dalton's combination of bold clarity and humility, especially in the following statement:

[12] The blind Gough is described by Wordsworth in the *Excursion*, Book vii.

I have been enabled to reduce a number of apparently anomalous facts to general laws, and to exhibit a new view of the first principles or elements of bodies and their combinations, which is established, as I doubt not that it will [be] in time, will produce the most important changes in the system of chemistry, and reduce the whole to a science of great simplicity, and intelligible to the meanest understanding.[13]

The famous Quaker chemist was made a Fellow of the Royal Society and was honored with doctors degrees by both Oxford University and the University of Edinburgh. He was granted a government pension in recognition of his discoveries and, in 1826, was awarded the first Royal Medal by the Council of the Royal Society. Though British Quakers have never established a separate college, they have long honored this great scientist and sought to continue his intellectual and spiritual heritage by the support of Dalton Hall as part of the University of Manchester. Modern English Quakerism has also contributed to the world of scientific learning both Silvanus P. Thompson (1851–1916), a distinguished writer in the field of electricity, and Joseph Lister, later Lord Lister (1827–1912), the famous surgeon who discovered the antiseptic method of treating wounds and for whom a well known antiseptic product is named.

The twentieth century has witnessed the appearance of a number of Quaker scientists, the most eminent being the late Professor Arthur S. Eddington (1882–1944), of the University of Cambridge.[14] Professor Eddington won great acclaim in the last decades of his life in his contributions to astrophysics, his major work being given as Gifford Lectures, with the title *The Nature of the Physical World*. His Swarthmore Lecture for 1929, *Science and the Unseen World*, has been more widely read and quoted

[13] J. P. Millington, *John Dalton*, p. 159. Dalton's new system was presented in two volumes, *A New System of Chemical Philosophy*, Pt. I, 1808, and Pt. II, 1810.

[14] Not to be confused with his cousin Arthur J. Eddington, of Norwich, one-time clerk of the Meeting for Sufferings of London Yearly Meeting.

than has any other Swarthmore Lecture since the inauguration of the series in 1908. When the lecture was given in London, every word was cabled to the United States and widely reproduced.

Eddington believed that Quakerism, in having strong convictions, yet no creed, was a religion especially attractive to the scientific-minded. He was too thoughtful to suppose that no reasonable defense of creeds is possible, yet he held "that Quakerism in dispensing with creeds holds out a hand to the scientist." He held that science, at its best, is more a process than an arrival, and this, he thought, was the dominant Quaker mood through the years.

Rejection of creed is not inconsistent with being possessed by a living belief. We have no creed in science, but we are not lukewarm in our beliefs. The belief is not that all the knowledge of the universe that we hold so enthusiastically will survive in the letter; but a sureness that we are on the road. If our so-called facts are changing shadows, they are shadows cast by the light of constant truth. So too in religion we are repelled by that confident theological doctrine which has settled for all generations just how the spiritual world is worked; but we need not turn aside from the measure of light that comes into our experience showing us a *Way* through the unseen world.[15]

Eddington's emphasis on experience gives us our best clue concerning the Quaker affinity for scientific endeavor. We must remember that Fox said of his most important insight, "This I knew experimentally." When we know that the key term is the synonym of "experientially," we are well on the road to understanding.[16] Quakerism begins with an experience rather than with a dogma and therefore can appeal to scientists because it is itself scientific-minded. It is no accident that so often the most impressive departments in the Quaker colleges are the departments of science. It is a revealing fact that, since the seventeenth century,

[15] *Science and the Unseen World* (London: Allen and Unwin, 1929).
[16] E. B. Castle, in his *Approach to Quakerism*, supports this judgment when he writes, "This emphasis on personal experience is the core of Quakerism" (p. 21).

the Royal Society has never been without Quakers among its Fellows.[17]

Of all Quaker scholars in three centuries of experience there is none who represents the type more clearly than Rendel Harris (1852-1941). In the 1880's, Professor Harris was one of the galaxy of scholars who made the recently established Johns Hopkins University the most exciting scene of intellectual life in the Western Hemisphere.[18] Though Harris used a variety of languages and seemed, in spite of his evident humility, to know everything, he taught Semitic languages, first at Johns Hopkins and later at Haverford College and Cambridge University. In 1903, Professor Harris and his wife reluctantly left their delightful life at Cambridge and declined an attractive invitation to occupy a chair at Leyden, in order to begin a new career. In this he was Director of Studies at Woodbrooke Settlement, established near Birmingham on the estate owned by George Cadbury and dedicated to a fresh kind of educational venture inspired by John Wilhelm Rowntree.

The important thing to say about Dr. Harris, as a Quaker scholar of the major tradition, is that he combined, in what seemed the most natural manner, the profundity of great learning with the faith of a little child. On the one hand he made signal archaeological discoveries in the Near East, while, on the other, he gathered his neighbors in his home for prayer, in which, quite naturally and unself-consciously, he would drop to his knees. Rendel Harris was as sure of the Life Everlasting as of his present life and he saw no inconsistency whatever in being both a tough-minded scholar and a tender-minded follower of his Savior. Once, walking at sunset with a beloved niece, Dr. Harris, in reply to a

[17] A list of names of Fellows is provided in *Friends Historical Journal*, Vol. VII, p. 30.

[18] In 1939, when Rendel Harris was eighty-seven years old, and as bright as ever, I asked him what was the secret of the powerful intellectual life at Johns Hopkins when he taught there. His laconic answer was, "We all attended each other's lectures."

question about the life everlasting, said, "Never worry over the way to Heaven, dear. Always remember it is a personally conducted tour." His mind remained alert and inquiring to the end, when he was eighty-nine, his favorite prayer still being, "Give us this day our daily discovery." He added greatly to the life of culture, but he made the addition tenderly and reverently. John Woolman represents the best of Quaker social concern, and Rendel Harris represents the best of Quaker culture.

13 / The Penetration
of the World

One cannot effectively keep the possessions that one has unless one has the courage to put them in circulation and devote them to fresh enterprises and ventures.

LEWIS MUMFORD

Of all of the ways in which primitive Quakers resembled primitive Christians, the most striking similarity was that of missionary activity. The earliest Quakers did not need to organize a missionary board or a committee because the entire movement was that of a missionary band. To ask, when did the Religious Society of Friends adopt a missionary program, is to state the question wrongly. Quakerism was a missionary movement before it was an organized religious society. The Quaker mission is older than the Quaker Church.

The more carefully we read the New Testament, the more we come to realize that the Christian Church, in its first phase, was essentially a missionary movement. The strategy was to turn mere disciples, i.e., learners, into *apostles*. This included both men and women, both learned and untrained. The focus of the early church was not the temple and its ceremonial requirements; neither was it the synagogue which was good, but not good enough. Both the temple and the synagogue were centripetal, drawing men from homes and businesses to a center. The early church was centrifugal, sending men into the world. The characteristic preposition, for the primitive Christian Movement, was "out" rather than "in." In what is a real watershed in the Gospel, after the relative failure at Nazareth, we read that Christ "called to him the twelve, and began to send them out" (Mark 6:7). Here was the new strategy.

The major figures of speech employed in the Gospel are figures of penetration, which means that the center of interest is always outside the individual Christian and even outside the Christian fellowship. The Christians are told that they are *salt*, and *light*, and *leaven*, the common feature of all of these figures being their function of penetration of what is around them. In the Kingdom of Christ that which is to be penetrated is the entire human civilization. The salt is to be the salt of the *earth*, while the light is to be the light of the *world*. The place for the leaven to operate is not in splendid isolation, but in the *lump*. This is why we speak today of Christianity as a "worldly" faith. If Christians are to go "into all the world" this means every phase of human civilization. No area is off limits for a Christian society which understands its own function and character. Where is the church? *The church is in the world!*

One of the most striking things about the Quakers who arose in the seventeenth century was that, without making such an analysis, the explosive character of the Christian mission seemed to be understood spontaneously and without argument. The logic was deceptively simple. If a man became a Christian in the important sense of being actually reached by Christ directly, in his own heart, there was no alternative to an explosive response which involved the effort to bring other people to a similar experience of newness of life. Consequently, each man had to find some way of engaging in missionary activity. Actually, then, the valid choices were only two. A man might, on the one hand, reject the appeal of Christ to his inmost being. He might, on the other, accept Him and, being consequently a changed person, try to change others. The one thing that a man could not possibly do was to have his life changed and keep it to himself. If a man keeps his faith to himself, that is ample evidence that it has not been genuine in the first place. It is self-evident that a person will try to share whatever he truly prizes.

Not every Quaker of the first generation made long journeys of a missionary nature, but an astonishing proportion did so. George Fox, writing from a foul prison to his associates, and urging all into missionary activity similar to his own, was only encouraging what was already being done. "Let all nations hear the word by sound or writing. Spare no place, spare not tongue nor pen, but be obedient to the Lord God and go through the world and be valiant for the Truth upon earth; . . . Be patterns, be examples in all countries, places, islands, nations, wherever you come, that your carriage and life may preach among all sorts of people, and to them." It was the total witness of both conduct and word that concerned Fox. Since the sweep of his world vision is intoxicating today, it must have been even more so when it was first expressed.

It is surprising to note how quickly, in spite of the slowness of travel, the early Quaker messengers reached remote parts of the world. Because the first Friends thought they had a universal mission, wherever there were men and women and whatever their cultural or spiritual background, there was a potential field of labor. William Dewsbury, writing from prison early in 1656, sent out an address which was ecumenical in its scope though it was inaccurate in its geography. "You people," he wrote, "scattered in Barbadoes, Virginia, New England and other islands thereaways and countries elsewhere, to you the mighty day of the Lord is coming and in his power is appearing amongst you." Whatever such a man as Dewsbury lacked, he did not lack gusto.

One expression towers above all others as a representation of this amazing missionary effort. This is the Letter produced at the Skipton General Meeting in 1660. The Letter describes the service beyond seas as going on in such "parts and regions as Germany,

America, Virginia, and many other islands and places, as Florence, Mantua, Palatine, Tuscany, Italy, Rome, Turkey, Jerusalem, France, Geneva, Norway, Barbadoes, Bermuda, Antigua, Jamaica, Surinam, Newfoundland, through all which Friends have passed in the service of the Lord, and divers other places, countries, islands and nations." Though we stand aghast at the geographical jumble of such a survey, and though we recognize an element of bombast in it, we cannot fail to be deeply moved by the clear statement of the reason for such far-flung labors:

> For England is a family of prophets, which must spread over all the nations, as a garden of plants, and the place where the pearl is found which must enrich all nations with the heavenly treasure, out of which shall the waters of life flow, and water all the thirsty ground.

Though the mixing of metaphors is bewildering, the sense of vitality is unmistakable. It is important to realize that such missionary action was the natural and spontaneous outgrowth of the vitality. The first Quakers could no more be held down than can a sprouting seed which may even break a hard surface. Of all of the autobiographical remains which help us to understand this vitality and its inevitable explosive effect, there is none which makes us see the logic of the situation better than that provided, in 1652, by that articulate and notorious man, James Nayler.

> I was at the plow, meditating on the things of God, and suddenly I heard a voice saying to me, "Get thee out from thy kindred, and from thy father's house." And I had a promise given with it, whereupon I did exceedingly rejoice that I had heard the voice of that God which I had professed from a child, but had never known him . . . . and when I came at home I gave up my estate, cast out my money; but not being obedient in going forth, the wrath of God was upon me, so that I was made a wonder to all, and none thought I would have lived. But after I was made willing, I began to make some preparation, as apparel and other necessaries, not knowing whither I should go. But shortly afterwards going a gate-ward with a friend from my own house, having on an old suit, without any money, having neither taken leave of wife

or children, not thinking then of any journey, I was commanded to go into the west, not knowing whither I should go, nor what I was to do there. But when I had been there a little while, I had given me what I was to declare.[1]

We are accustomed, in our day, to a missionary activity in which the work of missions is administered by boards and secretaries. People who feel led to volunteer for foreign service are screened carefully, given training if any is needed, and sent to faraway places with all expenses paid. Early Quakerism had none of this, but it did have, as has been mentioned in an earlier chapter, abundant financial support. With an amazing simplicity, funds were collected and disbursed without any office and with a minimum of organization.

After the first fires of enthusiasm had died down, Quakers still made some missionary efforts, but there were two important differences between the missionary work of the long quietistic period and that which preceded it. The first difference was that the large expectancy was gone. No longer did Quakers expect to see the world converted in a short time. The taunt applied by King Agrippa to Paul, "In a short time you think to make me a Christian!" (Acts 26:28), could have been leveled at the first Friends, but it was not applicable in the eighteenth century. What later Friends gained in wisdom they lost in vitality. The second difference was that the main missionary effort of later itinerants was *within* the Quaker communities. Visits like that of John Woolman to the Indians of Wyalusing were striking, precisely because they were uncharacteristic.

The Quaker missionary activity, in the modern sense, started only about a century ago. It owed a great deal to the prodding of an aged man, George Richardson, who wrote, on December 12, 1759, an open letter on missions which was printed and widely

[1] Nayler's autobiographical statement is printed in *Christian Faith and Practice in the Experience of the Society of Friends* (London Yearly Meeting, 1960).

circulated.[2] The first sentence of this letter states briefly the entire problem. "My mind has long been burdened with an apprehension that our Religious Society is not coming forward as it ought to do, but has shrunk from its true line of service, in reference to an endeavour to promote the extension of the kingdom of our Lord Jesus Christ in heathen lands." The author proposed the formation of an "Association for aiding in the Diffusion of Gospel Light," recognizing that it would be necessary to recruit persons who would be willing to engage in long-time residence in foreign parts, and that such persons would have to be supported financially by Friends remaining at home.

George Richardson died in 1862, being then in his eighty-ninth year, but he had already seen the rapid acceptance of the novel idea which he had proposed. London Yearly Meeting, of 1861, sent out an address which expressed the missionary spirit in no uncertain terms. The most striking sentence in the address was: "Christianity is in its very nature diffusive." The address showed that, since the objections against organized mission work were still powerfully felt, an effort was necessary if these objections were to be met. The critics of the missionary project held that organized work in foreign lands was incompatible with the basic Quaker dependence on the inward voice and the leading of the spirit. Many feared that an organized mission movement would lead to a pastoral system on the mission fields, and in this their judgment was correct. Though there are no pastors among British Friends, pastors have arisen in the mission fields which British Friends have established.

After the death of George Richardson, many younger voices were heard in support of the missionary idea. As early as September, 1865, an entire issue of The Friend (London) was devoted to the promotion of the modern missionary cause. The constitution of the Friends Foreign Missionary Association was drawn up in

[2] Richardson's letter may be read in the Appendix to his Journal (London, 1864).

1868, and soon Quaker representatives were sent to a variety of foreign fields.

The first concrete evidence of modern missionary enthusiasm among American Quakers appeared in 1867, when two devoted New England Friends, Eli and Sibyl Jones, made a visit to Palestine. The results of their labors were many, including the mission center at Ramallah, a few miles north of Jerusalem, which is active at the present time. At first each segment of American Quakerdom initiated its own foreign work, with Indiana Friends operating in Mexico, Iowa Friends in Jamaica, etc. Several Americans, feeling the need of strong organizational support, volunteered their services to the Friends Foreign Missionary Association of England, asking to be sent out under its auspices. As a result, leading English Quakers urged their American brethren to follow their example and to set up a central organization. This led, in 1894, to the formation of the American Friends Board of Foreign Missions,  which is now one of the constituent parts of the Friends United Meeting, with headquarters at Richmond, Indiana.

Though the work which emanates from the offices at Richmond, Indiana, is the largest Quaker work of its kind in the world, it does not include all American missionary efforts. For example, it has never included the work of Philadelphia Friends who, chiefly through their women members, started an important work in Japan, which has been effective for eighty years. The Women's Foreign Missionary Association of Friends of Philadelphia was organized December 12, 1882. One of the finest results of their work is the flourishing Friends Girl School in Tokyo. Local Japanese leadership soon developed to support the Philadelphia-based effort. Most influential of these was Inazo Nitobe (1862–1933), who wrote, in 1927, A Japanese View of Quakerism. At the foundation of the League of Nations, after World War I, Nitobe became its Under-Secretary-General.

Some of the missionary effort, which showed such vitality at the beginning of the twentieth century, has come to an end. There are many reasons for this. One reason is the doubt, in some minds, of whether it is right to disturb people of the other world religions by the introduction of Christian ideas. Sometimes this is merely the result of the superficial judgment that one religion is as good as another, but, in other minds, it arises from a more profound understanding of the way in which the Living Christ has, all along, been reaching out to all men, whether Buddhists, Moslems, or whatever. In India some Quakers have rejected wholly the idea of converting Hindus to Christ, and have sought to develop a new expression which is neither Christian nor Hindu. Even those who do not go this far find something of their missionary enthusiasm dampened by the recognition of obvious value in other religions. Very few contemporary Quakers believe that a devout non-Christian will be consigned to eternal punishment, simply because he is not a Christian.

Another cause of the decline in missionary zeal is the way in which so much of the idealistic urge of young Quakers has found expression in service projects and in new developments such as that of the Peace Corps. Once it was possible to recruit the ablest of young people for the missionary cause, under the inspiration of John R. Mott and other powerful leaders, but it is not possible now, except in isolated instances.

The general weakening of the missionary urge has occasioned an agonizing reappraisal of the entire effort. In Great Britain the separate mission work was given up in 1927, when the Friends Foreign Missionary Association joined with the Friends Council for International Service to form the Friends Service Council. This Council now supervises what is left of the old mission work, along with the work of service and relief and that of Friends Centers which have been established in various cities, especially on the European continent.

The general reappraisal has been, on the whole, a beneficent experience. As Quakers have reconsidered their basic missionary motive they see, with as much clarity as ever, that Christianity is, in its very nature, diffusive, but they are very eager to make sure that the act of diffusion must never seem presumptuous or imperialistic. The modern missionary goes not merely to give, but also to receive and, above all, to share. No one is so rich in spiritual resources that he can afford to neglect whatever he can learn from anybody who can teach him.

We are also helped today by the recognition that Christ's Gospel is not so much a matter of denunciation as of fulfillment. After all, Christ said, "I am not come to destroy, but to fulfil" (Matt. 5:17). If Christ can provide a fulfillment of what was only partly expressed in Judaism, He can do the same for Buddhism, Islam, etc. If we recognize, with the late Paul Tillich, that there are anticipations of the Gospel in all the world religions, this does not cut the nerve of missionary effort, but strengthens it. Men need the help of one another to bring to actuality what, without such assistance, is only potential. If Christ is already speaking to every man, we need to have the help of one another to learn more fully what it is that He is saying.

The consequence of this general reappraisal is that it is evident that missionary activity will go on. Indeed, the most successful of all organized Quaker missionary efforts is in contemporary existence in the new nation of Kenya. The work in Kenya began about 1900, with the powerful impetus of a few young men associated with Cleveland Bible Institute, in Cleveland, Ohio, but has, in subsequent years, attracted the support of a great variety of Quakers on both sides of the Atlantic. Since 1911, the African work has been under the care of the American Friends Board of Missions. The result is that East Africa Yearly Meeting is now the largest yearly meeting in the world. Much of the work is centered in schools, but it is increasingly spreading to work in agriculture and industry. The new mission work is directed to the whole life of the people. Without neglecting the inner life of religious experience, it stresses ways in which the total economy can be improved.

The same is true of other active mission fields. In Jamaica, for example, a great deal of the effort is concentrated on education, particularly in support of Happy Grove School, a patron of which is Sir Hugh Foot, the representative of Great Britain at the United Nations. The chief work of the Palestine Mission is the conduct of the two Friends Schools in Ramallah, one for boys and the other for girls, the majority of the students being Moslems.

If we read the signs aright we soon become aware that the missionary movement, instead of diminishing in our day, is actually undergoing enlargement. Perhaps the most vivid evidence of its enlargement is the general elimination, from our missionary vocabulary, of the word "Foreign." We see very clearly now that North America and Europe are themselves mission fields. The time has come again when, as in primitive Quakerism, every Christian can be and ought to be a missionary. If he is not, he has not rightly understood his vocation.

The secret of Quakerism, if there is one, lies in the close and constant marriage between religious experience and social concern. E. B. Castle, now retired from the University of Hull, tells how it was this aspect which struck him most forcefully when he was first introduced, in books, to Quaker life and thought. "What particularly appealed to me at that time," he has since written, "was the direct way in which the Quaker insistence on the quiet inward life became inevitably associated with its active outward expression in the world of affairs. In Quakerism I found the Christian and the social to be effortlessly intertwined."[3] The same author speaks of the penchant of Quakerism for "effortless penetration into every corner of life, into the intimately personal, but also into the social and political."[4]

It is not surprising, in view of the determination to hold the spiritual and the social in one context, that the concept of mission

[3] *Approach to Quakerism,* p. 10.
[4] *Ibid.,* p. 160.

has been both deepened and enlarged during the last century of Quaker experience. Over and over we have said that mission is not something added to the nature of a Christian society, but is intrinsic to it. The Church of Christ, when it understands itself and its relationship to its Lord, does not *have* a mission; it *is* mission.

While George Richardson encouraged Quakers, a century ago, to enlarge their sense of mission geographically, others have helped to enlarge it politically and economically. In no single way has this been done more spectacularly than in the work of service and relief. Though there had earlier been some public recognition of the work of Quaker relief, reconstruction, and international service, the great step forward, in this regard, came in 1947, with the awarding of the Nobel Prize for Peace. The award was given jointly to two organizations, the Friends Service Council, in Great Britain, and the American Friends Service Committee. In the presentation address it was said:

> The Quakers have shown us that it is possible to carry into action something that is deeply rooted in the minds of many people—a sympathy with others; a desire to help others; that significant expression of sympathy between men without regard to race or nationality. These feelings translated into deeds must provide the foundations of a lasting peace. For this reason they are today worthy to receive Nobel's Peace Prize.

The work of relief and reconstruction, the best-known single aspect of Quaker life, so far as the general public is concerned, has reached its peak in the periods of war, but is not limited to such periods. Though there are many examples of Quaker work in previous wars, the organized service work as it is known today began when in October, 1870, British Friends, who were deeply moved by the sufferings of civilians in the Franco-Prussian War, set up a Friends War Victims Fund. This was the period of the origination of the black and red star which is still employed as a badge of the Quaker relief worker. It is frequently worn today as a lapel button and thereby becomes a helpful means of identification, particularly in travel.

The work instituted in 1870 was given up when the need ended, but it was valuable in providing a pattern for renewed service in 1914, as soon as World War I began. The Friends War Victims Relief Committee was a revival of the organization which had been formed forty-four years earlier and again the black and red star was employed. The new committee was set up in September, 1914, by the London Meeting for Sufferings. At the same time English Quakers started a new venture, the Friends Ambulance Unit. This was especially appealing to young men who, though convinced that they were led not to fight, wanted to make sure that they were not following some safe or easy alternative. They welcomed the danger which ambulance work involved. The Ambulance Unit was revived in World War II and did valiant service in distressed Germany as soon as entrance by British workers was possible.

The American Friends Service Committee, established in 1917, on the entrance of the United States into the war, performed, so long as hostilities lasted, work similar to that of its British counterpart. The chief work included the conduct of hospitals and emergency housing for refugees, as well as the production and distribution of food. As soon as the war ended, the work of feeding, which was the one most desperately needed, was carried into Germany and Austria. A similar pattern was followed after World War II, with such widespread effectiveness that the term "Quaker Speisung" is still understood in Central Europe. So widespread was the reputation that Quakers were freely blamed for any poor quality donated food, whoever the donor might be.

It is important to know that this work of relief and reconstruction, like the work that has followed it to this day, is not financed solely or even mainly by Quakers themselves. All kinds of people, including a great many generous Jews, have given liberally to the

American Friends Service Committee through the years. Though the work is something for which Quakers must take responsibility, because of administration and the creation of policy, it is true to say that the majority of the money which makes the work possible is non-Quaker money. Also a great many of those who volunteer for service projects are those who are sympathetic with, but not members of, the Religious Society of Friends.

As the years of the twentieth century have gone on, more and more effort has been concentrated, not in healing the wounds which war entails, but rather in trying to work in areas of tension, to help to prevent war. The peace lover, if he is honest, is quick to admit that, when war actually breaks out, his cause is temporarily defeated. Picking up the pieces is indeed something, but it would be far better if such work were not required. Much of the emphasis of the Quaker social mission today is naturally directed into the Civil Rights Struggle, always with the hope of aiding in mutual understanding and thus forestalling violent conflict.

The best aspect of the Service Committee work has been the way in which programs are initiated with the expectation that they will eventually be taken over by others. A striking example of this process is that of selecting and training young people and sending them out to various points of need on a short-time basis. Most of these have no expectation of becoming full-time or professional service people, but they find great fulfillment in such temporary assignments in which they can, they hope, do some good and also learn a great deal. It has been obvious to many that this pattern of Quaker service is the essential one which the Peace Corps has since adopted. Indeed, the indebtedness has been freely recognized. Instead of feeling that they have been displaced and overshadowed by a glamorous governmental project, Quakers have a right to feel grateful that a good idea has been adopted and extended far beyond anything that a merely Quaker organization could ever do.

If the spiritual experience of Christ as the Present Teacher is to find expression by penetration of the social order, it is obvious that new avenues must be penetrated in as rapid succession as possible. Once the area of concern is slavery; once it is prison life; again it is civil rights. Always it must relate, in one way or another, to governments. For several decades, in the quietistic period, Quakers had almost no direct influence upon or membership in governments, but this has changed rapidly in the last few generations. For a long time British Quakers were legally barred from entering Parliament, but when, in 1828, there came the repeal of the Test Act and the Corporation Act, the obstacles were removed. Soon a North Country Friend, Edward Pease, was elected member from North Durham, though he refused to canvass or to incur any election expenses. Since that time there have been a number of Quakers in Parliament, the most famous being John Bright, who entered the House of Commons ten years after Edward Pease.

Though there was once a strong temptation to renounce politics and to keep themselves pure accordingly, Quakers have been enabled to reject this temptation partly because of the vivid witness of William Penn. Penn, we all realize, was forced to do many things in political life which he would have preferred not to do, and in the end his "holy experiment" failed, but in his very failure he performed a remarkable service. In Penn's brilliant work of preparing his *Frame of Government,* he stated the heart of Quaker political philosophy by saying, "Government seems to me a part of religion itself, a thing sacred in its institution and end."

Because, in contemporary Quakerism, there is a renewed appreciation of Penn's position, Quakers are beginning to urge their young people to prepare for government service. It is a natural step in the penetration of the world which is the Christian mission. Those who urge this are well aware of the dangers, and know that the personal price in each case is high, but they urge such a development because they understand some of the realities of power. As the race advances, and the power of government increases, it is the duty of committed Christians to try to be where the power is.

One relatively new Quaker development, involving a witness in and to government, came with the establishment, in 1942, of the Friends Committee on National Legislation, with headquarters in Washington, on Capitol Hill. While the organization is new, the essential activity is old and was brilliantly illustrated by Eliza Gurney when she met with President Lincoln in the dark days of the American Civil War.

The Quaker outreach is always symbolized by the conviction that the place of service is in the world, rather than the meeting-house. It is necessary to go into all the world, both extensively and intensively, because the only valid religion is that which is directly expressed in the common life which people actually live day by day. This is what we mean by worldly religion. Many have tried to say this, though it is doubtful if any have said it more impressively than the late Joan Fry (1862–1955). "Quakerism," she wrote in her Swarthmore Lecture, "is nothing unless it be a communion of life, a practical showing that spiritual and material spheres are not divided, but are as the concave and convex sides of one whole."

William Charles Braithwaite performed a service by calling the attention of his fellow Quakers to a striking passage in the *Epistle to Diognetus*, in which it is clear that the early Christians were being warned against any tendency to retire from the world, in order to remain untainted.

Christians are not distinguished from the rest of mankind either in locality or in speech or in customs. For they dwell not somewhere in cities of their own, neither do they use some different language, nor practise an extraordinary kind of life. . . . But, while they dwell in cities of Greeks and barbarians as the lot of each is cast . . . yet the constitution of their own citizenship which they set forth is marvellous and confessedly contradicts expectation. . . . They find themselves in the flesh, and yet they live not after the flesh. Their existence is on earth, but their citizenship is in heaven. They obey the established laws, and they surpass the laws in their own lives.

Here, from the early days of the Christian religion, we have essentially the same point said pithily, even though ungrammatically, by William Penn, as earlier quoted, "True godliness don't turn men out of the world, but enables them to live better in it, and excites their endeavours to mend it."[5] It is because Penn's admonition has been so often neglected and because so many people think, uncritically, of religion as something separated from common life, that Dietrich Bonhoeffer and others of our generation have felt it necessary to call for the emergence of a religionless Christianity. If the Quaker identification of religion with common life is accepted, such an emphasis as that of Bonhoeffer's last phase is unnecessary.

The ultimate position, to which the basic Quaker philosophy inevitably points, is the denial of the distinction between the secular and the sacred. What is done in the factory or the legislature or the household must be as much under Christ's immediate leadership as what is done in the prayer meeting. A recognition of the connectedness of the spiritual and the material has led Quakers to see business as a natural scene for religious witness. This found its first concrete expression in a reputation for scrupulous honesty and the primary reason for the use of the term "Quaker" in naming so many manufactured products, though the present usage may be so wide that the intended suggestion is lost. "It is to be noted," wrote William W. Comfort, "that the present day use of the term 'Quaker' in every sort of business may be taken as a tribute to the excellence of the products and the honesty of the dealings of the Quaker."[6]

Quakers have, in the past, done some pioneering in social reconstruction in connection with business. A vivid example is that of the Cadbury Brothers in the establishment of Bournville as a Garden Village, on the outskirts of the big city of Birmingham. When George Cadbury and his brother Richard took over their father's business, on his retirement in 1861, it was really a poor and struggling business. Partly because of the experience of the

[5] Works, 1726, Vol. I, p. 296.
[6] Quakers in the Modern World (New York: The Macmillan Company, 1948), p. 153.

brothers in the contemporary Quaker outreach through the Adult School Movement, they looked upon the workers in the small cocoa factory, not merely as "hands," but as fellow workers. Because they were sincerely concerned with the employees as persons, the Cadburys were the first employers in Birmingham to establish a regular weekly half-holiday.

The bold and unprecedented step which the brothers took, as soon as relative prosperity permitted it, was a movement of the operation into the attractive countryside, so that the workers could be surrounded by playing-fields, and homes with beautiful, though modest, gardens. Other industries have followed suit on both sides of the Atlantic, in subsequent years, but it is significant that the Bournville experiment was the pioneer one. One type of Quaker outreach, that of the Adult School, led to another, that of better housing and better working conditions. The sons of George and Richard Cadbury continued both forms of the outreach, Barrow Cadbury (1862–1958), Richard's son, continuing his teaching of an Adult School each Sunday morning into extreme old age, until shortly before his death at the age of ninety-six.

It is essential to the Quaker pattern of outreach that it be nonpossessive. The Adult School Movement was started in England, in the middle of the nineteenth century, not solely, but largely by Quaker imagination. It was intended to overcome, as much as possible, the appalling illiteracy of the working classes, and the schools were held on Sunday because that was the only free day. They were never exclusively religious, but did much to introduce eager minds to a wide variety of subjects, including poetry. A big step came when Joseph Sturge (1793–1859), a leading Quaker, opened an Adult School in Birmingham in 1845, but Quakers were soon outnumbered as leaders of the Movement and rejoiced in its ability to make progress in its own right.

The principle here exemplified may be termed the principle of multiplication. There is so much that needs to be done that some must be starters while others are developers and continuers. It takes a certain grace to start and to let go, but if we succumb to the temptation of possessiveness we can never realize the multiplication of effort which both the human need and the shortness of time require. We need people who can plant and also people who can nurture. Usually the one who plants is almost wholly alone, but his work will not be effective unless he can find or produce a dedicated group to go forward with the creative idea. "It seems to be the will of Him, who is infinite in wisdom," said Joseph Sturge, "that light upon great subjects should first arise and be gradually spread through the faithfulness of *individuals* in acting up to their own convictions." The Quaker hope is that, out of the intense experience of divine confrontation, such individual insight may arise and then that there will be many to recognize and develop such insight.

In practice, Quakerism is a religion of mission. Since the mission has taken many forms in the past, each being unrecognized before its emergence, we can be reasonably sure that this process will continue. At least we know that it ought to continue. A religious movement is untrue to its genius when it becomes fixed and ceases to move. We may not know what it is, but we have good reason to expect that there is new light to break forth. We accept, with humility and expectancy, the words of Jesus when He said, "I have yet many things to say to you, but you cannot bear them now" (John 16:12). "The field is the world" (Matt. 13:38) and, however big it may be, it is bigger than we know. The most inspired Quaker utterance on the subject of outreach is still that of John Woolman when he said, "To turn all the treasures we possess into the channel of universal love becomes the business of our lives."

14 / The Quaker Vocation

> They gathered sticks, and kindled a fire, and left it
> burning.
>
> ROBERT FOWLER's Log of the *Woodhouse*

How can we state honestly and truly the character of the Quaker
Movement? There is, in the nature of the case, no single authoritative statement to which all Quakers must subscribe. What is
possible, however, is to point to *experience*. Of all of the Quaker
experiences in more than three hundred years, one of the most
revealing is that of the voyage of the *Woodhouse*. This was a small
ship which carried to the New World a few Quakers, one of
whom, William Robinson, was destined to be one of the four
Boston martyrs. Even though it was known that any master of a
ship who should bring a Quaker into the Massachusetts Colony
would be severely fined, Robert Fowler, master-mariner of Brid-
lington, had a strong sense of calling. His vocation was that of
building a ship "in the cause of truth." He built a very small ship,
the *Woodhouse*, not really fit for ocean service, but, as he was
engaged in the building, he felt guided to offer her for a Quaker
voyage to New England. After he had sailed his little ship to
London, he found eleven Quakers, six of whom had already been
expelled from Boston, who were willing to make the venture
which was hazardous in more than one way. We get an added idea
of the courage of the little band when we realize that one of the
eleven, Humphrey Norton, had offered to change places with
George Fox when he was in the foul prison, Doomsdale.

The remarkable sentence, which stands as the epigraph of this
chapter, was the ship master's way of expressing what the little

company did when they landed, for a while, on the south coast of England. Even a short stay was employed for purposes of spreading the fire which was raging in their lives. Their Atlantic crossing, in 1657, was indeed an extraordinary one. Each day the Quaker passengers gathered to pray jointly for God's guidance in the steering of their course. The word which they all heard inwardly was: "Cut through and steer your straightest course and mind nothing but me." Perhaps the most revealing document of all is the log which includes this laconic statement, "We saw the Lord leading our vessel as it were a man leading a horse by the head." The actual landing was at New Amsterdam, where two of the women were arrested almost at once for preaching in the streets. After imprisonment, they were dispatched to Rhode Island, which served as a staging area for those intent on invading the Bay Colony. In the summer of 1658 William Brend, an elderly man who had been one of the *Woodhouse* passengers, was flogged almost to death in Boston. On hearing of this cruelty, the same Humphrey Norton, who had offered to change places with the imprisoned Fox, set out for Boston, where he, likewise, was imprisoned and flogged.

The Greek word "character" stood for the mark stamped on a coin, the quality of which was indelible. In this, the original sense of the word, there is no Quaker character, because the pattern is not fixed. What endures is the sense of vocation, the willingness to be divinely led, as the passengers and crew of the *Woodhouse* were led. Consequently, there is never a blueprint which is the same for all occasions. A changeless Quakerism would be a contradiction in terms. The only way to be loyal to the heritage of the pioneers is to pioneer, rather than to go on standing where the pioneers once stood. One of the most inspired of early Quaker writings was a postscript to an epistle written in 1656, at a meeting of elders at Balby, and directed to "the brethren in the north."

Dearly Beloved Friends, these things we do not lay upon you as a rule or form to walk by, but that all, with the measure of light which is pure and holy, may be guided: and so in the light walking and abiding, these things may be fulfilled in the Spirit, not from the letter, for the letter killeth, but the Spirit giveth life.

These great words which have often been neglected, have immense relevance to the task of Quakers today and tomorrow. It is good to pay close heed to what George Fox and others said three hundred years ago, but it would be a great mistake to suppose that the words of these pioneers are a sufficient guide for our feet or that the practices of yesterday must necessarily be the right practices tomorrow. Therefore, we must beware of making the Quaker system of life and thought into something too tidy. It is intrinsically open-ended, because Quakers believe that they live in an open-ended universe. There is profound truth, though also the strong possibility of misunderstanding, in the words of the late Edith Hamilton when she wrote, "If religion did not change it would be dead."[1]

The People called Quakers have seen great changes. Once no Quaker, not even George Fox, saw slavery as a deep and terrible sin. When Fox was on the Island of Barbados, he admonished owners of slaves to "cause their overseers to deal mildly and gently with their negroes, and not use cruelty to them, as the manner of some hath been and is; and that after certain years of servitude they would make them free." A hundred years later, at the death of John Woolman, the moral vision had altered so radically that slavery was seen as a sin, and emancipation as something required of any who sought to be followers of Christ.

Many other changes have come, and many more ought to come. When new proposals are made, each can be examined in the light of its own merits and some, when shown to be unworthy, should be rejected, but the fact that a proposal is novel will never be an adequate reason for rejection. When the pastoral system was instituted, as a Quaker novelty almost a hundred years ago, there were good arguments for it and there were good arguments against

[1] *The Greek Way* (New York: Mentor Books, 1960), p. 217.

it, but the argument that it was a departure from ancient Quaker ways was an argument wholly without validity. Any who had paid serious attention to the great words of the elders of Balby would have known that.

What is important to realize is that a people can be faithful to the spirit, even when there is a radical alteration in the letter. Outwardly, contemporary Quakers appear to be extremely different from the characteristic Quakers of two hundred years ago. No living Quaker dresses as the men of the eighteenth century dressed. Once Quakers did not sing; now almost all do so. Once all used the plain language, but today nearly all Quakers reject it, not out of unwillingness to make a witness, but because it is no longer plain, and seems merely affected or quaint. When a practice does not make the witness which it was originally intended to make, it should be abandoned. To speak of Sunday as "First Day" and to call Sunday School "First Day School" is to be guilty of a sectarian pride which hinders redemptive contact with the modern world. It is probable that some will go on with such linguistic practice, but, if they do, it is obvious that they are more concerned with maintaining the trappings of a sect than they are with the redemptive work of Christ in the world.

If we start with the central idea that Quakerism is nothing but "Christianity writ plain," we have an excellent beginning in the effort to know what the People called Quakers ought to do in the modern world. The task is to try to be faithful and intelligent Apostles of Christ in the world, the particular emphasis being determined in the light of each particular experience. Though both Methodists and Quakers must be emissaries of Christ in the world, there are some things which Methodists can say best, and there are other things which Quakers can say best.

A Christian, according to New Testament usage, is one who is *called*. This is why the Apostle Paul, writing to the Ephesian Christians, begged them to "lead a life worthy of the calling to which you have been called" (Eph. 4:1). The consequence is that "vocation" is one of the noblest words in the entire vocabulary of Christendom. That Quakers have begun to understand this is shown by the fact that the theme of the Friends World Conference at Oxford, in 1952, exactly three hundred years after the original burst of Quaker life, was "The Vocation of Friends in the Modern World." The uniqueness of the conference consisted almost wholly in the recovery of the idea of vocation. What was encouraging was that nearly all of the nine hundred delegates understood that, whatever the vocation may be, it must be one which refers to the world and not to the task of keeping alive, for its own sake, one more little Protestant denomination. The sense of vocation was nearly lost in the decades when Friends met, month after month, with a constant reduction in numbers, because they were always expelling from membership those who did not conform to a fixed pattern of conduct, but now the sense of vocation is being recovered.

It was the sense of vocation, we can see now, that produced the great change in the life and ministry of George Fox when that young man stood on top of Pendle Hill in 1652. Suddenly he saw the magnitude of his calling. We must remember how William Penn tells us that Fox "had a vision of the great work of God in the earth, and of the way he was to go forth to begin it. He saw people thick as motes in the sun, that should in time be brought home to the Lord, that there might be but one shepherd and one sheepfold in all the earth." The summit of Pendle Hill in 1652 was the scene of an ecumenical council with only one human being present.

Whatever the character of the authentic Quaker vocation may be, it must not be *sectarian*. The mere task of keeping up another little Friends Church, in competition with other churches, with a team in the bowling league, and a men's club which meets to eat, is so pathetically small that it represents treason to a great dream. The same can be said for those Quakers who are satisfied to have a feeble little gathering of old people half asleep, and then make the spurious claim that their meetings are kept up. Whatever the Quaker vocation may be, it cannot be genuine unless it involves something far bigger than the pattern for which contemporary Quakers are often satisfied to settle. The most vivid mark of contemporary Quaker failure is the slightness of the product that is sufficient to bring encouragement. The treason is not lack of accomplishment, but smallness of expectancy! The emphasis on vocation provides at least the beginning of a corrective.

One of the best effects of the serious acceptance of the idea of vocation is the way in which it transcends the differences among Christians regarding the relative importance of the inner and outer aspects of religion. There have always been those who have so stressed the inner experience that they have, in effect, neglected the work of service in the world, and there have also been those, on the other hand, who, impatient with the life of devotion, have hurried on to feed the hungry or to clothe the naked. The great significance of the central Quaker idea, however, is that it avoids this damaging separation by uniting, in an indissoluble bond, the inner and outer aspects of our faith. The experience is inner and spiritual, because it is God who *calls*, but the experience cannot be genuine unless it eventuates in *work*. Call is a verb which has about it a fundamental transitivity: the person who is called is always called *to* something: he has a calling and his calling is some form of service to his fellow men, who are likewise being called to membership in the body of Christ. In so far as Quakers have developed a theology, it has been one which gives equal emphasis to God's grace and to man's responsibility, and which stresses equally the roots and the fruits of religion, holding both in one context, in a manner so vividly demonstrated in the life and work of John Woolman.

There is no probability whatever that religion will come to an end. Even Lord Russell's prediction that the Protestant faith will not survive the twentieth century will obviously fail of verification, as so much wish-thinking does. Far from Protestantism dying, there is an important sense in which the Roman Catholic Church is becoming Protestant by degrees. Many Roman Catholic congregations now stress Bible reading and make public use of lay readers. One of the most encouraging of all facts about the Church of Christ is the way in which new life comes, when it is most needed, and comes by reformation from within. The salt almost loses its savor, but never loses it wholly. When the body of Christ seems almost lifeless, new powers suddenly emerge and vitality reappears. Whatever else may be the Quaker vocation, it is involved in this reappearance of vitality, not merely in the Society of Friends, but in the entire Church of Christ. The Quaker Movement exists, not for the sake of its own members, but for the sake of the Church Universal. But it is worth while to paraphrase Penn at this point in order to say that Quakers must be changed men themselves before they go forth to change others.

Though there is no probability that a Church, which has its own intrinsic means of renewal, will actually cease to be, it is only honest to admit that the Church, as we know it now, is a sleeping giant. That it is, externally, a giant is obvious. The official membership is very large, including, by any computation, well over a billion human beings. There are large investments, strong headquarters, and countless buildings, most of which, at least in the English-speaking world, are exempt from taxation. Large crowds can be assembled for some Christian gatherings, but in nearly all of them the men are fewer than the women and frequently the age level is so high that surprisingly few of the attenders are under twenty-five years of age. Thousands of Christian gatherings are made up primarily of spectators, with practically no sense of involvement or Christian commitment, and with no expectation of a real breakthrough of the Holy Spirit. Evidence of the mood is that, in the great majority of Christian gatherings, attenders prefer the back seats and are actually encouraged in this gesture of noninvolvement by the ushers who, for the most part, fill rooms from the rear. They are serving people who are performing a dull routine duty, with no expectation of any consequent change in their lives. It is not comforting to call attention to such weaknesses, but we dare not omit reference to them if we seek to report truthfully.

Even in supposedly Christian nations, those who are committed, rather than merely nominal Christians, now constitute a minority. Sometimes this minority is tolerated, and sometimes it is ridiculed. It is assumed, more widely than we ordinarily realize, that believers in the Living God, as truly a Person to whom men can pray and from whom they can receive guidance, are merely vestiges of a prescientific age.

The vocation of Quakers is that of contributing to the renewal of the entire Church. A little more than a hundred years ago, Thomas Hancock, in his remarkably perceptive essay, *The Peculiam*, pointed out the vast change in mood which had come in the Quaker Movement in two centuries. Whereas, at the beginning, he said, every Friend believed that the cause which he served was identical with the cause of the whole Church of Christ, by the middle of the nineteenth century, *no* Friend believed it. All had settled for something so modest that it was no longer really important. At the present juncture in history it is possible to outline a third way, not identical with either of the alternatives so brilliantly described by Hancock. The trouble with the seventeenth-century view was that it was lacking in humility, while the difficulty with the view of the nineteenth century was that it was lacking in magnitude. There must be a valid alternative both to arrogance and to triviality. What is it?

It is fundamentally wrong for Quakers to identify their own fellowship, as some of the boldest of the early Quakers did, with that of total Christianity. However good some of the Quaker ways have proved to be, they are not sufficient, and are not the only good ways. For example, there was a powerful development of Christian ideas on the part of some of the contemporaries of Fox, though he was hardly aware even of their existence. It is ridiculous to be contemptuous of the honest struggles devoted to theological thinking on the part of superlatively honest men through the centuries. It would be highly foolish for Quakers to limit themselves to the world of their own Quaker thinkers and neglect the contributions of such a man as Archbishop William Temple. It would be sinful to be so enamored of the plain beauty of the Quaker meetinghouse, as to neglect the beauty of the Greek temple or of the Gothic cathedral. To be so in love with Quaker silence that one could not appreciate an oratorio would be a needless and positively sinful impoverishment of the human spirit. And, in all honesty, it must be said that, if all Christians were Quakers, there would be no oratorios as there would be no cathedrals.

The third way of envisioning the Quaker vocation is to recognize that Quakers do not have all of the truth, but they do have a truth for all! The use of group silence, for example, is something which, to most Christians, of most denominations, is completely foreign. But, often, when once introduced to it, the people hitherto unfamiliar with it, find it as healing as did Caroline Stephen on the day which she described so memorably in *Quaker Strongholds*. The idea of holding, in one context, the roots and the fruits of religion, i.e., the close union of the life of devotion and the life of social service, is not unique to Quakers, but it has perhaps been more brilliantly illustrated in Quaker life than in any other. The notion that there is something better than the division of Christians into clergymen and laymen is not a new idea, since it was illustrated in the days of the New Testament, but it is a really fresh idea to millions of contemporary church members.

If these ideas are important and if they are good for all men, Quakers are disloyal to their vocation when they do not seek to make them widely available. Therefore, the Quaker who has some hint of the nature of his calling will not be satisfied merely to speak with and to his fellow Quakers. Ideally he will find ways to reach both his fellow Christians of all denominations and the multitudes of Christ's contemptuous despisers. The understanding Quaker will, accordingly, write more for the world than for his own little group. He will be more eager to publish the truth which he sees in secular than in religious magazines. He will accept opportunities to speak publicly to non-Quakers. By so doing he will recover the heritage of Fox and his colleagues, and, at the same time, fulfill the tasks relevant to our time of trouble and of hope.

A highly significant step in loyalty to the Quaker vocation was that taken by the late Rufus Jones when he began to give sermons far and wide, particularly in the great universities. He spoke in hundreds of pulpits of all of the major denominations and proved to be acceptable. It was not unusual for him, in his later years, to preach in as many as twenty college chapels each year. It is difficult for us now to realize how shocking this bold Quaker outreach was to many of the Quaker contemporaries of Rufus Jones. His practice was condemned as un-Quakerly because, in promising to preach a sermon in a college chapel, he obviously had to think in advance concerning what he would say, and some considered this to be "creaturely activity." How could such a practice, they asked, be made consistent with the Quaker idea of the ministry as arising directly out of the meeting for worship, by the leadership of the Spirit? So great was the criticism that it was many years before the ministry of Professor Jones was fully recognized in Philadelphia, even though he taught at Haverford College.

The pattern of outreach in the ministry, of which Rufus Jones was the chief inaugurator, has now been widely accepted, but it has not been sufficiently followed. There is now need for an emergence of a new guild of Quaker evangelists, penetrating the world around them at every possible point, both with the written and the spoken word. A start has been made with the loose formation of a Guild of Christian Writers, under Quaker leadership, but it is not enough. The shame is not that the kind of evangelism which Rufus Jones exemplified is not adequately done, but that, for the most part, it is not even considered. It is indeed easier to be sectarian. To be loyal to their heritage, contemporary Quakers will necessarily begin to perform a function in the total Christian Cause similar to that of the Valiant Sixty, who, in the seventeenth century, spread out from northern England to varied sections of the globe. The Valiant Sixty did not address themselves primarily to fellow Quakers, for the very good reason that these were nonexistent in many of the places to which they felt called to go and to minister.

The Quaker Movement has a peculiar opportunity at the present time because of the degree to which various types of Christians are willing and eager to listen to a message from Quaker lips. There are several reasons for this, the most obvious being that Quakers are so small numerically that they do not constitute a threat. In short, though the great denominations, in spite of ecumenical talk, are frankly in competition with one another for the loyalty of the same people, Quakers do not appear to be competitive. This situation helps to clarify the precise nature of the Quaker calling. The need is not, primarily, to get more people to join the Religious Society of Friends, though such joining is welcomed. The need is to spread, to as many sincere seekers as possible, those insights which have emerged in the course of the Quaker experiement and which all men need, whether they recognize their need or not.

Though it is important for Quakers to know the general nature of their vocation, it is equally important for them to know the conditions which must be met if the responsibility to the future is to be fulfilled. These conditions become increasingly clear when we analyze the lessons of experience. They relate both to faith and to practice, and they relate to both together. In the matter of faith, one of the clearest lessons is to the effect that Quakerism cannot be faithful to its vision and to its consequent task unless it is truly evangelical. By this we mean that Quakers are not likely to recover and maintain vitality unless they are both Christ-centered in religious experience and evangelistic in religious practice.

This point is so important that it requires some elaboration. There have been times when Quakers have been evangelical, in this double sense, and there have been other times when they have not, but under the latter conditions the Quaker life has always tended to wither. Partly because Quakers have never had a creed, there has naturally been wide latitude in belief and sometimes Quakerism has tended in the direction of a mere ethical culture society, but the invariable end of that road is death. A movement of this kind cannot even survive and provide its own leadership, let alone shake the world. Over and over the sections of Quakerism which have tended to move in the antievangelical direction have been forced to turn to those nurtured in an evangelical atmosphere in order to have adequate leaders for themselves.

Any honest study of the life of Quakers in the exciting days of their origin cannot fail to show how exceedingly Christ-centered they were. The experience of Fox and Burrough and Penn was not religious experience in general or the flight of the Alone to the Alone. Quakerism began, not with the inference that there was in the universe an Oversoul, but rather that Christ could be known directly. In the most quoted of all of the insights of George Fox, he did not even report that he knew God; he said that there was one, even Christ Jesus, who could speak to his condition. Fox and his associates, as E. B. Castle has said so vividly, "never remained in rapt and self-satisfying contemplation of an infinite Beyond." Instead, they centered their attention on Christ as their practical Teacher in the practical world of concrete events. Castle is very clear when he says, "This unhesitating Christian emphasis is important, for it established firmly the fact that the founders of Quakerism had no doubt whatever that their faith was Christ-centered and Christ derived."[2]

[2] Castle, *Approach to Quakerism*, p. 26.

On the American side of the Atlantic, Douglas V. Steere has recently called attention to the place of Christ in the Quaker faith, particularly in an address, given in the spring of 1965, to Philadelphia Yearly Meeting on Worship and Ministry and printed by the Yearly Meeting. Professor Steere recognizes the danger involved in the influence of good people who are spiritual refugees, in Quakerdom, coming from churches in which creeds are overarticulate and binding. The danger he sees is the danger that they, in their new sense of emancipation, will leave out Christ.

We have now and I predict that we shall have increasingly in the future, many men and women in our ranks who treasure our tenderness with those who, out of inner honesty, dare not formulate the cosmic redemptive scene in even as rigid a way as I may seem to have done in this swift statement. I should be the last one who would want to crowd or to compel these precious seekers whom God may have called into our company to go beyond what their integrity or their experience up to now has disclosed to them as valid. But I would not want these persons to be deprived of facing the fact that the Quaker experience of the centuries, joined with that of other Christians over the years, has found this windowing of God's own nature in Jesus Christ of compelling significance.

A syncretistic world religion might have a number of adherents and it might include many truths, but there is grave doubt whether it could maintain its vitality. In any case it would not be remotely similar to the mainstream of Quakerism. A Christ-centered faith provides the requirement of concreteness and, in consequence, is immeasurably superior to "religion in general." There is a movement in our day which encourages those who are conscious of the values of world religions to suppose that concentration on Christ is an unnecessary limitation, and some, with this in mind, are drawn to the Quaker Way of Life, supposing that a creedless Quakerism provides them with a vehicle for their purpose. Tender as we may feel toward such people, and noble as their motives undoubtedly are, their supposition about Quakerism is entirely mistaken. It must be a shock to those who have rebelled against orthodox Christian belief and who have turned hopefully to Quakerism, on the supposition that it provides an emancipation from such belief, to discover, when they begin to read, what the mainstream of Quaker faith has been.

There is every reason to conclude that George Fox accepted, with sincere conviction, every item of the Apostles' Creed. Indeed, his letter to the Governor of the Barbados, which has been such an embarrassment to those who try to explain it away, was virtually a paraphrase of the Apostles' Creed. The important theological point is that Fox believed in the Apostles' Creed and *more*. Because it was this *more* that was significant, Fox did not bother to argue for the basic faith with which he began and which he shared with his Christian neighbors, but he did argue for the *extra* which seemed to him to give life to the dry bones of mere belief. Far from doubting Christ's atonement for sinful men, Fox believed in it so fully that, to the horror of his Christian neighbors, he interpreted Christ's revelation as actually "retroactive,"[3] and thus universal in time as well as in space. Though Fox, being no scholar, did not know it, he was reaffirming the faith of Justin Martyr, of whom Rendel Harris remarked that when he saw Socrates, struggling in the sea, he was not content merely to throw him a rope to assist his salvation, but he hauled him on board the ship of Christian faith, and bade him make himself at home with the crew.

As we have already seen in Chapter 4, characteristic Quaker thinkers have been able, by reference to the Logos Doctrine, to combine an evangelical emphasis with genuine appreciation of extra-Christian or pre-Christian insights. The Divine Word means God in self-revelation. Since this self-revelation is not limited temporally or spatially, it is not limited to the incarnation in human history even though perfectly expressed by that event. No

---

[3] We owe this clarifying term "retroactive" to the Japanese Quaker, Inazo Nitobe (1862–1933): "His grace was retro-active, so that it was He who enlightened all the seers of old." (*A Japanese View of Quakerism*, 1927, p. 7.)

Quaker has stated this central Quaker faith more adequately than
did the famous Archbishop William Temple.

> All that is noble in the non-Christian system of thought, or conduct,
> or worship is the work of Christ upon them and within them. By the
> Word of God—that is to say, by Jesus Christ—Isaiah, and Plato, and
> Zoroaster, and Buddha, and Confucius, conceived and uttered such
> truths as they declared. There is only one divine light; and every man
> in his measure is enlightened by it.[4]

The earliest Quakers took very seriously Christ's parable of the
Vine and the Branches. Never, except in extreme instances, did
the first Quakers identify themselves with Christ, though even Fox
was accused of this heresy. They were not Christ, but they had
found, by experience, that they could be engrafted in Him. "The
difference between Christ and themselves was the difference between the absolute and the relative."[5]

We can be sure that we shall never know, in full measure, the
relationship between God and man, for this is a great mystery and
we are limited to the finite predicament, but we have enough to
provide a basis for commitment when we see that God, who is
always seeking to reveal Himself, did, at one point in history,
reveal Himself fully. The means by which this occurred are not
part of our knowledge, but, as we confront the Christ of the
Gospels, we stand in awe, because we see One who suffered as
men suffer, and more, yet exemplified a kind of life which we
simply do not exemplify. A Christian is one who, in all humility,
becomes a recruit in His Cause.

In what is perhaps the most moving of his essays, Rendel Harris,
the eminent scholar with the faith of a little child, expressed the
conviction of Quakerism with beautiful clarity.

> We do not know any other way. We do not know any other light to
> follow. We do not know any other face or any other embrace, except

[4] *Readings in St. John's Gospel* (New York: St. Martin's Press, 1959).
[5] Castle, *op. cit.*, p. 36.

that beloved face and embrace which is in the arms of everlasting love and says, "Come to me, all ye that labour and are heavy laden and I will give you rest."[6]

It is this aspect of the gospel, as Augustine and Pascal tell us, which distinguishes it from the speculations of merely philosophical writings.

That such a faith should be evangelistic is inevitable. The disciple who has truly heard the word "Come" will also hear the word "Go" and then he will be more than a disciple, for he will be an apostle. Those who get any glimpse of truth must, if the experience is genuine, seek to publish it. They do this, not because they are arrogant, but because they are humble enough to see that it is their function to be instruments. What they are publishing is not truth about themselves, but truth about their Teacher.

If anyone would understand the historical phenomenon known as Quakerism, he is well advised to begin primarily with persons rather than with doctrines. There have been, by common consent, a few individuals who have represented the Quaker life with fidelity. Most outstanding of these are George Fox, John Woolman, Stephen Grellet, Joseph John Gurney, Elizabeth Fry, and Rufus M. Jones. As we study the lives of these six people we soon notice an important feature which they have in common. All were committed, in practice, to the traveling ministry. They visited, they aroused, they taught, they preached. A common characteristic was that, having been set on fire by Christ, they were enrolled in the incendiary fellowship of those who carried the fire, in order to enkindle others. It may be truly said that the central and similar Quaker experience through the centuries has been that of the baptism by fire, which John predicted (Luke 3:16).

There is no probability of a genuine recovery of Quaker vitality unless the practice of the traveling ministry is revived and broadened. In seeking to recreate this redemptive pattern, we do well to learn from past experience, and one of the best models is provided

[6] *The Sufferings and the Glory* (London: Headley Brothers), p. 65.

by the career of Stephen Grellet. The life of this amazing man is worthy of close attention because of his constant sensitivity to divine guidance, his obedience to the divine voice when heard, and his ability to stir up life in others. It was noted, in Chapter 8, that it was Stephen Grellet who was the one to provide Elizabeth Fry with the immediate inspiration to inaugurate her famous prison work, but this was only one out of many instances of Grellet's ministry of lighting fires in others.

There are, undoubtedly, some Christians who ought to stay at home, because that is where their service can best be rendered, but many should be more open to the ministry of cross-fertilization than they now are. This ministry must be carried on between congregations, between denominations, and between faiths. The golden text of such a vocation is Colossians 3:16, "Let the word of Christ dwell in you richly, as you teach and admonish one another in all wisdom." The reason for our need of one another is our inadequacy while separated.

What is it that Quakers have to teach and admonish their brethren? Unless there is something of this nature and unless such a vocation is followed, there can be no reasonable justification of the continued separate existence of the Religious Society of Friends. What is the basis of this justification? There is no justification at all, in an age of church union, if Quakers are merely another one of the competing churches of Protestantism. Real justification of continued existence comes, if it comes at all, along a totally different road. The existence of Quakers makes sense if Quakers actually become a redemptive factor in the Church Universal. Quakers ought to be the most ecumenical of Christians for, though they seldom repeat the Apostles' Creed, they do most emphatically believe in the Holy Catholic Church. One of the most eloquent of Quaker spokesmen, T. Edmund Harvey, who was a long-time member of Parliament, a scholar, and a warm-hearted Christian, spoke for many when he expressed his belief in the Church:

282/ THE PEOPLE CALLED QUAKERS

But the words of the old Creed, "I believe in the Holy Catholic Church," express a great reality. We can get the greatest help from this belief in the dark hours of the soul, and in all times of transition to fuller knowledge of the truth, if by belief in the Church we mean belief in the whole body of those who have come into touch with God through Christ, and through his spirit, and who can be recognized as his disciples because they bear in their lives his likeness. And as we believe in the Church in this sense, we shall strive to feel the inner bond of union that connects together the good and holy of all creeds and nations, and to bring our lives into harmony with the same spirit of unity.[7]

The ideal of ecumenicity, as expressed by Isaac Penington, is so well adapted to our new situation that it seems wholly contemporary, as it is wholly satisfying. The major statement of Penington is as follows:

And oh, how sweet and pleasant it is to the truly spiritual eye to see several sorts of believers, several forms of Christians in the school of Christ, every one learning their own lesson, performing their own peculiar service, and knowing, owning, and loving one another in their several places and different performances to their Master, to whom they are to give an account, and not to quarrel with one another about their different practices (Rom. 14:4). For this is the true ground of love and unity, not that such a man walks and does just as I do, but because I feel the same Spirit and life in him, and that he walks in his rank, in his own order, in his proper way and place of subjection to that; and this is far more pleasing to me than if he walked just in that track wherein I walk.[8]

Quakerism is at its best when it is passionately loyal to the Church Universal, yet fully aware that it is not by any means identical with that grand totality. It functions best, not as another denomination, but as an *order* in the great Church which is coming into being. By a wise instinct Quakers have, for the most

[7] A *Wayfarer's Faith* (London: Wells, Gardner, Darton & Co., Ltd., 1920), p. 130.
[8] This and more to the same effect is printed in *Christian Faith and Practice in the Experience of the Society of Friends* (London Yearly Meeting, 1960), section 222.

part, refused to call themselves a Church, reserving that wonderful word for something far bigger than themselves. Instead, Quakerism, in its periods of vitality, has seen itself in the modest role of a "religious society." Now the point is that a society can be the same as an order, as the Jesuits have demonstrated. There is nothing amiss in speaking, accordingly, of the "Quaker Society of Jesus." An order, though it is not the Church, exists to serve the Church. Its purpose is to produce something which otherwise might be forgotten, lost, or minimized. To such a vision Quakers are called.

APPENDIX A /

Quaker Organization

The terminology of Quaker organization is easily understood. The essence of the system is that the smaller units meet more frequently, while the larger units meet less frequently. In most parts of the world, the smallest unit, which is often a single congregation, is called a "monthly meeting." Normally, a single monthly meeting conducts one or more periods of worship each week and one business meeting each month. The business meeting is presided over by a person who is called a clerk, who may either write the minutes himself or have the assistance of another who performs this task.

In the characteristic business meeting of Quakers all over the world, the decisions are made without voting, and without adherence to ordinary parliamentary rules of order. The hope is that the clerk will be a highly sensitive person who can find the "sense of the meeting" without a show of hands. He is supposed to try to search for essential unanimity and to judge by "weight," rather than by mere numbers. When there is a clear division, the usual practice is to postpone a decision for at least a month or to settle into a time of worship and prayer. Frequently, the effect of such waiting verges on the miraculous. It does not always succeed, but it succeeds so often that there is no serious doubt concerning the wisdom of the method. One beneficent effect is the avoidance of 51–49 decisions which almost always leave a residue of bitterness. The Quaker method of reaching decisions is slow and outwardly inefficient, but the results are often healing. That it has not always been faithfully followed is evidenced by the few unhappy divisions which Quakers have experienced in the course of more than three centuries.

What is called a "quarterly meeting" is a geographical unit covering an area in which representatives of local congregations gather four times a year. A "yearly meeting" is a unit which refers to a still larger area and which constitutes the major legislative and administrative body among Friends. The clerkship of a yearly meeting is a demanding position of great influence, though it never involves any financial remuneration. Yearly meetings vary greatly in numbers of members, the differences arising from historical and geographical considerations. Seldom are the divisions identical with those of states and governments. Some, such as the yearly meetings on the European continent, are very small, while those called "London," "East Africa," "Philadelphia," and "Indiana" are comparatively large. London Yearly Meeting, which usually gathers in London in May of each year, though it may meet elsewhere in Great Britain, reports about twenty thousand adult members. This number includes some in Australia and in New Zealand. The term "yearly meeting" refers both to the actual gathering, of a few days' duration, and to the total organization, which, for legal purposes, is incorporated. Thus the yearly meeting can own property, though it is not taxed.

Since it is obvious that decisions need to be made during the long intervals between the annual sessions, all yearly meetings have executive bodies. Some are called "permanent boards," and some "executive committees." In Great Britain, the ancient and appropriate name which is retained for the executive body, which meets monthly, is "meeting for sufferings." This body tends to become, so far as the British public is concerned, the official voice of Friends on public issues. Sometimes the meeting for sufferings addresses messages to heads of states. The terminology is reminiscent of the days when Quakers suffered persecution, but can easily be extended beyond this to the suffering of any people.

During the last century there has been a repeated concern for wider unity among Quakers. This has taken several forms. One form is represented by the planning and conduct of Friends World Conferences, of which there have already been three. The first was held in London in 1920, the second near Philadelphia in 1937, and the third at Oxford, in 1952. The fourth is scheduled at Guilford College, North Carolina, in 1967. Each conference has been attended by representatives of all of the farflung yearly meetings. Another form of united action is that involved in what was originally termed the "Five Years Meeting" and is now called "Friends United Meeting." This meets every three years, usually at Earlham College, and maintains executive offices on Quaker Hill, Richmond, Indiana. Friends United Meeting does many things, especially in the field of publication, which the separated yearly meetings, which make it up, could not do alone.

Somewhat comparable is the Friends General Conference, which unites several Quaker bodies on the eastern seaboard of the United States, with offices in Philadelphia and a conference every two years at Cape May, New Jersey.

The Friends World Committee for Consultation has the broadest base of all Quaker organizations. With a central office in Birmingham, England, and regional offices elsewhere, it is the only continuing Quaker world organization. As such, it is permitted to appoint nongovernmental representatives to work closely with the Assembly of the United Nations. The good offices of this committee are useful in the planning and conduct of the world conferences. There are also a great number of auxiliary organizations such as the service agencies already described in Chapter 13. Many of the organizations have come into being because of particular "concerns" felt by a few individuals. In Quaker language "concern" is something about which someone feels so deeply that he is moved, almost against his will, to do something about it. Organizations which arise in this way are so numerous that they cannot be mentioned.

Annotated Bibliography

Since the number of books by and about Quakers is extremely large, any useful list must be severely selective. There are, for example, more than fifty of the printed Swarthmore Lectures, the small volumes which represent the closest approximation to an authoritative statement of Quakerism in the twentieth century. These Lectures have been printed annually since 1908, with the exception of 1948, when no Swarthmore Lecture was delivered. All Swarthmore Lectures are published in London by George Allen and Unwin and include lists of all past titles. A useful classification of Quaker books is as follows:

HISTORICAL WORKS

The most ambitious of modern Quaker histories is called the Rowntree Series. The relevant titles are:

William C. Braithwaite, *The Beginnings of Quakerism* (London: Macmillan and Company, 1912). The second edition, revised by Henry J. Cadbury, was published by The Cambridge University Press in 1955.

William C. Braithwaite, *The Second Period of Quakerism* (London: Macmillan and Company, 1919). The second edition, prepared by Henry J. Cadbury, was published by The Cambridge University Press in 1961.

Rufus M. Jones, *The Later Periods of Quakerism*, in two volumes (London: Macmillan and Company, 1921). These volumes carry the history to the time of World War I.

Besides the Rowntree Series, four contemporary works of history require attention. These are:

Hugh Barbour, *The Quakers in Puritan England* (New Haven and

London: Yale University Press, 1964). This is the substance of Dr. Barbour's doctoral dissertation at Yale.

T. Edmund Harvey, *The Rise of the Quakers* (London: Headley Brothers, 1905). A very brief, but highly reliable account of Quaker beginnings.

Elbert Russell, *The History of Quakerism* (New York: The Macmillan Company, 1942). This book, which won the Mayflower Cup Award, is now, unfortunately, out of print. Where available it provides the best one-volume history.

Elfrida Vipont, *The Story of Quakerism* (London: The Bannisdale Press, 1955). The author, who in private life is Elfrida Foulds, lives in the area where Quakerism began and understands the original scene better than any other living person.

BIOGRAPHIES

Margaret Fell, Mother of Quakerism, by Isabel Ross (London: Longmans, Green & Company, 1949). The life of the most influential Quaker woman of the seventeenth century is told by one of her descendants.

Elizabeth Fry, Quaker Heroine, by Janet Whitney (Boston: Little, Brown and Company, 1936). A highly readable account which, upon publication, quickly became a best seller.

Joseph John Gurney, by David E. Swift (Middletown, Conn: Wesleyan University Press, 1962). This is a long overdue account of the life of the most influential Quaker of the nineteenth century.

Elias Hicks: Quaker Liberal, by Bliss Forbush (New York: Columbia University Press, 1956). A full-length and scholarly biography of the man whose name came to be associated with the division of 1827.

Friend of Life, the Biography of Rufus M. Jones, by Elizabeth Gray Vining (Philadelphia: J. B. Lippincott Company, 1958). Though Rufus Jones wrote of his own life superbly and though others have undertaken to write about him, Mrs. Vining's book provides the most nearly complete treatment of his entire career.

William Penn, a Topical Biography, by William I. Hull (London and New York: Oxford University Press, 1937). A highly satisfactory account of the various phases of Penn's life, including that of author as well as colonizer. The list of all of Penn's writings is particularly valuable.

The Journal and Essays of John Woolman, by Amelia Mott Gummere (New York: The Macmillan Company, 1922). This volume is the best single introduction to the life of Woolman, partly because of Mrs. Gummere's biographical introduction.

PRINCIPLES OF QUAKERISM

A. Neave Brayshaw, *The Quakers: Their Story and Message* (London: George Allen and Unwin, 1953). More skillfully than any other contemporary author, Neave Brayshaw combines history and theory.

Howard H. Brinton, *Friends for Three Hundred Years* (New York: Harper & Brothers, 1952, and Pendle Hill Paperback, 1965). Though the title suggests historical treatment, the book deals primarily with principles, special reference being made to those accepted in the unprogrammed meetings.

E. B. Castle, *Approach to Quakerism* (London: Bannisdale Press, 1961). An unusually vigorous attempt to relate Quaker ideas, from the point of view of an English Quaker, to the current scene.

Harold Loukes, *The Quaker Contribution* (New York: The Macmillan Company, 1965). A short book by an English Quaker which, though it is concerned chiefly with Quakerism in Great Britain, has general relevance.

T. Edmund Harvey, *A Wayfarer's Faith* (London: Wells, Gardner, Darton & Co., Ltd., 1920). A short book written by a member of the House of Commons who was also deeply versed in historical theology. The intention is to present Quakerism as a live option for modern man.

Walter R. Williams, *The Rich Heritage of Quakerism* (Grand Rapids: William B. Eerdmans Publishing Company, 1962). This book fills a long-felt need. Whereas so many Quaker books of the twentieth century have represented only a minority of Quakers, though an articulate one, this book represents what is probably the majority of living Quakers, those with a frankly evangelical mood.

Index

Format by Katharine Sitterly
Set in Linotype Electra
Composed, printed and bound by American Book–Stratford Press, Inc.
HARPER & ROW, PUBLISHERS, INCORPORATED